Second Edition

TAPWORKS

A Tap Dictionary and Reference Manual

Second Edition

TAPWORKS

A Tap Dictionary and Reference Manual

Beverly Fletcher

A Dance Horizons Book
Princeton Book Company, Publishers

A Dance Horizons Book
Princeton Book Company, Publishers
P.O. Box 831
Hightstown, New Jersey 08520

Cover and layout design by Lisa Denham

Library of Congress Cataloging–in–Publication Data
Fletcher, Beverly.
    Tapworks: a tap dictionary and reference manual / researched and compiled
by Beverly Fletcher.
        p. cm.

    ISBN 0-87127-247-4
        1. Tap dancing—Dictionaries. 2. Tap dancing—History. I. Title.

GV1794 .F555 2002
792.7'8—dc21
                                                    2002034572

CONTENTS

I offer a very warm thank you to the people who have made this book a reality: to my father and mother, Charles and Hazel Fletcher, who nurtured my love for dance through the years, and to my two daughters, Bambi Feuz and Robin Bishara who, with their families, gave me the space, time, guidance and encouragement to complete this project.

To these friends I am deeply indebted for their encouragement, help and optimism: Tom Ralabate, Barbara Denny, Suzi Hayes, Patti and Sam Viverito, and Diane Sheehan. I thank the Dance Masters of America for their acceptance of *Tapworks* as its official reference book, and Rhee Gold, the national president, for suggesting that this book might be used for that purpose.

To all of those dance teachers who donated facts, steps, definitions and combinations to the *Tapworks Dictionary:* many thanks for your irreplaceable contributions.

Beverly Fletcher

PART I

AN HISTORICAL LOOK AT TAP

An Historical Look At Tap

America has given birth to many firsts—minstrelsy, vaudeville, dance marathons, the Big Apple, radio, the Lindy, movies, T.V., the Charleston, ragtime, jazz music, jazz dance, and tap—all of them as American as apple pie, all of them "Made in the U.S.A." But why here? Why not Europe, Australia, or the Orient? What special set of circumstances was needed to produce such a myriad of contributions that would be seen and imitated throughout the world?

The Beginnings

Historically, we know that one major factor lies in the 17th century, when large groups of people left England and migrated to America. They came in search of a new land and a new home, one as yet unpolluted by years of war, politics, and finances, a country open to the ideas of freedom and individual choice.

Concurrently, there was another great exodus, this one from Africa, not filled with the anticipation or the exhilaration of the first. These people came unwillingly. They were sold into servitude, some by their own, most by profiteering slave-traders. They were heading for an unknown destination and for a future that was out of their control. Yet their coming contributed to the growth of dance and the birth of tap in this country. All of these races and nationalities brought with them not only their belongings, but also their traditions, customs, and beliefs. America was to become a cocoon for the preservation of the old and a melting pot for the development of the new.

By 1607 the English had created a settlement at Jamestown and in 1620 the Puritans arrived at Plymouth, Massachusetts. Most English colonists were Calvinists who had a rigorous and merciless religion. Where dancing and gaiety were frowned upon and most music, with the exception of sacred hymns, was banned, pleasures were few. Life was harsh and this was particularly true for the poor. For the rich, life was

only briefly interrupted in transit to the new land, and then, upon arrival, it returned to its former state. These more affluent European settlers brought with them a highly developed system of music, including a twelve-tone scale, tonal melodies, harmony, and counterpoint. Along with them came their social dances, complete with the proper attire and impeccable manners. Thus, there were three different immigrant factions taking up residence in the New World: the wealthy, whose minuets, gavottes, and quadrilles would no longer be hidden in the ballrooms and palaces of Europe; and those of moderate or less than moderate means, who would bring with them their jigs, reels, and clogs, resplendent with sound; and finally, the Africans—whose energetic, percussive, into the ground dancing defied description. Together, they would become the birth parents of tap.

Other colonists soon followed; the Dutch Protestants found their way to New York (then called New Amsterdam), the Quakers to Pennsylvania, the Anglicans to Virginia and the Carolinas, the French and the Spanish to Louisiana, and the Moravians to Pennsylvania and North Carolina. Each brought with them wonderful gifts, which in time would become an integral part of the American lifestyle. The waltz, for example, arrived as a social dance; although it came from Vienna, it had its early roots in the folk dances of Germany. During the Napoleonic invasions of that country, it was brought to Paris, where it crossed over to England. England considered it indecent and of loose character because of the close hold with which the male held the female. Society had dictated that one must see "a candle's width of light" between the couple when they assumed dance position—an impossible request, as the vigor and the twirling quality of the dance made a firm and close embrace not only important, but also a necessity. It is interesting to note that this newly introduced 3/4 time would eventually become the basis for our own waltz clog.

Scotland contributed its reels, complete with bagpipes, danced high on the balls of the feet, and the Highland fling, which received its name from performing on one leg while flinging the other about. Germany contributed the schottische, a gayer and more active version of the waltz, while Bohemia brought the polka, and Poland the polonaise and the mazurka. England, Ireland, and Wales introduced the hornpipe, a step dance now associated with sailors and their manual tasks while on shipboard. Later it would become a favorite stage dance. The list is endless, but one should not forget the Lancashire clog from England or the jig from Ireland, for when they combined with the contributions of the black race, tap became a reality.

CONTRIBUTORS

The Old World contributed two of the most influential dances to the beginnings of tap. The Lancashire clog had its roots in England, where workers in the factories would often take their lunch breaks outside on the streets. Here, where the cobblestones acted as a sounding board for their wooden clogs; they would hold contests and competitions to see who could produce the fastest and most innovative sounds and rhythms—a very pleasant way to acquire recreation and financial reward simultaneously. Because of the wooden shoes that were worn and the county from which it emanated, the dance became known as the Lancashire Clog, and the sounds that they produced were called "shoe music."[1]

The Irish jig may have taken its name from the French word *gigue*, a kind of fiddle used for its accompaniment. Although credited to Ireland, the dance was common to Britain as well. The early Irish peasants' shoes were hard, possibly as protection from the inclement weather or in order to last. The jig's tempo was lively, with highly complex footwork. The upper body remained erect and rigid with the arms down by the sides or lifted in a horizontal line to the shoulders, with the lower arm bent upward. The jig, like the clog, became a highly competitive form of dance, with contests held frequently in various regions of the country. Such performances required three sets of judges: one for style adjudication, which was done from the orchestra pit; a timing judge, who remained in the wings; and a third judge who sat beneath the platform to listen to the clarity of the feet, never seeing the contestants! Such competitions are still held today in the United States and Canada.

It might be advantageous at this point to discuss shoes, as without them tap would indeed become a vanishing art. Clog shoes, or sabots (pronounced sah-BO), were the common footwear for all public dancing and dancers (courtiers found a softer shoe). Cut from one continuous piece of light wood, with the inside scooped out, clogs were practical, durable, and good for a lifetime or until your feet grew. By the 1800s leather was readily available, but when it became the footwear of performers, it still sported a wooden sole and heel for producing sounds. Maple was, and is, the wood of choice. Later, just the wooden heel was used. It

should be noted that true cloggers, even in minstrelsy and early vaudeville, always wore wooden clogs, while jig dancers wore leather shoes with thick wooden heels. Metal taps for the toes and heels were not available until 1915, but even then many dancers preferred wood to metal.

AFRICAN HERITAGE

Agnes de Mille, in her book *America Dances*, states that in the 1600s and 1700s alone, more than eight million slaves were brought to the shores of America. Slavery, unfortunately, was not a new occurrence, as the Europeans had participated in it before the sailing of Columbus and the Portuguese had a slave trade market as early as 1441.[2] However, with the introduction of Africans into America, we were one step closer to the development of tap.

The African people came from many territories and settlements, some extremely isolated, others heavily populated. Most African communities, with the exception of large cities, developed independently from each other, and although their dances contained great similarities, they also bore noticeable differences; some tribes were known as leapers and jumpers, others spinners and turners, yet others specialized in highly skilled body isolations. Unfortunately, through the years the white man would perceive the blacks as being all the same, regardless of their territorial heritage, their final point of residence in the United States, their occupation, or their social status.

African dance was and is energetic, vigorous, and athletic. The people danced for the joy of it as well as for their beliefs. They brought with them a highly complicated and developed system of syncopated rhythms. Later, we would see these expressed in our own music—ragtime, jazz, and swing—and in the feet and souls of our great traditional tappers. Marshall and Jean Stearns, in their book *Jazz Dance*,[3] point to six basic characteristics that help us to identify the African presence in America:

1   It was performed flatfooted, barefooted, and on the naked earth, as opposed to the European style of using shoes to create sounds against hard surfaces.

2   The dancing was done by leaning forward, with the knees bent and in a crouched position, as opposed to the upright stance of European dance.

3   It was very imitative of the animals and wildlife found in the environment; they, like the American Indian, copied in accurate detail those things which surrounded them.

4   Improvisation and the idea of self-expression played a dominant role in their dance and rituals.

5   Their dance was centrifugal, exploding in an outward direction and from the point of origin, (i.e., the legs from the hips, not the knees, and the arms from the shoulders, not the elbows).

6   The dance itself had a constant, consistent, pulsating rhythm, which gave it a swinging quality later to be found in Jazz music.

Africans brought with them lutes, drums, and gourds strung with animal hair and instruments made from hollowed wood, covered with parchment or skin. Also included was the banjer, described as a variation on the Spanish guitar. It was also known as the banza, banja, or banjello and believed to be the forerunner of the banjo, the most favored instrument of minstrelsy.

The passage to America was arduous, appalling, and cruel, often taking four to six months to accomplish. The men were kept below deck, while the women were allowed to roam freely, thus becoming easy prey for the ship's officers and crew. If there was any redeeming feature about this journey, it could be the following event: to keep the captives healthy, they were brought to the top deck and exercised before the ship's personnel, which in reality meant that they performed their native dances, accompanied by the beating out of rhythms on an overturned bucket or the sides of a pail. Likewise, the ship's personnel exercised by performing their country, step, and folk dances along with their favorite jigs, reels, and flings. Thus, in the middle of an ocean and perhaps for the very first time, these two groups, each with a totally different perspective of dance, caught a fleeting glimpse of the other's heritage. The crew witnessed undulating bodies in a crouched position performing unbelievable feats of acrobatics and spontaneity, while the slaves, amazed, heard percussive sounds emanating from the feet of men who danced in an upright, almost static position. What a marvelous moment for all! Strangely enough, a similar incident would take place many years later in a dwelling called the Old Tenement House in New York City, but on this occasion it would occur between the freed slaves and the Irish, and it would lead to a change of roles and style on the stages of America.

In America

The slave buyers distributed their human cargo in both the North and the South as well as in the West Indies, Cuba, South America, and parts of the Caribbean. Depending on their surroundings and their circumstances, different degrees of blending took place. In the American South, many became field or farm workers and many others became house servants, literally becoming part of the family. They lived in the main house, raised the children, cooked the meals, and entertained their owners. In turn, they had the opportunity to view at close range the European dances of the plantation owners. From this set of circumstances was born the famous cakewalk. The black servants, tilted in a backward stance, pranced and strutted, mimicking the pompous manners and courtly look of their white owners performing the minuet and the cotillon. Much to the enjoyment and dismay of the white family members, the couples added kicks and flourishes of their own.

The dance and its exaggerated style became so popular that competitions rapidly appeared, usually pitting one plantation against another. In the South, these were held each Saturday night at the town square on a small wooden structure used for community events. Each proud master would present his dancers in the hope of becoming the victor. The prize was actually a cake, the winner to share it with the other participants. Eventually, the cakewalk would reach America's ballrooms and, before the turn of the century, it would appear on the stages around the country. Thus we have direct evidence that a recreational dance became a social dance, and in time reinvented itself into a dance for theatrical performance. Another example of blending occurred when Katherine Dunham, a well-known authority on black dance, realized while participating in a Jamaican dance, that what she was really doing was the Maroon African version of the quadrille, which in turn was a European social and society dance. Others claim that the cha-cha from Cuba was a combination of steps from Africa and contained the hopping and leaping patterns of the European schottische. The blending process was beginning to take effect.

In New Orleans, the mixture of dance and music occurred much earlier than it did in other sections of the country, likely because of a number of factors: the lack of segregation of the black race from the white; the large family plantations; and Latin-Catholic traditions. In other words, Southern whites and blacks had a different kind of relationship with each other than did blacks and whites of the North. The blending of races in the South would see Creoles of color sending their children abroad to be educated, while they themselves looked to European culture and dance. While this was happening in the city, the larger outlying plantations kept African dance and customs alive and current. However, in the North the black race was free, yet isolated, from white socialization, making the blending process much slower and more difficult—if possible at all.

The year 1740 saw the infamous Slave Law enacted in Stono, Virginia. The owners, fearing insurrection, forbade all slaves from beating drums, blowing horns, singing, or playing instruments, theoretically stopping all possibilities of message-sending and communication among them. Faced with this new circumstance, the slave substituted hand clapping, body patting, foot stomping, and vocal intonations for the musical instruments, using as accompaniment the tambourine and/or the clacking of bones. Most of these adaptations were for their own entertainment, but they were also initiated to keep in touch with the family through prearranged signals. As in all other things, these changes also became an integral part of their dances, a new addition to an already expansive vocabulary, which we would later see in the minstrel shows of the country.

By 1774 two dance masters had established schools in Philadelphia. Teaching dancing as a profession was well accepted, but the performing aspect was frowned on. Dance masters were expected to teach the social dances of the day as well as the social graces and deportment. Proper etiquette was a must for colonial living.

Before the Declaration of Independence was signed, the entertainment industry was not exactly flourishing in the New World. There was a sparse performing population, widely scattered, with only two or three hundred persons at best representing the show-business field. Furthermore, very few towns had performance areas. Usually, all touring companies made do with the dining rooms of taverns or the blacksmith's shop, where soap boxes, barrels, and pails could be used for seating. In the New England colonies, the Calvinists still held sway and all entertainment was strictly forbidden. However, as the 18th century progressed, there were a few shining lights on the horizon. The Williamsville Theatre opened in Baltimore as well as the Nassau Street Theater and the John Street Theatre in New York City. Wandering bands of jugglers and magicians plus wagon and medicine shows appeared in all the colonies, and in 1793 John Bill Ricketts presented a full-scale circus in Philadelphia, the nation's capitol, with President George Washington in attendance.

In 1789 one of the first American dancers to attract attention on the stage was a white male, John Durang, born in Lancaster, Pennsylvania. He became an actor, author, dancer, and manager. Durang played the role of Friday in the pantomime of *Robinson Crusoe* (also known as *Harlequin Friday*), where he appeared in blackface and performed his specialty, the hornpipe. Notes discovered on this routine included ballet terms such as glissade and terre-à-terre, but they also included double shuffle, back shuffle, side shuffle, and heel toe shuffle, which may or may not be the shuffle as we know it today. However, it opened new avenues of discovery. Durang was cognizant of the way in which the Negro danced and injected some of this knowledge into his own work. His performance inspired others to look to the black man's dancing as a possible source of new material. Unfortunately, this source would be very abused within the next few years.

By the mid 1800s the entertainment picture was much rosier. Waterfront towns were visited by floating theaters, later to be called showboats. With the building of the Erie Canal in 1825, an entertainment passageway was created between Albany and Buffalo, and boats were transporting performers up and down the Ohio and Mississippi rivers as well.

THE BIRTH OF THE MINSTREL SHOWS

In 1829, while touring with a theater company in Kentucky, a professional white dancer, Thomas Dartmouth Rice,

became exceedingly interested in watching a slave perform his tasks at a livery stable behind the theater. The slave, "Old Daddy," suffered a deformed right shoulder and had a limp produced by a stiff left leg, permanently bent at the knee. He had been renamed Jim Crow after his master, a rather common practice of the day. As he went about his chores, he would sing a little song, ending each verse with a crippled jump that culminated on his heels. The verse was "Wheel about, turn about, do jis so; and ebery time I wheel about, I jump Jim Crow."[4] Rice, after watching the slave's movements for several weeks, donned a porters outfit, blackened his face with burnt cork, created a few new verses to the song, upped the tempo, and developed one of the first dances in that era based strictly on Negro material. He then presented it to the Louisville audience, who were so enamored of his performance that they gave him twenty curtain calls on opening night. The jumpin crow dance would become a national craze and a worldwide success, and under his new stage name, Daddy "Jim Crow" Rice, Thomas Dartmouth Rice had set the blackfaced prototype for the minstrelsy. Black and white had come together, popularized by a white man but at the expense of the black man.

By the 1830s, black dance had developed into a highly complicated and rhythmic form. Agnes de Mille stated about black dancers of that period that "they let go, in face, in voice, in fun and when they danced they yelped, called, giggled, laughed and moaned. White folks were taught never to do any of these things, the black folk danced with more personal expression and invention and they enjoyed themselves while they did it."[5]

In the 1840s, two major events swept the country, both of which would blend white and Afro-American dance together. However, they would take place in two separate arenas—a white and a black one. Each would influence the other, but not under the same roof.

The first event occurred in 1845. The potato famine in Ireland caused thousands of Irish families to flee their country as they watched whole villages succumb to starvation. Upon entering the United States, they settled throughout the country, with a large number of them remaining in New York City, their port of entry. Many took up residence in a rather ancient and somewhat decrepit structure known as the Old Tenement House, or the Old Brewery, in the infamous Five Points neighborhood.[6] Here, owing to their lack of finances and for recreational purposes, they would find empty spaces within the building and fill their evenings with their own jigs, reels, and songs. Also residing in this building were an almost equal number of black families, who enjoyed the same pastime and, unfortunately, the same poverty. Eventually, the two groups met, and from then on spent evening after evening watching the other perform dances of their origin, a scene fairly reminiscent of those days in the mid-Atlantic in which the slaves and the crew indulged in the same pastime. This time, however, it was voluntary. How lucky we are, for all those evening dance sessions would produce the tap sounds and steps that today we call tap dancing. Upon viewing the footwork of the Irish, the blacks learned the material quickly and changed it to a more syncopated beat. Likewise the Irish, with their sense of humor and flair for the spectacular, began to incorporate their bodies and arms into their own dancing—a real deviation from the original. The stage would soon see the blacks performing the Irish jig and the Irish performing the black Virginia Essence. Out of both of these would come the Buck and Wing.

The second event, the minstrel show, would become the most popular entertainment form of its day. It began as whites in blackface imitated the blacks, then blacks in blackface imitated the whites imitating the blacks! It had a life span of approximately 55 years (1845-1900), but its heyday was in the first fifteen years. Starting in the United States, it soon spread all over the world. It would provide a true blending ground, where African-American dance would mix with Irish and British dance in the United States. The dances most affected by this integration would be the hornpipe, clog, and jig.

Why were these shows so appealing? Some felt that Daddy Rice's characterization of the black man coincided with the viewpoint held by most whites that blacks were sometimes devil-may-care, smart-talking, and gaudily dressed. At other times they were viewed as lazy and lackadaisical, childlike and irresponsible, but always fun-loving, good humored, and had a gift for music, dance, and song. Still others felt that America was open to nonserious entertainment after experiencing the hard colonial years, and that the transportation and communication systems were developed sufficiently to support this idea. Some pointed to the fact that the 19th century saw a falling apart of the social molds and principles that had existed, giving way to an emergence of the individual and his right to free expression and thinking. For whatever reasons, minstrelsy would provide a place where the African-American style of song and dance would forever be a part of American culture.

By the 1850s the minstrel show, whose basic instruments were the banjo, the tambourine, and the bones, had developed a pattern of presentation that began with a parade through the town, commencing at 11:45 a.m. and leading to the performance area. The show then followed this pattern:

- The presentation began with a musical overture and opened with the entire company seated in a semicircle, with Mr. (Brother) Bones and Mr. Tambo at either end. In the center was a dignified interlocutor (the straight man) who carried on a question-and-answer session with the two comic endman. This was followed by sentimental and comic songs and culminated in a Walk-Around, a dance that had a challenge section performed by the entire company as they processed in a semicircle.

- The Olio, as it was called, was next. It contained a number of singing, dancing, and speaking roles, which in vaudeville became the variety acts.

- The conclusion of the show was the Afterpiece, at first a dramatic presentation, but later a burlesque on some serious drama of the day. The Grande Finale was the cakewalk, performed by the entire company and done to the thunderous applause of the audience, which by this time was on its feet.

White or blackface minstrel shows ruled supreme as long as minstrels were in existence. No black performer was allowed in white minstrelsy in the U.S. Therefore, black minstrels (black men in black face) emerged. This did not begin until after the Civil War (1860–1865) and, when it did, its managers were usually white, basically creating a white monopoly. It is also interesting to note that the minstrel stereotype established by the whites—the corked face, the enormous, grotesque white lips, and the kinky black wig that could be made mechanically to stand on end—was such a strong minstrel image that the black minstrels had to adhere to it as well, including the corking of the face. The black performers were forced to seek employment in poorer areas of town, where saloons and brothels were abundant.

Again, because of their poor economic situation, Irish and African–Americans found themselves residing side by side as they had in the Old Tenement House. For both, the living conditions were far from desirable, but for dance the conditions were ideal. There is no doubt in the minds of historians that these two groups, more than any others, were heavy contributors to the field of tap.

In the early 1840s appeared a young black male, William Henry Lane, professionally known as Juba.[7] He would come to be known as the greatest dancer of his time. A nineteen-year-old freeborn slave from Providence, Rhode Island, he would long be remembered as the greatest dancer of his time. Lane had studied with an Irishman, William Lowe, a master of the jig. It was said that a proficient jigger could produce at least 15 sounds per second. Juba more than met this challenge and became noted not only for his style and technical skills, but also for the brilliance of performance. A critic in the *London Theatrical Times* said, "There is an ideal in what he does that makes his efforts at once grotesque and poetical, without losing sight of the reality of representation."[8]

Juba's nearest rival was Master John Diamond, a white dancer, small of stature and considerably older, who prided himself on his skill at Negro dancing. As a final determination, and to prove who was the best dancer, the two were pitted against each other in a series of three challenge matches. The first match was declared a draw. After the second and third competitions, Juba was announced the winner and proclaimed King of All Dancers. Ironically, shortly thereafter, in Massachusetts, having defeated a number of formidable challengers, Juba was given the title The John Diamond of Boston.

As a young man in 1848, Juba joined Pell's Ethiopian Serenaders, a white minstrel show established in London. Remarkably, he was the only black man ever to perform with white minstrels. He was again honored overseas as the most influential performer of the nineteenth century. In his lifetime he opened a dancing school for whites who were interested in exploring the early Negro dances. Unfortunately, he never lived long enough to fully understand the extent of his fame, he died in London in 1872. (Because of their exclusion by whites, many black performers migrated to Europe, where they developed forms of jazz music and jazz dance. In this new setting, they were viewed as talented and innovative and were received more readily than at home. Their interest in Europe was also spurred by the ending of the Civil War—its outcome gave them freedom but often left them homeless and jobless—when the rift between the black and white races was at play again.) In retrospect, writers of dance have stated that Juba's work was as much jazz and eccentric dance as it was tap, and that in every tap dancer's repertoire, including today, the elements of his work are present. If Daddy "Jim Crow" Rice created the stereotypical `darky' for the minstrels, Juba fused Negro and white dance.

THE SOFT SHOE

The minstrel stage became the performance arena of the day and fostered a type of entertainer who would become the variety act in vaudeville, which in turn would provide the material for the silver screen musicals of the 1930s. These shows were masculine, family-oriented, and predominantly a Southern art form that fostered an Afro-American style of dance very reliant on solo performance and improvisation. These performances supported four main dances: the jig, the clog, the hornpipe, and later the essence of old Virginny, which in its final form would become the soft shoe. The first two were the most influential, but the last would remain throughout the minstrel era, find its way into vaudeville, enter films, and exert its importance on the dance of today. It is interesting to note that the jig actually outlasted all of minstrelsy and, up to the present, has remained unchanged in its performance or structure. The clog became absorbed by and absorbent of many other dance forms. Harland Dixon, a recognized soft shoe exponent, claimed that the hitting together of the toes and the heels (toe-heel clicks) originated with the clog. Barney Fagan, the first to syncopate the clog, claimed that the buck and wing had done nothing but hurt the famous old dance. Dixon's comment on Fagan was that Fagan's work was so intricate that neither the audience nor the other dancers could decipher what it was about.

The soft shoe, often called "song and dance," came into being and received its name from the soft shoes in which it was performed. It had been conceived from the gentler and less abrasive parts of the Virginia Essence, which some claimed was a dance characteristic of the rude and untutored blacks of the old plantation. One of the leading exponents of this new form was George Primrose, an Irishman whose real name was Delaney. He became a master stylist and when he performed to *Swanee River*, according to soft shoe dancer Willie Covan, "with every movement he made a beautiful picture."[9] Dancer Billy Maxey said, "everybody was influenced by Primrose, he was the only true stylist of the time."[10] Others credited with contributing to this style of dance were Dan Bryant, a blackface (white) minstrel who performed it to a very slow tempo; George More, who is credited with its invention; Eddie Girard, who used old-fashioned black steps as its basis; and Eddie Leonard, who was more imitated then Primrose because his steps and style were easier.

The variety acts were just what they claimed to be: a diversity of ideas of every type and description. For example, Harry Bolger performed slap-shoe dancing, later to be used by the clowns in the circus; Eddie Foy, the hand dance; Eddie Horan, the cane dance; Harry Pilsner ran up the proscenium wall and flipped off backwards long before George M. Cohan introduced it; Al Leach was tap dancing on a staircase in the 1880s, which Bill Robinson popularized many years later. Billy Kersands, a headliner with black minstrels, used to wow them by singing *Wait' Til the Clouds Roll By* while peeling off twelve vests and delivering a terrific Virginia Essence; he later performed a monologue with a mouth full of billiard balls.

What led to the death of the minstrel shows? There seem to be many reasons for its demise: the white minstrels had their classic period from the 1830s to the 1860s, and many concluded that after the Civil War its format had grown tasteless and rude. The black image had changed in the eyes of whites; essential qualities that had existed before were now dated. Others felt that minstrel performances had become cluttered and incongruous with ballads too sentimental, and comedy too slapstick. It had also remained a very masculine form, with little if any sex appeal. It is interesting to note, however, that when women were introduced, no matter how talented they were, they, too, felt and looked out of place next to male entertainers. For all minstrel men a job on the stage was mostly successful, but life off stage was sheer drudgery: fatiguing hours on a train, long work schedules, and very little pay. The job had become very unglamorous, exceptionally tedious, and totally uncreative.

By now, musical comedy companies had begun to appear largely owing to the opening of an extremely popular extravaganza, *The Black Crook* (1866). This production would be the forerunner of the American music hall, the variety theater, vaudeville, and later the musical theater. The final straw was not a stage happening, but a musical one—ragtime—which emerged in the 1890s. This form would slowly, but surely, take the country by storm and become the rage of the 1920s—the Jazz Age.

Thus, the minstrel shows bowed out in the late 1800s and America was ready for a change of entertainment, one that would be as popular, if not more so, as its predecessor. This genre would see that tap became known and recognized as a true American form—its name was vaudeville.

ENTER VAUDEVILLE

The term "vaudeville" is of French origin, from the word *vaux-de-vire,* which referred to the popular, satirical songs that were composed and presented in the valleys (*vaux*) near the French town of Vire in the 15th century. Vaudeville, to most, means a variety show comprised of many different kinds of entertainment. However, some theater buffs protest this definition, stating that the term "variety" is better used in connection with the old beer halls, where alcohol was sold and whose main patronage was male. Vaudeville was respectable, they claimed, always being held in a theater, where no alcohol (at least then) was obtainable and where the audience was both male and female. Regardless of this difference in understanding, eventually the terms variety and vaudeville became synonymous under the careful supervision of Tony Pastor.

Pastor is credited, in 1880, with opening his 14th Street Theater in New York City and with it taking the variety acts out of the beer halls and into a theater setting. Immediately after that, Benjamin Franklin Keith opened The Gaiety Museum in Boston, where he ran continuous entertainment. In 1884 Keith was joined by Edward F. Albee and together they would build a theatrical empire. Vaudeville quickly climbed onto the bigger stages of the country. If one really had one's act together it could be done clear across the country, then changed slightly and especially with different wardrobe, could come back across the country again using the same material.

Vaudeville was conceived with the idea that it would focus on the working class and present a popular, yet inexpensive, form of entertainment. It maintained its status as show-business kingpin because it gave people what they wanted. It also kept in mind the family. Strict censorship was exercised on its stages, so that any member of a family could attend a show without risk of being offended. Although circumvention of censorship codes was common,[11] the clean image of vaudeville basically remained intact. As a matter of fact, vaudeville had such a strong cultural influence on American society that the public clung to its moral view long after the medium expired, transfering censorship to the motion picture, radio, and television industries.

By 1894 the Keith Theater had two shows a day, with no reserved seating, a ten-cent admission charge, and no competition in sight. In the late 1890s Keith had so perfected the entertainment concept that all the smaller houses would run continuous entertainment, while larger theaters maintained a two-a-day schedule. Eventually, only the Palace Theatre in New York was limited to a smaller number of shows; the rest did a full schedule because of popular demand.

And what was happening on the vaudeville stage? Everything! There were "dumb acts" (anything that didn't use the spoken word), which included dancers, acrobats, bicycle acts, animal acts, rough-house, legomania, eccentric, Hawaiian, ballet, toe tap, Russian, Scotch, and Apache as well as the "animal dances" of the day: the grizzly bear, the turkey trot, the horse trot, the bunny hug, and the kangaroo dip. Along with the clog, still being performed in wooden shoes, or at least wooden soles, were the jig, now with authentic tap sounds as well as the original jig sounds; the pedestal dance, which presented a dancer, juggler, or acrobat in a tiny dance space suspended atop a column; a sand dance, where a small cup of fine sand would be carefully spread center stage for the performer, who would then produce swishing and scraping sounds to an orchestral background; a soft shoe, an offshoot of the sand dance, in which the dancer, in soft leather shoes, produced no sounds but captivated the audience with slides, glides, turns, and flowing images.

THE BLACK CIRCUIT

Unfortunately, instead of a joining of African-Americans with whites on the entertainment circuit, there was white vaudeville in the form of the Loew's, Orpheum, and Keith and Albee circuits (the latter included the Palace and possible connections with England and Europe), and there was the Theatre Owners Booking Association for black artists. It was also referred to as TOBY or T.O.B.A., which was more commonly known as Tough on Black Artists or, in some cases, Tough on Black Asses. As the white performer began to excel at his craft, he would find his way to one of the major or minor vaudeville circuits that crisscrossed the United States. But, as explained by Dewey "Pigmeat" Markham, a black dancer who, by sheer will and hard work, finally appeared on the *Ed Sullivan Show,* "Show business for a colored dancer was like going through school, you started in a medicine show (kindergarten), then to a gilly show (grade school), if you had something to offer, you went to a carnival (high school) and in college you became part of a minstrel show or Broadway or vaudeville—some never left the tent."[12]

There were many white and black artists who contributed abundantly to vaudeville. On the white circuit there was Thomas Patricola, who, while playing the ukelele, created new dance steps and performed a new form of blackface. There was Pat Rooney, known for his waltz clog and popularizing the Shuffle Off to Buffalo and Falling Off a Log steps. There was Eddie Horan, who laid the foundation for song and dance acts with the use of a cane and the performance of his walking waltz clog.

White families also abounded on the stage: the Four Fords, known as the Greatest Dancing Family; the Purcella

Brothers, dressed like convicts with their legs linked together, complete with ball and chain. There were the Cohans, George M. being the most famous, who introduced Americanism to the stage; the five Kellys, among them Fred, who directed attention to fast tap dancing along with his brother Gene, who went on to fame in the movies. And let us remember the Condos brothers; Steve Condos was the originator of practice drills called tap rudiments. Similar to a drummer's rhythm with his sticks, the rudiments produced innumerable variations and numbers of strikes on each foot.

On the Black circuit, there were many notable contributors. Most black performers had a number of skills: singing, acting, dancing, patter, jokes, skits, etc. Leonard Reed, the creator of the famous Shim Sham Shimmy, could dance, do the Charleston, tell stories and somehow pass for white owing to his interracial background.

The T.O.B.A. circuit was founded by a black comic and actor, Sherman Dudley, who, before World War I, bought up many theaters, primarily in the South and the Southwest. He was so successful that he formed a theatrical circuit through which black artists could perform in more than three hundred theaters, across the United States from the South through the North. The talent it produced was remarkable: Ethel Waters; the superlative dancing of Toots Davis; Eubie Blake, the yet to be famous pianist-composer; and John Bubbles, who in 1922 would be the creator of rhythm tap, a highly complex, syncopated, and stylized form of the art. Together with these notables was Peg Leg Bates, a marvelous one-legged dancer who incorporated flash steps with tap and never missed a beat. He was such a fine performer that many, after seeing him, forgot that he had only one leg. Another sensational performer was Baby Laurence, a great master of close to the floor tap work.

Probably one of black vaudeville's most outstanding and innovative teams was that of John Bubbles and pianist Ford Lee "Buck" Washington, known as Buck and Bubbles. They created a new style of tap with a simple appearance and a complex sound, which gave the impression of being controlled and dignified. One of the most influential dancers of the time was King Rastus Brown, a flatfooted buck dancer, heavily involved in syncopated rhythms, rhythms basically unknown and unused by the European and white dancers. There was Eddie Rector, a great soloist and stylist who had added arm and hand movements to the soft shoe; Jack Wiggins, a dancer and choreographer who brought the "class act" to the circuit, from which it never left. The class act consisted of a duet or trio, usually male, in full evening attire—top hat, tails or tux, spats, and sometimes sporting a cane—presenting a suave, smooth routine in identical precision that created an atmosphere of grace and elegance. The master dancer Honi Coles and his partner Cholly Atkins were one of the most famous of the class acts, as well as Rufus Greenlee and Thaddeus Drayton. The class act helped to change the black man's image from shiftless, happy-go-lucky and devil-may-care to suave, sophisticated, and dignified. Its influence would be felt much later.

Some acts who were already stars skipped the T.O.B.A. circuit entirely and went directly into the white theaters. Others formed their own circuit, such as the Whitman sisters (Alice, Alberta, May, and Essie) who had not only a terrific act, but were also considered the foremost leader and promoter of black talent on the circuit. Eventually they joined the T.O.B.A. because they were able to get top billing and demand extremely high salaries. Some black performers had passed from the minstrels into vaudeville, and a few would pass from vaudeville onto the silver screen: Bill Robinson did.

Although vaudeville was generally a man's world, this era saw the arrival of women on the stage. As dramatic skits were part of the entertainment menu, so was Ethel Barrymore; so was Gertrude Hoffman in her "Salome" dance of the seven veils, and Eva Tanguay, who promptly tried to rid herself of the veils in her Solome, but was prevented from doing so by the management.

THE CHORUS LINE

In this mélange of vaudevillian achievements, one should not overlook the faithful chorus girls of the stage, that spectacular line of females who made the heart beat a little faster with each high kick and new formation. Formerly known as the Tiller Girls—the predecessors to the Rockettes—they were named after their trainer in England, John Tiller, and brought to America to perform in white musicals. Prior to the Tiller line, the chorus lines of the country had been described by writer Cecil Smith as "gigantic chorus ladies with their Amazonian marches and drills."[13] The Tillers, on the other hand, were a trained precision line of dancers who performed in unison and who ended their routine with a flourish of high kicks. They became a welcome addition to any show and changed the American concept of what a chorus actually did. Later, Charlie Davis, a fine buck and wing dancer turned coach, was asked to create some material for a Tiller line. Finding the look of the line rather sweet and tame, Charlie, in his own words, "took out the kicks and put in taps . . . and then drilled them until they could all do it together."[14]

It was during the vaudeville era that old and new steps were being discovered, explored, and in some cases standardized or at least popularized. This was a natural consequence of dancers who, while traveling on the road, had an opportunity to view each other's work and even exchange ideas, combinations, and steps. Thus, there was a great deal of dance exposure both for performers and for spectators. Audiences became capable of recognizing and anticipating certain well-known and frequently used movements, such as the time step, the Buffalo step, and falling off a log.

THE TIME STEP

The basic structure of the time step was identical in both black and white vaudeville circuits. Most black performers preferred working flatfooted, with feet close to the floor, in a crouched Afro-Cuban stance with little or no arm movements. White dancers tended to perform on the balls of the feet, in an upright, Irish jig-like position. It was during this period that the black performer would begin his time step on the count of 8 with a stomp or step scuff and substitute chug or heel drop for the hop, while the white performer, being weaned on jigs and clogs, was executing a shuffle on the eighth count and an articulate, clear hop on the 1 count. These very time steps would become our present buck (rhythm) and standard (basic) time steps, and the difference in the rendition, style, and motivation would lead to the separation of the traditional tap dancer from the contemporary one.

THE BUFFALO STEP

The Buffalo step was conceived for a line of Tiller Girls who were performing at Shea's Buffalo Theater, in the city of the same name. When the director refused the choreographer the privilege of a blackout for exiting, the latter rose to the moment by having the girls stand, place their arms around the waist of the girls on either side of them, look to the right, and exit stage right while doing the soon-to be famous step. It was so unexpected and inventive that it became a common exit of the day, not only with chorus lines but also with acts of all kinds. Incidentally, other steps named after cities of their origin are the Cincinnati, the Charleston, and the New Yorker.

FALLING OFF A LOG

Falling off a log was an imitative movement of loggers as they loosened log jams and rolled their product down the river, using only their sense of balance and very nimble footwork. Falling downstairs was invented by an eccentric dancer/comedian who needed an effective and quick exit.

Many steps derived their name from the look or the action of the foot or leg, or the direction of the movement; for example, slap, click, pullback, cut-out, treadmill, slide, draw, stamp, etc. Little emphasis was placed on whether the step carried weight or remained weightless. Therefore, there was no difference between stamp and stomp, flap and slap, or heel drop and heel stand. Perhaps the first to confront this problem were the English, who used the word "cramp" to indicate the bearing of weight, and the word "beat" for not carrying the weight. These terms are in existence today in the form of heel cramp and heel beat, toe cramp and toe beat, etc. But one must remember that in the very early beginnings of tap, steps were named after the number of

sounds they produced: 1 = step, 2 = shuffle, 3 = shuffle step, 4 = shuffle ball change, 5 = waltz clog. A 6 has been debated—some say that it is two running shuffles, others that it is a double waltz clog (flap, shuffle ball change). These simple terms actually existed and were used into the 1930s. It is also interesting to note that some claimed that the terms tap and clogging were interchangeable, therefore identical, not recognizing that a new style had been born.

Certain dances brought with them steps that were already ingrained in their framework. For example, from the jig and the clog we obtained the terms shuffle and heel; terms also found in steps and complete dances of African origin. The hornpipe produced the well-known sailors' rock and the bell, while traditional dancers offered the rundown, the chug, and the roll as well as the family of roll steps. Yet other steps were taken from the dancer and skill or his work, such as the Maxie Ford break, the Abe Kabbible, the Ruby Keeler time step, the Ann Miller break, the Bill Robinson break, and the Shirley Temple.

Our vocalization of tap steps usually has the same number of syllables as the sounds being made; for example, step, shuffle, shuffle hop step, heel toe, spank step ball change, etc. In the beginning this was not true, for example, the term toe (i.e., hit the top of the R toe crossed back L) was called toe tip or toe strike. It is probable that the dancing teacher changed this procedure because verbal commands are very connected to the step's rhythmic content: the structure of a step, its rhythm, and accompanying verbalization all match to emphasize the step's execution. So conscious of this thought are we as teachers that, in uttering of the simple phrase "flap ball change," we will resort to "a-flap ball change" or "fah-lap ball change" to ally the rhythm with each section of the step.

THE BUCK AND WING

Vaudeville launched a new style of dance: the buck and wing. James McIntyre introduced this dance on the New York stage in 1880. This new dance was a mixture of jigs and reels. "buck" got its name because dance in general, and tap in particular, was a masculine art; therefore, as the male of many animal species was known as the buck, so was the dancer. The term "wing" was derived from another source. This step, discovered in the 1880s, did not reach solid acclaim until the 1930s. Some say that its origin was an old Afro-folk step, the pigeon wing, which involved a foot-shaking movement executed by the early minstrel dancers. Others say that it came from a wild flapping and circling of the arms of the performer during its execution. Either way, it has been part of the tap vocabulary for more than one hundred years. For many years, the wing was considered a flash step, which normally was quite acrobatic. Flash steps appeared at some strategic point in the routine, usually at the end or during a particularly loud and vigorous section of the music, the effect producing a flash or brilliant outburst strictly meant for applause. Flash steps would come to include trenches, coffee grinds, Russian splits, etc.

The buck and wing was danced on the balls of the feet by most, an Irish influence. However, some preferred to remain flatfooted, an African influence. It contained fast foot work comprised of heel and toe drops and variations on the time step, which, because of its familiarity and its syncopation, was often used by the performer to cue the orchestra. But owing to the cost of rehearsal time or the unavailability of either the performer or the orchestra to rehearse, this was often accomplished on stage during the performance.

The vaudeville era helped to popularize and standardize terminology that still exists today. The term "hoofer" came into existence. To most it meant a flatfooted style of tap; to others it included all tap dancers. Some terminology came from other fields. Riff and paradiddle are probably associated with drumming and the brisé cramproll from combining the ballet brisé with tap cramproll. The shimmy and shorty george added tap sounds to movements from social dances of the era, which in turn were created in response to music. Essentially, the vaudeville era founded and categorized most basic steps—flash steps, time steps, and breaks—that we teach today. The only new additions would be those stylized from music produced in the 1940s, 1950s, 1960s, and on, and new areas in tap created from combining tap with other dance forms, such as ballroom, ballet, and jazz. Vaudeville definitely established tap as an American product and placed it high on the list of firsts.

The early dancers, unlike contemporary dancers, were not trained by dance masters in a dancing school, nor were they exposed to the proper classes in ballet, ballroom, or creative movement. The profile might have read: from a middle-class or poorer economic level, probably black but occasionally white, with a tap education received from a brother or a sister, a friend, or an acquaintance on a street corner or at a bar. As the tap vocabulary increased, the dancer would consider himself a musician, countering the music, adding fullness to a bass section, or syncopating a break. He was part of the music. He would be performing not only for an audience, but also for other musicians. With or without music, he would create "conversations" with his feet by controlling accents and shading. He was a jazz artist who loved jazz music and was at one with it. The motion picture *Tap* probably best expresses this philosophy of a traditional tapper: the involvement they had with each other, the music, the challenges, the dedication, and the art.

BOJANGLES

Born in 1878, at age twelve Bill "Bojangles" Robinson appeared as a "pick" on the minstrel stage. Picks, a short term for pickaninny, were young children who were hired to surround a black female singer on the stage, contributing to her maternal look and increasing the authenticity of what was, usually, a plantation setting. The picks were frequently

used throughout a production to sing, dance, and add gentleness and atmosphere to the stage.

On May 9, 1927, at the Liberty Theatre in New York City, a play called *The Blackbirds of 1928* opened. Although the production itself was not a success, Bojangles was. (Bojangles is a contraction of the words "bone jangler," one who creates wonderful rhythms while playing the bones). At that time he performed a stair dance that would make him famous for all time.

Some think that his idea for the stair dance was born by accident. While he was closing a solo dance at the Palace Theatre, he saw some friends in the audience. Simultaneously, he spotted the four steps that lie on either side of the stage, leading down into the audience so that the actors could enter or exit from the stage during a play. Bo ad-libbed a little dance down the stairway, shook hands with his friends, and danced back up. It was so well received by the audience that he kept it in the act and had his own stairway built.

Robinson, a self-taught dancer of the streets, was a magnetic and irresistible performer. Unlike the current dancing, he stood erect and performed on the balls of his feet. His taps were clean and neat, with no flash steps and uncomplicated footwork. He was deeply influenced by the white dancers Eddie Leonard, James Barton, and Jack Donahue. In his lifetime, he produced dozens of time step routines, using breaks to separate one from the other. As a performer, he was pleasant and charming, captivating the audience with his personality and smile. He was almost fifty years old when he became the first black star on Broadway. Bojangles would continue his career in films, where he would be teamed with, and become the teacher of, Shirley Temple. They would become the first interracial team on the screen and the most successful to ever play in any entertainment medium.

In 1950 the Copasetics came into being, "a benevolent organization dedicated to the memory of Mr. Robinson,"[15] whose favorite saying was "everything's copasetic" (in those days meaning that everything's fine, great, terrific). The original group was comprised of people, many of whom were the top dancers of the day—Buster Brown, Ernest Brown, Leslie "Bubba" Gaines, Charles "Cookie" Cook, and Honi Coles. As a further tribute to Bojangles, Congress instituted National Tap Dance Day on May 25, 1989, in commemoration of Bill Robinson's birthday. Had he been alive he would have been 111 years old.

THE HOOFER'S CLUB

One of the most famous meeting places for dancers in the 1920s was the Hoofer's Club at 131st Street and 7th Avenue in New York City's Harlem. It was described as a fifteen-foot square back room behind a pool hall (some say it was a comedy club, but it really doesn't matter, as both offered gambling). Here, old professionals and young aspirants as well as nondancers who just loved tap would congregate. The new arrivals sat on benches that lined the walls and, by some unspoken word, knew that they were to remain stationary, expressionless, and become part of the wallpaper. They were there to observe, watch, and learn.

Dancers such as King Rastus Brown would drop in and casually execute a time step or two. That night, the eager benchsitters would go home, practice what they had seen, change it a little, and call it their own. Another possible way of gaining material, if you were a rather well-known dancer yourself but in need of something new, was to allow the performer to do his step and then immediately interject, "Oh, I saw it this way" or "Here's another variation." This would be quickly followed by a short rattling of the feet that would slightly resemble the step that had been originally done, in hope that the dancer would demonstrate the material again. Marshall and Jean Stearns state, "Protocol at the Hoofer's Club fostered the invention of new steps and the unwritten law was 'Thou Shalt Not Copy Another's Steps—Exactly' which meant that … you could imitate anyone inside the club, and it was taken as a compliment. But you must not do so professionally (that is in public or for pay)."[16] Some of the notables who frequented the room were John Bubbles, Ralph Brown, Baby Lawrence, Bill Robinson, Leonard Reed, Honi Coles, Raymond Winfield, Eddie Rector, and Warren Berry. The Club sadly saw its last days in the early 1960s.

OTHER PERFORMANCE AREAS

Fortunately, vaudeville was not the only source of employment for entertainers. There were many revues, ranging from the *Flora Dora Girls* of the 1900s, to the *Passing Show of 1918,* featuring Adele and Fred Astaire, *George White's Scandals of 1920*, and Florenz Ziegfeld's numerous *Follies*, which created such stars as Fanny Brice, Ann Pendleton, and James Corbett. Broadway saw George M. Cohan's second musical, *Forty-Five Minutes from Broadway,* and hit shows such as *Shuffle Along* and *Of Thee I Sing*.

Because of Prohibition, much entertainment literally went underground and resurfaced in the form of speakeasies, which provided liquor, dancing, and live performances. Later, many legitimate clubs supported this same idea but were far more elegant than the "speaks," especially those in Harlem that invited the uptown white trade to come out for an evening of food, liquor, entertainment, and beautiful girls. Clubs such as Harlem's Cotton Club were extremely popular in the early 1900s. They employed many acts plus a full chorus line, and profitably survived through the end of vaudeville.

In the past, especially on the vaudeville circuit, dancers created their own material. With the arrival of the big revues and Broadway shows, choreographers, known as dance directors, were in great demand. They became jacks-of-all-trades, having the responsibility of not only the auditioning and casting process, but also many times having to fully train the dancers, most of whom were selected for their beauty

and not for their talent. Later, they might have to create an imaginative and suitable concept for each star act or act, being sure that every gesture and movement was harmonious with the image to be created. This was followed by the staging of background chorus routines. Choreographers then focused on explosive dance numbers for the main stage. They were also responsible for special effects and the creation and development of an elaborate wardrobe. Choreographer-dancer Gemze de Lappe said to me one day that every time someone hit a note on the piano, she would jump to her feet, for she knew that was her cue to create something else. (See the section in this book Dance Director and/or Choreographer)

NED WAYBURN

The basic formula for such a production consisted of popular stars, beautiful girls, comedy, memorable songs, and dance numbers that stopped the show.[17] Ned Wayburn, a popular dance director from 1900 to 1930, stated that regardless of the type of show to be presented, he stuck to the following format: Step 1, the entrance and traveling step that got the dancers on stage; Steps 2–9, a variety of steps and kicks executed in a variety of angles; Step 10, the exit, developed to elicit as much applause as possible from the audience. While still in a directorial position, Wayburn wrote down set routines and codified the kicks, turns, and poses that were placed in them. An example was a hitch kick: "any kick that was able to extend fourteen inches above the head". He was also responsible for the famous Ziegfeld walk, which he devised as a protection for the dancers while descending the steep stairway of the set. This involved stash walks using the hip and shoulder in opposition. Wayburn was a very successful dance director who retired from the stage and opened a dance studio, whose slogan was "Health, Beauty, Fame, Popularity, and Independence"—a decided theme for the times.[18]

VAUDEVILLE COLLAPSES

By the early 1930s vaudeville had reached its peak and its descent would be rapid and permanent. The reasons for its decline were many, but the primary death blow was delivered by the movie *The Jazz Singer* in 1927. Produced by Warner Brothers Pictures, it was the first "talkie." It not only hurt vaudeville, but also collapsed the market for silent films as well. Following immediately upon its heels were technological advances in radio. Even though the medium had been discovered in the 1920s, it was far from perfected. With the formation of the National Broadcasting System in 1926 and the Columbia Broadcasting System in 1928, vaudeville's fate was sealed. Eventually, those families who had gone to vaudeville together could be seen gathered around the radio set, enjoying broadcasts from London and Europe and the songs of Rudy Vallee—without ever leaving their house.

Other events were also in the works. The motion picture industry had been packaging stage shows for many years, and owned most of the major theaters that presented vaudeville. It became less expensive for them to put together their own shows than to use the acts that had been previously performing. To add to this bleak picture, Edward Albee, from the Keith-Albee circuit, met John E. Kennedy (father of Robert, Edward, and John) who, through shrewd investments, had bought controlling interest in the Keith, Albee, and Orpheum franchises. Kennedy, having little interest in vaudeville, promptly sold his shares to the Radio Corporation of America, breaking Albee financially and creating RKO, a new movie company.

Vaudeville was ending. Performers were jobless as the American public flocked to see and hear larger-than-life actors talk on the bigger-than-life screen. They traded their vaudeville life for a new career. Many returned home or settled in larger cities like Buffalo, Boston, or Philadelphia, where there was still work. Others tried the new media; George Burns and Gracie Allen, Jack Benny, Milton Berle, Fred Allen, and Ed Wynn became pioneers in radio comedy. Still others joined big bands that were becoming famous. The team of Coles and Atkins went to Europe; Dale and Dean, Dynamite Hooker, and Hyde and Seek sought work in nightclubs. Some, such as Betty Kean, Lee Dixon, and Florence Covan, went to Broadway, while others became teachers or choreographers, like Louis DaPron, Ernest Carlos, Stanley Brown, and Henry LeTang. Some became movie stars: Bill Robinson, Ray Bolger, Ruby Keeler, Fred Astaire, and James Cagney.

By 1935 vaudeville was virtually invisible, but not yet gone. The Palace Theatre was doing two-a-day shows in the eight-act format into the mid 1950s. A few theaters in other cities were also holding on. The era had seen the standardization of music and stop time, the establishment of intermission in Broadway shows, ragtime and all its dance crazes, World War I and its introduction of new dance steps such as pulling the trenches, over the tops, and drumrolls (cramprolls), which would become part of the vocabulary of close to the floor tap, already in progress. Vaudeville had accomplished what it set out to do: create entertainment for the family. Now it was a new day, a new time, a new era. Technology would advance and the motion picture screen would slowly change the image of tap. Between Broadway and Hollywood, a different type of dancer would be born.

Social Dances

Dance has always followed lines parallel to, and in accordance with, the music of the era. In turn, the music follows dance. Prior to 1900 social dance basically found its joy in the development of steps and the fun of movement. Through the end of the 1920s, the Dixieland movement and syncopated beat created by ragtime had spread from New Orleans to Chicago and then to New York. From the day in 1913 when the Original Dixieland Jazz Band decided to stay in New York, it took only a short time for jazz to dominate the field of popular movement and music. Through the widespread use of the gramophone and then radio, jazz rhythms and jazz attitudes quickly spread. After World War I, jazz sounded like freedom, good times, and the abandonment of the mores and taboos of a previous generation. It was the Jazz Age and the Charleston more than any other dance that seemed to epitomize the feeling.

Named after the town in South Carolina from which it emanated, the Charleston was originally conceived by blacks who danced it to ragtime music. It was directly traceable to African roots. People became immediately crazed with it. For the first time it allowed partners not to hold on, not to accept the lead from the male, but to dance separately while still dancing together. It required kicking, turning, shaking, shimmying, and crossing the hands on the knees while they were rapidly opened then closed. It was fast, wild, frantic, and totally unorthodox. It fit the era and the time. In the first decades of the twentieth century more than a hundred new dances developed, but only the Charleston, the black bottom, and the shimmy left an indelible impression. These would embed themselves stylistically in both tap and jazz.

During the Depression years, huge dance marathons with cash prizes for the couple who stayed on their feet the longest would become the rage. Exhausting spectacles that became endless feats of endurance, endangering both the contestants and the audience, they lasted from two to three days. Contestants, desperate for money, would barely be able to stand at the end of such a match.

There was also a new kind of music, called swing, which would lead to the jitterbug, the lindy, and the boogie woogie. It was quickly spread by the formation of Big Bands, which would give the public what they wanted to hear—a blaring, big sound.

America's answer to the Depression was the movies, in particular the musical. It offered an escape from reality. Fun, light hearted, whimsical, with song, dance, music, and a couldn't-possibly-happen plot, it was available each Saturday afternoon for one dime—and that included a double feature, a serial, and two short subjects or a cartoon.

The Film Musical

The film musical knew no bounds or confines. It experimented with choreography, color, collaboration, and camera angles.It treated all of these with imagination and inventiveness, for it had but one purpose—to entertain. As it was based on the format of the stage musical, many stage stars, such as Maurice Chevalier, Jeanette MacDonald, George Jessel, Eddie Cantor, and Fanny Brice, easily and quickly made the transition into films. So did a young vaudeville and Broadway dancer, Fred Astaire.

FRED ASTAIRE

Astaire, having had many years of ballet, tap, and ballroom training, introduced to the screen an air of elegance, grace, and sophistication. He established a new image for the tap dancer of control, smoothness, and polish. He was a tireless perfectionist, rehearsing each movement and each small detail of every step countless times. How did it sound? Where was the placement of his arms? What was the camera angle? Could it be done more satisfactorily or in any other way, in any other direction?

His partner, Ginger Rogers, not acclaimed as a dancer, together were box-office magic. As Katharine Hepburn once said of them, "Ginger gave Fred sex appeal, and he gave her class."[19] Together they are credited, as was the third member of the team, choreographer Hermes Pan, with creating ballroom-tap, a combination of the two dances blended into one.

HERMES PAN

Hermes Pan, an excellent dancer himself and assistant to dance director Dave Gould, was hired by MGM to work with Astaire on his dances in *Flying Down to Rio* (1933). The match was one made in heaven: their styles were remarkably similar, as was their interest in clarity and exploration. They both believed that the dance should be shot from a distance and include the whole body, not just the head and feet, and that the musical rhythms and the tap rhythms should match and/or counterpoint each other. Furthermore, they were insistent that the control of all elements surrounding the dance numbers be in their hands, not in those of the film director. Fred Astaire and Hermes Pan became lifelong friends, choreographic partners, and collaborators. Strangely enough, they were the same height and build, and because of the similarities in their styles they were often difficult to distinguish if they were dancing together.

OTHER PERFORMERS

It is impossible not to mention again Bill Robinson and his famous partner, Shirley Temple. Their two 1935 films, *The Little Colonel* and *The Littlest Rebel*, created film history and made her "America's Little Sweetheart." Similarly he became Hollywood's "first black superstar." Other 1930s favorites include George Murphy, a chorus boy on Broadway, leading man in the films, and later a U.S. senator from California; Buddy Ebsen, a comedy-eccentric soft shoe dancer from vaudeville, later to do films and television; and James Cagney, a buck and wing dancer, who won an Academy Award in 1942 for his outstanding acting and dancing in *Yankee Doodle Dandy*, a portrayal of George M. Cohan. Others who were prominent in films were the Nicholas Brothers, Harold and Fayard, tap acrobats who performed not only in Harlem and in other New York nightclubs, but who were also considered the *flash dance artists of the 1930s*.

Ray Bolger, an eccentric, soft shoe, legomania specialist, could slowly, inch by inch, sink to the floor in a split, and while going through the process in reverse, would suddenly fall to the floor again with the words "oh, my goodness." Bolger soon made the transition from show dancer to expressive artist. He will never be forgotten as the Scarecrow in *Wizard of Oz* (1939) or for his comedic talents in the Broadway hit *Where's Charley* (1948).

Ruby Keeler, a charismatic, pretty, and talented buck dancer, made her debut and won fame as Peggy Sawyer in the film *42nd Street* (1933). She appeared later that same year in a movie with James Cagney. In 1935 she starred with her husband, Al Jolson, and in 1936 completed a movie with Paul Draper as her dance partner. She is best remembered as film's "first female dancing star."

Eleanor Powell introduced to the screen close to the floor tap work, complete with hundreds of spins and turns. Beginning as a ballet dancer, her entrance into tap was a necessity for the procurement of work in New York. Jack Donahue was her instructor, and with him as her inspiration and Fred Astaire as her idol, she became a Broadway hit in 1928 and a Hollywood star and top dancer in *The Broadway Melody of 1940*.

Although not well known for his work in films, Charles "Honi" Coles was, and is, a legend in dance and has long lived up to the nickname his mother gave him in childhood. A tall, lanky, sweet "honey" of a person and as a dancer, he spanned the years from the 1930s well into the 1990s when he was proclaimed a master of tap. His specialty was rhythm tap. While in New York in 1931, he made the decision to go back home to Philadelphia and practice technique, clarity, and speed. After spending more than a year and a half alone in practice sessions, lasting between ten and thirteen hours daily, he returned to the dance profession and received the title "The Fastest Feet in Show Business."

In 1939 he met Cholly Atkins, also a well-known solo dancer, and they formed the highly successful team of Coles and Atkins. Together they became the best, greatest, and last "class act" in the business. They were well known for performing the slowest soft shoe imaginable and providing with each glide, slide, and sound pictures of precision and perfection.

MUSIC OF THE DAY

The 1920s made ragtime its music, and now ragtime was giving way to the swing of the 1930s. This new music would inspire such dances as the jitterbug, the boogie, and the Lindy hop, the latter said to be named in honor of Charles Lindbergh and his solo flight across the Atlantic (a truism perhaps for whites, but blacks claimed they had been doing it for a long time before it was so named).

The Lindy's inventiveness and popularity is credited to a black marathon dancer, George "Shorty" Snowden, who often won cash prizes in Harlem's dance contests for his virtuosity and imagination. It is said that one day, in the heat of the dance, he flung his partner aside and improvised a solo section of his own. It was an automatic success and was incorporated into the Lindy as the breakaway, the section in which a couple leaves each other and creates his or her own movement. The Air Lindy, in which one of the partners, usually the women, is tossed, turned and/or thrown into the air while being guided by the man, was also developed in a Harlem ballroom.

The Lindy bred the boogie, which was quite different having to do with the swinging of the knees and the isolation of the hips and shoulders. It created a new musical style—8 beats to the bar—replacing the normal 4 beats to the bar and extending the 8-measure phrase to one of 12 measures. Stylistically, it still remains in the tap vocabulary with such steps as the boogie walk, the sugarfoot, and the Shorty George. Young people responded eagerly to swing music, and, with our entry into World War II in 1941, jitterbug spread to every port in the world where the American forces were sent.

The swing of the 1930s helped to produce the Big Band era that was looming on the horizon. It had been started by Benny Goodman and his clarinet, Duke Ellington's band playing "It Don't Mean a Thing If You Ain't Got That Swing," and musicians such as Tommy and Jimmy Dorsey and Count Basie. Swing emphasizes a simple melody, which allows the different instruments to take solo improvisational leads. It became a heyday for traditional tappers.

Other striking events also occurred at this time. Paul Whiteman had begun to produce the sound of symphonic jazz. Using semiclassical and classical music as the basis, he brought to it syncopation and a new sound. Almost simultaneously, George Gershwin created the score for *Porgy and Bess* in 1935 on Broadway. Gershwin insisted it was a folk opera that he hoped depicted the richness despite poverty in black lives. Unfortunately, white critics "abhorred its operatic tendencies and comedy elements,"[20] while black critics were offended by the characters perceived as stereotypes. Later, most have concluded that the reviewers were wrong.

Meanwhile, Harlem's Savoy Ballroom, The Home of Happy Feet, had nightly dance contests to the music of the Big Bands. It was the largest ballroom in the world, occupying one complete block, and for thirty years the music of the day had its home there. Other bands were playing what was considered crossover music—a popular style of jazz played in many clubs.

The 1930s was an energetic and creative period, a golden day for tap and one in which the dance and music worlds would be closely related for a few more wonderful years.

BIG BANDS

The early 1940s started out with the same high enthusiasm as did the 1930s. Big Bands were spreading the message of jazz throughout America and each one carried on tour its own dancer. Honi Coles was with Cab Calloway, Baby Lawrence with Duke Ellington, the Condos Brothers with Benny Goodman, Teddy Hale with Louis Jordan, and Bunny Briggs with Earl Hines, Count Basie, or Charlie Barnett.

As this music lent itself to solo instrumentation and interpretation, so it lent itself to dance improvisation. A tap dancer could create rhythms and counterrhythms with or against the melody or the bass, sometimes becoming a solo instrument himself or at other times taking the role of a percussionist. It was a time of great creativity, invention, and discovery.

Because of big bands, large ballrooms, huge dance halls, and lavish nightclubs were built. The Lindy, jitterbug, and boogie had become the American pastime.

The movie musical was riding the crest as well, with many new names appearing on cast lists, both as dancers and as dance directors. Gene Kelly was among these notables.

GENE KELLY

Gene Kelly, born in 1912, came from a dancing family, the Five Kellys, patterned after the famous Seven Little Foys. They appeared often on the stages of their hometown, Pittsburgh, and opened a family-operated dancing school there. Eventually, Gene left for Broadway and, while performing in *The Time of Your Life*, was offered the lead role in *Pal Joey*. Brother Fred came to New York to replace him, thus allowing Gene to move on to other roles. Shortly Gene did move on—to Hollywood.

He rose to stardom quickly in the movies, and in 1944 his "alter ego" dance in *Cover Girl* was acclaimed as the first dance ever to enhance and further the storyline of a musical. Other successes followed: *The Ziegfeld Follies* in 1945, the only time he teamed with Fred Astaire, *The Pirate* in 1948 with Judy Garland and the fabulous Nicholas Brothers, and *On the Town* in 1949, inspired by Jerome Robbin's ballet *Fancy Free*. However, his true recognition would come with two musicals produced in the 1950s. *An American in Paris* (1951) featured his twenty-minute ballet, which not only explored the plot, but also used the element of abstraction. Kelly based the scenery, costumes and style of each section on the particular style of a famous French painter. In 1952 he sang, danced, and co-directed with Stanley Donen the brilliant hit *Singin' in the Rain,* which contained his classic umbrella/rain number, performed to the show's title tune.

Kelly inspired more men to dance than perhaps any other male dancer. When *Singin' in the Rain* appeared the sale of tap shoes increased threefold. He was charismatic, energetic, and athletic, and his talents as a dancer and as a director influenced dance studios and helped change the style of dance in musical theater.

DANCERS IN FILM

Donald O'Connor spent many years on the stage performing with his siblings, mother and, relatives—they also were a family act. He was a superb vaudevillian and a noted comic. He said at a young age, "If you keep doing the time step long enough, people applaud."[21] He was a tireless worker, yet one who never seemed to be working while he was performing a routine. He added much humor and professionalism to many minor films of the 1940s, but his talent was seen at its peak in *Singin' in the Rain* with Gene Kelly, when the two of them performed such dances as "Moses Supposes" and "Fit as a Fiddle." And who could forget his brilliant work in "Make 'em Laugh" in the same motion picture?

Other outstanding male dancers in this era were Gene Nelson, who started as a tap dancer, switched to ice skating also studying ballet, and then returned to tap to be remembered as a fine technical dancer, singer, and actor; Johnny Coy, Canadian-born, who had come to Hollywood during World War II. He would become known as a classical tap dancer extraordinaire. Certainly not to be forgotten, is the song-and-dance man Dan Dailey, who starred in so many movies of the 1940s and who continued into the 1950s with *Meet Me at the Fair* (1952), *The Girl Next Door* (1953), *There's No Business Like Show Business* (1954), and *It's Always Fair Weather* in which he co-starred with Gene Kelly and Michael Kidd.

The women on the scene were not so numerous, but the top tappers of the era were Ann Miller, Eleanor Powell, and Vera-Ellen. Unfortunately, Ann Miller was always vying with Eleanor Powell for the title of the world's fastest tap dancer. Strangely enough, each began her career when she was very young. Ann Miller, at age 11, was already dancing professionally and was known as a rapid-fire tapper. At 15 she was on Broadway in *George White's Scandals*. She left for Hollywood in her late teens, where she worked for RKO Studios for many years.

When Miller arrived in Hollywood, Eleanor Powell was already a star, receiving $250,000 for each movie. She remained at the top until she married actor Glenn Ford, when she hung up her tap shoes and retired from show business at age thirty-three. At age forty-eight, she appeared once more to fulfill a one-month engagement at the Latin Quarter in New York. She was not a hit but a smash, dancing just as well as ever and with the same marvelous figure she had sported fourteen years earlier.

Vera-Ellen, who co-starred with Ann Miller in *On the Town* and Danny Kaye in *Wonder Man*, was a fine ballet, tap, and acrobatic dancer who made films in the 1940s and 1950s. She had been a specialty dancer on Broadway and was a member of the Radio City Music Hall Rockettes. Her films include

Three Little Words, Belle of New York and *Call Me Madam,* in which she co-starred with Donald O'Connor in 1953.

Dance directors were constantly working to full capacity to roll out the movies of the mid-century. Such dancers as Nick Castle, Eugene Loring, Robert Alton, Michael Kidd, Jack Cole, Gower Champion, and Bob Fosse became well known in the film industry, and many would go on to star on the Broadway.

The world was also being influenced by the writing, dancing, and choreography of Katherine Dunham and Pearl Primus. These black leaders in the concert dance world would, in turn, influence another generation of choreographers—Alvin Ailey and Talley Beatty. Thus would be born a new breed of dancers and dancing, no longer one of "song and dance," but one trained in many areas, including modern and ethnic dance.

DANCE DIRECTOR AND/OR CHOREOGRAPHER

As culture continues to develop there is always a time when the old and the new are seen existing simultaneously. So it was for the early 1930s through the mid-1950s with the dance director and the choreographer. Each, basically in the business of "making dances", as Doris Humphrey has so concisely put it,[22] but each approaching it in a different manner and from a different viewpoint.

The dance director's golden era was in the early shows on Broadway, in variety shows, and in the great movie musicals. Movies demanded large, spectacular, theme productions complete with lavish costumes and countless dancers. Busby Berkeley was at the head of the list for such extravaganzas. A master at camera angles and a chorus girl's (and guy's) dream because of the number of dancers he employed, Berkeley was a marvelous director, but unfortunately he himself couldn't dance a step. Because of this, he was often the dancing star's nightmare. Such was the plight of Ann Miller in her picture *Small Town Girl*. In 1953, Miller had a huge dance number to "I've Got to Hear That Beat" and her director was to be Berkeley. Because of this she begged for help, so Willie Covan, a marvelous tap dancer and member of the Four Covans, was brought in as a collaborator. Willie thought of the idea of arms reaching up through holes in the stage with musical instruments in their hands, while Ann danced through and between them. It was one of the most brilliant numbers produced in that period. Unfortunately, Willie Covan was known only as a dance coach and received no credit for the number whatsoever—not an uncommon practice.

The choreographer was originally thought of only in connection with ballet. He was normally a dancer, many times of notable reputation, who, because of his own training, was well aware of the performance technique, style, and manner of presentation. The task of creating for other dancers was a matter of drawing upon his own reservoir of knowledge and personal experience.

Broadway occasionally needed the expertise of a choreographer who was capable of working with actors as well as dancers. For this, the person of choice was Clarence "Buddy" Bradley, a fine dancer (although he never performed professionally) and a respected and recognized teacher whose students included Adele and Fred Astaire, Lucille Ball, and Eddie Foy. He was also a man of tremendous vision and creativity. One of this finest achievements was that for actor Clifton Webb who, in *Little Show of 1929*, imitated Earl Tucker's snake-hips dance as singer Libby Holman sang "Moanin' Low." Buddy did what every good choreographer hopes to achieve: further the plot and extend the character through movement and dance.

Agnes de Mille, in 1943, changed the concept of the Broadway musical with her choreography for *Oklahoma!* She expected the world from her dancers: they must act, sing, and be highly trained in all forms of dance. Dance and drama were intertwined and united by a serious plot. Then it was presented to an audience that had been used to lightness and froth. Its success can only be measured by the fact that it played around the world for thirty seven years and is still revived. With this production, she set the future pattern for musical theater and the Broadway stage. By melding ballet with Western themes, she saw to it that each dancer must be of high caliber and trained in all aspects and phases of theater.

Agnes de Mille would not be the only choreographer that Broadway would come to know and recognize. Jerome Robbins, at age twenty-five, began his notable choreographic career in 1944. He enjoyed many successes, most notably with *West Side Story*, which he conceived, directed, and choreographed in 1957. This stands as a monument to his talents and genius. He brought ballet, jazz, and realism to the stage.

THE 1940s

The early 1940s saw tap dancers everywhere. When the war ended Broadway was booming, perhaps as a necessary relief from the strains and sorrows of war. But as the good times were rolling, so was technology and it was about to give birth to a brand new invention of great magnetism—television. Live entertainment would flourish for several more years and then TV would take over. Again, as with the introduction of radio years before, when people stayed home and listened, they were about ready to stay home and watch.

Post–World War II saw the decline in Big Bands because of a rise in the interest and production of recording companies. The young could purchase a record, go home and dance for hours, and not pay or travel to hear music. At the same time, smaller combos took over a number of recordings and became dominant in the industry. Jazz had become more cerebral and intricate; it demanded to be listened to, not danced to. For the first time in their long association, dance and music became disassociated. Because they parted company, the world would view each of them with a more serious eye. It was in this era as well that jazz dance became

recognized as a professional dance form and allowed itself to be influenced by ballet and modern dance. On the New York scene, Luigi had perfected his technique, as had Matt Mattox, while Gus Giordano was developing jazz dance in Chicago. Tap, however, had not felt the jazz influence as yet.

The 1930s had left music that could be played in stop time, allowing the sounds and rhythms of the tap dancer to be heard and enjoyed. The music of the 1940s added energy and athleticism to the form, while swing invited the dancer to become an orchestra member, a musician whose rhythmic patterns went along or contrasted with, or could even defy the beat.

The 1950s would usher in rhythm and blues (still a tolerable mixture for the tapper); rock and roll, a combination of hillbilly, blues, rock, and gospel (no possibility here for improvisation or creating new footwork); and Elvis Presley, whose hip undulations and isolations were no encouragement for tap.

THE 1950s

The music of the 1950s was promoted, pushed and marketed by the record companies and disc jockeys of America. It was get up and dance time but not get up and tap time. Tap speaks through sound, through wonderful rhythms, melodies and syncopations created by the feet.

In the 1950s, both Hollywood and Broadway produced some great musicals. The former, along with the films that have been previously mentioned, produced *Seven Brides for Seven Brothers* (1954), *Oklahoma!* (1955), *The King and I* (1956) and *Funny Face, Silk Stockings* and *Porgy and Bess* in 1957. Except for Astaire's few soft shoe dances in *Funny Face* and Gene Nelson's "Everything's Up to Date in Kansas City" in *Oklahoma!*, tap was not often found in these hits—jazz, ballet modern, and ethnic dance were predominant.

The Broadway stage was slightly kinder to tap. *Call Me Madam* (1950), *Where's Charley?* (1951) and *Gypsy* (1959) contained an occasional essence or trench. However, after Jerome Robbins choreographed (and directed) *West Side Story* in 1957, tap shoes became silent on the Great White Way. The image and composition of the musical, whether it was from Broadway or Hollywood, had changed form and concept so that the contemporary dances first presented by de Mille in *Oklahoma!* were firmly established.

However, the art was visible in nightclubs, at Radio City Music Hall and on TV variety shows. Other entertainment rooms around town included specialty acts such as Betty Bruce, Johnny Coy and the team of Bobby Van and Elaine May. There were also rehearsal halls around the city, like Michaels on Eighth Avenue, where one could rehearse for one whole hour for one small dollar, or, if you preferred a larger space, one dollar and fifty cents. Agents often roamed these studios in the hope of scouting out new talent. Knowing this, beautiful girls haunted the premises, hoping to be chosen for a job at famous clubs like Copacabana or the

Latin Quarter. Many had not studied dance in any form, but this was not crucial because these big clubs, as those in Las Vegas, employed two companies of women—showgirls and dancers. Agents were searching for tap dancers for single or double acts in smaller clubs or for the Roxie Theatre, which offered a motion picture plus a stage show, and for the two-a-day semivaudeville theater around the corner. Most of the dance openings, unfortunately, were for men unless the woman was already part of the act. As Billie Mahoney has written, "With few exceptions, tap dance in the 50's was a white man's game. Ray Malone, Georgie Tapps, Johnny Coy—and, of course, Paul Draper appeared in concert halls. For the male dancer in the 1950s, ballet-tap was the popular form in which to excel."[23]

Paul Draper (1909-1996) was not just a fine tap dancer, he was an intellectual, a photographer, an accomplished writer, and a teacher. He had very few tap lessons, catching people here and there to show him what they knew, and finally studied dance (at the age of twenty-three) at the School of American Ballet. He started his career in London, then performed at Radio City Music Hall and for years in night clubs around the country, where he danced on top of a small round marble-topped pedestal. he began to combine tap with classical music, dancing to Bach, Vivaldi and Handel, *creating a classical art form, ballet tap.* He became widely respected in the American dance community and between 1940 and 1949 appeared with harmonica virtuoso Larry Adler - a spellbinding match not heard before or since. Both artists were blacklisted in 1948 by the infamous House (of Representatives) UnAmerican Activities Committee, and Draper's career suffered. Draper and Adler were reunited at Carnegie Hall in 1975 to thunderous applause.

In 1953 Danny Daniels, a classic tap dancer, held classes called Tap for Ballet Dancers. It should be remembered that in the early 1950s the various kinds of dance, such as tap, ballet, and jazz, were entirely separate from each other. The words "ballet tap" and "jazz tap" were just coming into being. Also it was common practice for those nontappers to rush to dance studios prior to an audition in an attempt to at least approximate the look of the usual steps required, the favorite being the time step. At this time as well, Paul Draper encouraged composer Morton Gould to create music meant for the tap dancer alone. Through Draper's insistence, Gould created the *Tap Dance Concerto,* a composition comprised of four sections: a lively Toccata, followed by a slower and more subdued passage; the Pantomime, with the last two sections a Minuet and a fast and exciting Rondo. The concerto was first performed by Daniels, and later by Michael Dominico, an excellent dancer from Buffalo, New York. Unfortunately, tap had begun to decline in popularity and, after several performances with philharmonic orchestras, the concerto was temporarily laid to rest until it was performed by the Jerry Ames Tap Dance Company in the late 1970s.

The 1950s saw the development of New York City dance complexes in which the student could study many different dance forms, such as ballet, tap, modern dance, jazz, Spanish, acrobatic, and ethnic dance—all housed under the same roof. Jack Stanly's studio, located in the old Roseland building, was one of these facilities. Jack Pottiger taught ballet, Paco Cansino (Rita Hayworth's uncle), Spanish, Johnny Plaza, acrobatic, and Stanly himself, tap. A student could remain in the same building all day and never have to leave in search of lessons.

Another such complex was June Taylor's Studio at 56th street and Broadway. Financed by her friend and employer, Jackie Gleason, it also offered classes in a variety of forms, plus additional classes by well known professionals who sought extra income, fame, practice in teaching, and a place with willing bodies to test their ideas. Such dancers as Michael Bennett, Hal Loman, David Winters, Tanya and Timmy Everrett, and Bob Hamilton were part of this schedule. These classes would be held on a day-to-day or week-to-week basis, decided by class attendance and their popularity. The studio would take a monetary percentage for rent and cleaning; the teacher had the experience and the money, the student worked with the young and potentially famous. In a way, these classes were successful because they were a great experimental playground for a great experimental time in dance history, especially for jazz. In other ways, it was a very destructive period, for most of the teachers were dancers who, though marvelous at their craft, knew only their own body, not the proper procedure or treatment for the many body types that faced them each day. Injuries were thus prevalent, some of them lasting. But in the heat of the class, it didn't really seem to matter.

During the same period, there were many well-established teachers who had their own spaces: Henry LeTang, Ernest Carlos, Jane and Roye Dodge, Danny Hoctor, Bill Gary, Paul Draper, Luigi, Matt Mattox, and later Charles Hughes, Phil Black, and Charles Kelly, to name only a few. New York was a learning mecca. However, in the next few years there would be a reshuffling of teachers into other dance spaces because of the large increases in rent and the demolition of many of the older buildings. Some of these new spaces were Carnegie Hall studios, Morelli's, and the Clark Center on 8th Avenue.

Today, we are seeing a repeat of history with dance complexes such as Broadway Dance Center and Steps in existence as well as individual teachers who have dance studios elsewhere in the city. However, there is a major difference in the individual studio locations: they are no longer clustered in the Broadway area, but have moved farther out to the peripheral sections that offer more affordable rents. Thus, the student must travel greater distances when seeking these lessons.

The end of the 1950s saw Nick Castle choreographing for TV, Sammy Davis Jr. appearing in *Mr. Wonderful* in 1956, and the tap show *Hit the Deck* in 1960 starred Gene Nelson and in the chorus were Bob Audy, Bob Fitch, and Billie Mahoney.

If the 1950s produced true teenage music, then the psychedelic 1960s would concentrate on carrying it farther, developing such concepts as don't touch your partner, everybody do his and her own thing, and let's explore the whole body, not just one part. The era promoted free-style dances of all types, the birth of the twist, the frug, the hitchhike, the pony, and more. The positive impact of this period was that much improvisation took place, many dance halls temporarily reopened, and through TV one was exposed to the latest music and dance trends—a great period of social dance and jazz creativity. The bad news was that tap, professionally, had vanished. However, there were sporadic important events, all of which would have a lasting effect on dance.

THE 1960s

In 1962 Marshall Stearns, co-author of *Jazz Dance*, asked a group of tap dancers to perform at the Newport Jazz Festival. It was Stearns's hope that watching tap, people would recognize and help to promote this traditional form of American dance. Legendary figures like Honi Coles, Pete Nugent, Baby Lawrence, and Chuck Green performed. It was Stearns's belief that these men were the sole carriers of this art, and that all the information would die with them if it was not passed on. It is the same cry that we hear from Gregory Hines today.

Six years later, Leticia Jay, a former dancer and one who always professed that tap dance was the ethnic dance of America, sponsored *A Tap Happening*. This event was held at the Burt Wheeler Theater in the Dixie Hotel, on 43rd Street and Broadway in New York on four successive Mondays. The first half was devoted to individual performers, while the last half was a "tap jam," in which everyone could show their wares—a custom that harked back to the street corners of Boston and Philadelphia, to the Hoofer's Club, and to the Shim Sham Shimmy days when Leonard Reed invited the whole audience to dance on the stage at the show's conclusion. The presentation opened with a marvelously mixed cast of people, like Chuck Green, Sandman Sims, and Jerry Ames. It was so popular that it returned for eight more weeks of performances and led to the formation of the Hoofers, a group of dancers who opened at the Mercury Theater on July 29, 1969. Tap was exposed to the critical audience of New York for a short, but productive, time. Everyone who hadn't experienced the thrill of jazz tap at its best, did that evening—it will be long remembered.

Another short-lived but important event was a concert tour of Duke Ellington's band featuring Bunny Briggs as its solo performer. The band appeared in large cathedrals and halls both here and abroad in a series of sacred jazz concerts—tap was in yet another setting.

Tap had fled undercover to the dancing schools of America. What perpetuated its disappearance from the stage? Some believed that the expense of producing musicals in Hollywood or on the Broadway stage had become astronomical; others felt that tap had failed to change with the times. Still others said that it had no performance arenas in which to learn or to experiment. It was also suggested that tap technique had never reached its full potential, that it had ignored the classics as well as the concert stage, and finally that the music of the period did not allow the tap dancer to tap but merely to stylize. Whatever the reasons might be, the local dancing teacher has never lost sight of its worth or potential. Whether tap is doing well on the screen or stage or is not even there, the younger dancer and the advanced student will always find the studio door open and class in session.

THE 1970s

In the 1970s the tap world came alive with the revival of *No, No Nanette*, an old 1925 Broadway musical. Its star was Ruby Keeler, then age 62. It was the break that those who owned tap shoes had waited for. Tap also found its way onto the university and college campuses of the North and the Southwest, and performing arts high schools were created.

Bob Fosse began as a teenager in vaudeville and burlesque. He considered himself a song and dance man and was awed by the razzle-dazzle of show biz. Much of his work bordered on surrealism and sensuality, using elements of commercialism and the eccentric qualities of people, situations, and dance. He looked to the format of Jack Cole, rather than to the ballet background of Jerome Robbins, and his style was distinctive and exaggerated. His productions, such as *Pippin* (1972), the 1972 film of *Cabaret*, and *Dancin'* (1978), began to interject some elements of tap.

Gower Champion, a choreographer-director, found fulfillment on the Broadway stage in New York after appearing in many Hollywood film musicals. He was directly responsible for reintroducing tap on to the Broadway stage with the show *42nd Street*.

Michael Bennett had been the choreographer of *Company* (1970), and the co-director of *Follies* (1971) when he conceived and choreographed *A Chorus Line* in 1975. It was an instant success, spontaneously producing three touring companies within a few months and immediately grossing $600,000—a whopping amount for that time. The show brought tap back into focus for a younger audience, who may never have experienced a chorus line of dancers.

Other events, including the Broadway shows *Dames at Sea* and *George M.*, MGM's release of *That's Entertainment* (1974) and its sequel *That's Entertainment Part II* (1976), allowed young people to see excerpts from classic movies such as *Anchors Aweigh*, *The Band Wagon*, and *Singin' in the Rain*. In the late 1970s Jerry Ames had a touring tap company and in 1977 wrote *The Book Of Tap*, one of the few books available on the subject. In that same year, Lee Theodore founded the American Dance Machine, dedicated to the reconstruction and preservation of important works from the Broadway stage. All in all, in the 1970s tap saw some very good and productive years.

AFTER THE 1970s—INTO TODAY

One of the nicest occurrences in recent years has been the frequent appearances of Gregory Hines and his vested interest in the field of tap, especially in his relationship to the older tap dancers who are now in their sixties and seventies, and to new stars such as Savion Glover. He truly expresses his feelings in his writing of the foreword to the book *Tap,* an excellent piece by Rusty E. Frank. In it he states, after a three-hour chance meeting with Bunny Briggs, how lucky he was to be born at this time so that he could see the greats of this era, Gene Kelly, Gene Nelson, and the greats from the past era, such as Bunny Briggs and Baby Lawrence.[24] It is an insight into his compassion.

The film *Cotton Club,* (1984), reminded America of the jazz and energy of tap during the 1920s. A current work, *Bojangles,* about the life of Bill Robinson, should help to reestablish the name of tap. The films *Tap* (1989) and *White Nights* (1985) offered two different aspects of the field. The first demonstrated the feelings, caring, and devotion of the traditional dancers to their art, while the latter placed ballet and tap, in the persons of Mikhail Baryshnikov and Hines, side by side in wonderful dance passages created by Twyla Tharp. Other good tap happenings included the Broadway shows *The Tap Dance Kid, My One and Only, Crazy for You, 42nd Street, Bring in 'da Noise, Bring in 'da Funk,* and Michael Bennett's *Chorus Line. Jelly's Last Jam* featured Hines and the extraordinary Savion Glover.

Because of great advances in technology, it is now possible to present films to the individual or educational institution at an affordable price. Some of those that are most valuable to the tap field are the rental films *Tap Dancin'* by Christian Blackman, *No Maps on My Taps* by George Nierenberg, and the videos *The Dancin' Man: Peg Leg Bates, The Jazz Hoofer: Baby Lawrence, Great Feats of the Feet: The Copasetics,* and *The Shim Sham Shimmy* by Leonard Reed. Books include *Jazz Dance* by Marshall and Jean Stearns, *Inside Tap* by Anita Feldman, and *Tap!* by Rusty E. Frank, and two other books which are out-of-print at the time of this writing, *The Book of Tap* by Jerry Ames and Jim Siegelman, and Beale Fletcher's *How to Improve Your Tap Dancing.* All have contributed to our knowledge. *Inside Tap* by Anita Feldman is a fine resource book and Acia Gray's *The Souls of Your Feet* gives a wealth of information about building tap skills. Brenda Bufalino, founder of The American Tap Dance Orchestra, has been a long–time performer, educator, and promoter of tap. Documentation of tap, its technique and history, is increasing.

TODAY

This era has produced excellent tap companies, such as Manhattan Tap, The American Tap Dance Orchestra, Rhapsody in Taps, Rhythm in Taps, Tap America Project, Tapestry Dance Company, Flying Foot Forum, National Tap Ensemble, and many, many more. Most are self-sustaining groups, receiving little if any federal funding. The *International Tap Dance Association Newsletter,* a wonderful publication, acts as the glue for the field, reporting on everything and everyone that is making tap news, plus presenting articles on its history and its historymakers.

We should remember to credit individual dance teachers, studios, and organizations that have the responsibility of producing the dancers of tomorrow. They not only have kept the core of dance alive in their students, but also have made many contributions to its progress.

We are indeed at an interesting crossroad in the field's history where we can see the reflections of the past in the present. Many traditional dancers, such as Honi Coles, Steve Condos, Jimmy Slyde, and Leon Collins, have passed on, but we see images of their work reflected in performances of such greats as Gregory Hines and Savion Glover who honors tradition but is making tap hip again. It is wonderful to know that there are many dancers/educators/teachers, who are exponents of the work of traditional tappers, who are continuing to pass down their steps and philosophy. We see on the stage today that history does repeat itself: *Tap Dogs* displays traditional flatfooted tap from its African roots, while *Riverdance* reintroduces us to the look and feel of the Irish jig. "Tap dance is the tempo of America," said Steve Condos. So to move forward, we must concentrate on the knowledge of the past and have creativity and imagination for the future. Tap is not only an American invention, it's an American heritage.

ENDNOTES

1.   Frost, Helen. TAP CAPER AND CLOG. (New York: A.S. Barnes, 1932), pp. 1–2.

2.   De Mille, Agnes, AMERICA DANCES. (New York: MacMillan Publishing Co., Inc., 1980), p. 14.

3.   Stearns, Marshall and Jean, JAZZ DANCE: THE STORY OF AMERICAN VERNACULAR DANCE. (New York: Schirmer Books, 1968; rpt. New York: daCapo Press, 1994).

4.   Also known as *Rockin De Heel*.

5.   Agnes De Mille, AMERICA DANCES, p.14.

6.   Ambiner, Tyler. FIVE POINTS: The 19th Century New York City Neighborhood that Invented Tap Dance, Stole Elections, and Became the World's Most Notorious Slum. (New York: The Free Press, 2001).

7.   *Jube* and *Juba* are slave names, associated with dancers and musicians.

8.   LONDON THEATRICAL TIMES, 1848, p. 7.

9.   Stearns, p. 51.

10.   Ibid.

11.   In Troy, New York, the words *Ferry Street* were forbidden; in Louisiana, *nightshirt* and *hotdog* were banned.

12.   Stearns, p. 63.

13.   Ibid., p. 131.

14.   Ibid., p.147.

15.   Ibid., p. 261.

16.   Ibid., p. 338.

17.   Kislan, Richard. HOOFING ON BROADWAY, (New York: Prentice Hall Press), 1987, p. 41.

18.   Ibid., p. 47.

19.   Frank, Rusty E.: TAP, (New York: William Morrow and Company, 1990.), p. 70.

20.   Wilk, Betty, THE FILM MUSICAL, Md.: Digon Press Inc. p. 191.

21.   Frank, p. 147.

22.   Humphrey, Doris. THE ART OF MAKING DANCES. (New York: Holt, Rinehart and Winston, 1959; rpt. Princeton Book Co., Publishers, 1987).

23.   Billie Mahoney, "WHAT WE TAP DANCERS WERE DOING IN THE '50S," International Tap Association Newsletter, Vol. 5, No. 6, November–December 1995.

24.   Frank, p. 8.

PART II

STEPS AND STYLES OF TAP DANCE

A CHRONOLOGY OF STEPS

Tap styles, footwork, and presentations changed through the influence of music, culture, and the events of the day. It is important for us as teachers to recognize the steps that were developed and the time in history in which they were popularized. Many of the steps and movements listed below will appear in more than one category.

TAP BEGINNINGS

From the early days of minstrelsy and through the vaudeville era, many different types of dances existed on the stage. The Irish jig, Lancashire clog, hornpipe, cakewalk, Virginia essence, softshoe, buck, and eccentric were among those that greatly influenced and helped to create our present field of tap.

EARLY TAP

1920s

Influences

The end of World War I, the Roaring Twenties, the Jazz Age. Ragtime and Dixieland moved to Chicago.

Performers

Pat Rooney, Eddie Rector, John Bubbles, George M. Cohan, King Rastus Brown, Max Ford.

Military Tap

(2/4, 4/4, 6/8) Dance in a military manner, with clean, clear patterns.

military time steps	falling off a log	drumrolls
trenches	pivot turns	running shuffles
over the tops	buffalo steps	

Buck and Wing

(moderate 4/4) Energetic, vigorous, showy, a combination of jigs & reels. The wing was developed in 1900 and later added to buck dancing, creating the buck and wing. However, by 1921, the buck and wing was considered old fashioned.

time steps	Maxie ford	bombershay
buck and catch	shave and a haircut	wings (single, double)
scissors	flash steps	hip wings

Waltz Clog

(3/4) (soft, rhythmic)

waltz clog	step toe hop	step brush hop
3-step turn	scuff hop step	brush off toe

Soft shoe

(slow 4/4) Originally done in soft shoes and sand. The more graceful parts of the Essence of Old Virginny became the soft shoe. Both were originally done to a 6/8 tempo, now 4/4. George Primrose popularized it. It was known as picture dancing.

front essence	soft shoe time step	short essence
back essence	long essence	Virginia Essence

Rhythm Buck

(4/4) Appeared around 1910, when ragtime and syncopation had reached their height. However, it remained flatfooted and in contact with the floor, dwelling for the most part on the guttural sounds such as stamp, stomp, heel drops, chug, or draw.

buck time step	chugs	heel drops
breaks	stamps	side travels

Rhythm Tap

(slow 4/4) Close to the floor work, involving many rhythm patterns of sounds or accents, the use of syncopation and accenting, and heel and toe work. John Bubbles was its originator in 1922.

heel and toe work	riffs	time steps and breaks
toe / heel clicks	paradiddles	flash steps
paddle & rolls	tanglefoot	

1930s—Mid-1940s

Influences

Introduction of talkies, the collapse of vaudeville, big bands, swing. Chorus dancing had reached its height, as had the idea of integrating the sets, costumes, and dancers into spectacular theme numbers. The era also saw the rise of dancing stars in films and chorus dancing.

Performers

Fred Astaire, Shirley Temple, Bill Robinson, Eleanor Powell, choreographers Busby Berkeley, and Buddy Bradel.

Lindy, swing, jitterbug, boogie

(moderate to fast 4/4) Steps from social dance with tap added underneath, highly stylized, and energetic.

basic Lindy	trucking	shorty george
suzy Q	camel walks	kick ball changes
sugarfoots	kimbo	boogie walk

Eccentric

(any tempo) Usually done in comedic vein; may include elements of contortion, legomania, and shake dancing. It is a catchall phrase for dancers who have their own nonconforming style and personality.

Performers

Ray Bolger, Buddy Ebsen, Harland Dixon.

french twist	slides	bells
legomania	soft shoe	splits

LATER TAP

1945-1970s

Influences

The end of World War II, and jazz was influenced by modern dance and ballet.

1943	*Oklahoma,* by Agnes de Mille and *Fancy Free* and *On the Town* by Jerome Robbins came to Broadway. Tap begins to fade from the Broadway stage.
1950s	Elvis Presley popularized rock and roll.
1960s	Fad and social dances: pony, twist, jerk, monkey.
1970s	Disco and funk.

Tap temporarily absorbed all of the above styles, then slowly two new forms emerged: ballet tap and jazz tap.

NEWER CATEGORIES

Ballet or Classical Tap

The term ballet tap, also known as classical tap, had strong exponents in dancers such as Paul Draper, Johnny Coy, Danny Daniels, and Michael Dominico. They accurately combined the technique of ballet with controlled and delicate footwork. Their choices of music were basically classical, but included soft shoe, jazz, swing, and old standards. Appearing in films and in concert halls, they were a unique blend of the old and the new.

progressive cramprolls	waltz pickups
assemblé cramprolls	riffs
brisé cramprolls	shuffle wings

NOTE: See Gail Grant, *Technical Manual and Dictionary of Classical Ballet.*

The following ballet terms are often used in the execution of ballet tap:

arabesque	passé
assemblé	pas de bourrée
attitude	pirouette
balancé	port de bras
battement	relevé
brisé	renversé
cabriole	rond de jambe
changement (de pieds)	sauté
développé	sissonne
en dedans	tendu (tendue)
en dehors	tombé (tombée)
fouetté	tour en l'air
glissade	

Jazz Tap

To the traditional tap dancer, this was indicative of the jazz music to which he performed. To us, it refers to the practice of combining tap sounds with port de bras, style, and movements found in jazz dance. This category also includes the early or "era" jazz (Charleston, jitterbug, Lindy) as well as the style and look of today.

Its exponents are varied, ranging from Shorty Snowden and Patricia Burch to Gregory Hines and Savion Glover. Today's hip and body isolations may be accompanied by alternating cramprolls, jazz turns with riffs, pickups, and wings, while jazz port de bras is used extensively in jazz runs, walks, and across the floor progressions and combinations.

There are many other forms, styles, and types of tap work that have not been discussed here (i.e., those done on the musical comedy or theater stage; those using other rhythms, such as Latin, Afro-Cuban; those done in tacit). The exploration of different and diverse possibilities can only lead to the advancement of the tap field, its teaching, and its dancers.

STYLES AND DANCES

Alphabetically listed below are descriptions of some of the more recognized types and styles of dances that have influenced or combined with the field of tap. Many are still in fashion, others are obsolete, still others have recently come into existence. All of them reflect the absorbent nature of the tap field. Some of the entries in this glossary are in the Dictionary of Tap Terminology (Part III), which explains how to do a step or group of steps.

Acro-Tap

Very popular in the 1930s; combines two entirely different dance forms—tap and acrobatic; therefore, no blending process takes place. Tap combinations and rhythms are used in between and while performing acrobatic tricks. It is often used in dancing schools and competitions for students who are versatile in both forms.

Ballet Tap

Founded in the 1940s and 1950s; also referred to as classical tap. It united the technique of ballet and the sounds of tap and, through such dancers as Paul Draper, Danny Daniels, and Michael Dominico, began to explore classical music as a possible source of its accompaniment. Ballet tap is a true blending of the two techniques and has led to the development and rise of our contemporary dancer. See CHRONOLOGY OF STEPS: Newer Categories

Ballroom Tap

A form of dance introduced and popularized by Fred Astaire and Ginger Rogers in their films of the 1930s and early 1940s. It was a fine blending of the steps and style of ballroom dancing and the sounds and rhythms of tap, and it lent itself well to both camera angles and the medium.

Black Bottom

Based on African source material it became well–known in 1926, at which time it replaced the Charleston in form and popularity. It was described as dancing on the after-beat (the syncopated beat). By the 1930s it had combined with tap.

However, because it involved some "feminine" content, such as slapping one's rear, it was seldom executed by men.

Buck Dancing

Described as a mix of folk dance, flatfoot dancing, and close to the floor shuffles, twists, and grinds. It was highly individualized, full of legomania steps, very eccentric. Some of its combinations later developed into what we now recognize as the time step and, although breaks were also added, they were always improvised. Because of its flatfooted quality, chugs and heel drops were substituted for hops, and all dancing took place from the hips down with little, if any, arm movement or upper body activity. The form derived its name from the fact that the male of many animal species is known as the buck, and dancing at that time was most often performed by males. Although later both George M. Cohan and Bill Robinson were recognized as fine buck dancers, even though they both performed on the balls of their feet, King Rastus Brown, a flatfooted bucker was eventually credited with the title Greatest Buck Dancer of All Time.

Buck and Wing

A mixture of jigs and reels. It took as its basis the buck dance, with one new addition, the 3-point wing, our regular wing. This wing was used in a number of ways: as an addition to the time step; performed by itself on one and both feet; and added to other steps that involved hopping or changing from one foot to the other. It eventually led to the discovery of the hip and pendulum wings as well as the 5-point wing, which is accredited to Frank Condos. It is said that the wing was so named owing to the action of the working foot and the circling and flapping of the arms during its execution.

Cakewalk

This dance originated and found its its popularity with the black house servants of southern plantations. They were exposed to the polite, prim, and proper European dances of the white plantation owners; thus, in mockery and with tongue in cheek, they took the erect stance, tilted it backward, thrust their chin up high, and added struts, prances, and stylish kicks. They paraded the new routine before their white "family members." It was an instant success and became a point of competition between plantation owners. The prize was a cake, which the winners were expected to share with the other contestants.

Cane Tap

The use of a cane with tap is considered a novelty routine and has a long and varied history. It was often incorporated into a dance to establish a particular character or image, for example, George M. Cohan added it to his famous walk to add vitality and energy; Fred Astaire's cane gave him a sauve and sophisticated air, which was also true of the Class Acts. On the other hand, a hooked cane suggests vaudeville. King Rastus Brown used his cane to create rhythms along with his feet.

Challenge Tap

Usually involves two dancers but may also be done by a group. Most of the matches are friendly competitions that include a great deal of improvisation and seeing who can produce the cleverest, most intricate, most syncopated steps and combinations. These sessions are the pride and joy of the traditional dancer and are well portrayed in the film *Tap*. Another type of challenge routine is one that has been choreographed, leaving certain sections in which one dancer performs a solo or challenges the other.

Character Tap

The use of character steps, attitudes, styles, and music that are associated with a particular country or ethnic group such as Hungarian, Russian, or East Indian. It may also be used in connection with the portrayal of a particular character, such as a sailor, Charlie Chaplin, or Elvis.

Charleston

A social dance of the 1920s that had a large impact on the dance field. The Charleston arose from West African dance, the Obolo of the Ibo tribe. It derived its name from Charleston, South Carolina, where it received its impetus and its popularity. First seen on the American stage in Ned Wayburn's *Ziegfeld Follies* (1923), it had become a national craze by 1925. Its steps evolved around the twisting in and out of the feet and knees and its style was inspired by the ragtime music of Scott Joplin. The Charleston ushered in the jazz age, women's liberation, rolled-down hose, and prohibition. As a dance, it reached its peak in *Runnin' Wild* (1923), and it would make two public innovations as well: the first time a step was taken over and performed by both men and women; the first time a dance went from being watched to being performed. However it was quickly replaced by the black bottom.

Class Act

Generally performed to a slow soft shoe tempo, complete with full evening attire: top hat, cane, spats, and gloves. It seemed to glide and float and the whole idea of control and polish was emphasized. Some feel that the class act was conceived from a desire of both black and white performers to present an air of elegance and refinement. It found its fame in the early 1910s and was often performed by two dancers in perfect precision and unison. Its most famous exponents were Coles and Atkins (Honi Coles and Cholly Atkins), who performed a twelve-minute routine - all of it a class act.

Classical Tap See BALLET TAP

Clog

Beginning as a country step dance, the Lancashire clog found fame in Lancashire, England, during the Industrial Revolution (see chapter one). Clog dancing was performed in solid wooden shoes, from which the dance took its name. Cloggers continued to use these shoes throughout the era of minstrelsy. The clog, along with the jig and the hornpipe, were on the stage by 1840. Originally it contained no syncopated rhythms until Barney Fagan introduced them; Willie Covan was credited with adding punch and grace to this old form.

Close to the Floor Tap

This style of tap was introduced by John Bubbles in 1927 and became known as rhythm tap. It embraced all those steps in which the feet are held close to the floor, including toe heel work, side travels, chugs, etc. Eleanor Powell and Ann Miller were both exponents of this style of tap. See CHRONOLOGY OF STEPS: Early Tap, 1920s, Rhythm Tap

Contemporary Tap

A style of presentation rather than a dance. In contemporary tap, the dancer has studied other dance forms such as ballet, jazz, modern, or acrobatic. This term may also mean tap that is performed to current music.

Eccentric Dance

Embraces comedic movement; odd or individual interpretation; satire; and all styles and presentations that are of a nonconforming nature. It may be as subtle as Chaplin or as blatant as a circus clown. Many times it evolves around a character or a situation and is usually performed without words. The terms legomania and rubber-legs are often coupled with this dance form. See CHRONOLOGY OF STEPS: Early Tap, 1930s–Mid–1940s

Essence

The step most commonly associated with and used in the performance of the soft shoe. It is often called a soft shoe time step and the soft shoe (meaning the dance). Both are incorrect, as the essence does not fit any of the criteria of a time step and is a step of the dance, not the dance itself.

Essence of Old Virginny (Virginia)

Originally based on the African shuffle and used extensively in black minstrelsy. It was considered raucous, rude, and impolite by many who saw it in performance—especially white audiences. However, that did not prevent others from taking the softer, gentler parts of the dance and molding them into the soft shoe as we know it today.

Flash Tap

A popular form in the 1920s and leaned heavily on flash steps. These steps were used strictly for applause and to give a moment of excitement, surprise, and brilliance to a section of the routine. They included trenches, over the tops, coffee grinds, etc. and occurred when there was a loud section of music or one that needed a boost, and always for the ending. Flash steps were usually acrobatic in nature and had few, if any, taps; wings were the exception.

Giouba (Juba)

A dance of Africa that appeared in America in some form wherever there was a black community. It no doubt became the famed juba dance of the Carolinas and Georgia, and in many ways resembled the jig. Its influence was seen in the stage dances of minstrelsy and vaudeville, and, as was the case with the famed dancer William Henry Lane, the name juba became synonymous with dancer.

Highland Fling

A lively folk dance of the Scottish highlands that emphasizes the precise stretching of the feet and legs. It received its name from its place of origin and the manner in which the legs are flung outward from the body.

Jazz Tap

Introduced in the 1920s, it referred to the music being played and not the dance being performed. Today, jazz tap refers to the type of tap executed by traditional tap dancers as well as that which is performed to jazz music of all eras. Thus, the black bottom, Charleston, jitterbug, and Lindy are as viable as bop and rap. See CHRONOLOGY OF STEPS: Early Tap, 1930s–Mid-1940s

Jig

Born in Ireland but known in Wales and Britain as well. Its main characteristics were and are an erect torso, with hands on the waist, down by the sides, or at right angles to the body. The accent is on precision and brilliance of the footwork, the accuracy and clarity of the sounds, and the adherence to strict rules regarding its execution. The jig has remained the same throughout its history, not accepting the influence of time or place. The competitions and rules that prevailed during the early years are still present. There are three judges: the style judge, who sits in the audience; the timing judge, who is located in the wings; and the third judge whose position is underneath the platform, where he judges the clarity of the feet. When the jig combined with African dance, tap was born.

Juba See Giouba

Jump Rope Tap

A novelty form of tap founded in the 1920s and very popular as a variety act in vaudeville. It required skill and timing. This kind of routine was usually executed as a solo by a female, but

occasionally was done with a whole chorus of dancers. One of the most spectacular acts involved six dancers executing a fast tap while sharing the same rope.

Latin Tap

A catch-all phrase embracing not only Latin, but also Afro-Cuban rhythms regardless of its source or place of origin. Thus, it includes bossa nova, cha-cha, samba, tango, rumba, lambada, etc. The Latin influences were strongly felt in the 1930s with the large influx of ballroom teams into this country, and tap dancers found its rhythms, counter-rhythms, and syncopations exciting and inventive.

Military Tap

WWI produced a rash of military routines and a redefining of tap terminology that pertained to the event. Cramprolls became known as drumrolls; trenches were discovered as a flash step and assumed the name pulling the trenches or through the trenches; over the tops and the military time step achieved great popularity and were used frequently. See CHRONOLOGY OF STEPS: Early tap, 1920s

Musical Comedy

In the beginning, a combination of steps suitable for the ingenue or juvenile and considered to be of the lowest common denominator. Eventually, the term embraced a particular style of dancing seen on the stage that was part of a musical revue or production. It included soft shoe, tap, character, ballet, and any other form of dance that offered entertainment or was used to further the plot. Examples of this may be seen in the works of Agnes de Mille, Jerome Robbins, and Bob Fosse.

Novelty Dances

Popular in vaudeville as variety routines, these dances include the use of props, such as canes, tambourines, chairs, etc. They are also routines that carry a novel idea, such as the use of magic, creating a tall figure by placing one dancer on the shoulders of another, or hiding small people under a large hooped skirt.

One Man Dance

This routine is performed by several people, pressed against each other, front to back and dancing in absolute unison and precision. It was also known as contact dancing.

Pedestal Dancing

Evolving at the time of the hornpipe and the waltz clog, it was primarily performed on a four-foot round marble platform supported by a pedestal base of three to four feet. The interest lay in the clear, crisp sounds of the taps against the marble and the ability of the dancer to remain atop such a small space. It was totally on-the-spot dancing.

Picture Dancing

Credited to George Primrose and his execution of the soft shoe; It was said that when Primrose, an exceptional stylist, performed in his slow and graceful manner, he created beautiful pictures. Many others tried to emulate him; few succeeded.

Rap Tap

Part of the jazz tap category that was developed to rap music which is basically spoken and has a regular recurring beat with little musical content or melody. Thus, it can provide a good accompaniment for close-to-the-floor and syncopated foot work.

Rhythm Buck

Making its appearance around 1910, although it included a more rhythmic content, it was still performed in a flatfooted fashion, danced into the floor, and used guttural sounds, such as stomps, stamps, drags, and chugs. See CHRONOLOGY OF STEPS: Early Tap, 1920s

Rhythm Tap

The credit for rhythm tap is given to John Bubbles (John "Bubber" Sublett) who, at age 10, teamed up with 6-year-old, Ford Lee "Buck" Washington, a pianist. Together they became the famous team of Buck and Bubbles and by 1922 rhythm tap was born. It contained complex, syncopated, close-to-the-floor footwork and combinations, which Mr. Bubbles presented in an easy–going and almost nonchalant manner. He chose a moderate 4/4 tempo which allowed him to produce more sounds to the beat than if he had worked to a 2/4 beat. It is said that he provided the link between the Lancashire clog and buck dancing. See CHRONOLOGY OF STEPS: Early Tap, 1920s

Rhythm Waltz Clog

A form of the waltz clog that became popular during the ragtime period. It incorporated a more advanced and syncopated use of rhythmic patterns, including heel drops, clicks, and travels.

Sand Dance

Considered a novelty or specialty dance, extremely popular in vaudeville and a forerunner to soft shoe dancing. Fine-grained sand was spread center downstage, and the dancer, wearing soft shoes, scraped his/her feet in various rhythms, while executing glides, slides, and spins. Many times there was no musical accompaniment. Exponents of this form were Dewey "Pigmeat" Markham and his partner Enoch Baker, Alice Whitman, and Eddie Rector who performed it in the revival of *Shuffle Along* in 1952. It was the stagehand's dilemma!

Shim Sham Shimmy

This was a complete routine created in 1927 by Leonard Reed and his partner Willie Bryant (others have claimed credit for it as well). It was born from a comedy routine they called "Goofus" and created a finale to their act in which the whole audience could participate. It used one standard chorus of music: 32 measures, or 4 steps of 8 measures each. Step 1 was the shim sham; Step 2, the crossover; STEP 3, the tack Annie, and Step 4, the half break.

Soft Shoe

Named after the soft shoes worn for its performance, it uses as its main step the essence in all forms: single, double, triple, front and back, etc. Originally it was called song and dance (see SONG AND DANCE) and was born of the less abrasive sections of the essence of old Virginny. George Primrose was its well-known exponent, dancing to very slow tempo (See PICTURE DANCING) and adding a genteel air to its presentation. Jack Wiggans and Willie Covan had a more aggressive approach, while Coles and Atkins (Honi Coles and Cholly Atkins) returned it to its pure and more beloved state. They performed more slowly than any other team, with the emphasis on style and control, and claimed that it was correct only when it sounded as good without as with musical accompaniment.

Song and Dance

This form was popular in minstrelsy and vaudeville. It could mean (1) a song followed by a dance, or (2) later synonymous with soft shoe because, as this dance was being performed in the foreground, it was often accompanied by a chorus of singers in the background.

Stair Dance

Usually required a set of five or six steps that led up to an elongated platform and descended on the other side with an identical set of stairs. It was constructed of a hard wood. The space under the steps and the platform was critical because they acted as a sounding board for the taps. Bill Robinson was not the first to use them, but certainly boosted their popularity because of his clean, light footwork and opulent personality. Actually, Al Leach used them in the 1880s and Max Roach and King Rastus Brown used them occasionally in their act.

Toe Tap

This form of tapping while on pointe was discovered in the early days of vaudeville and paid little attention to the technique or principles of ballet. However, it paid a great deal of attention to flash steps and made it look difficult. It was rather limited in tap to shuffles, hops, and toe taps and leaned many times on the circling and swinging of the arms for effect and balance. A popular theme was military, often using flags and batons to extend the idea.

Traditional Tap

Also known as hoofers and jazz tappers, includes such people as Savion Glover, Gregory Hines, Buster Brown, Leon Collins, Cookie Cook, and Diane Walker. They are from the original school of tap: dancing flatfooted, passing work down from one to another, experimenting with the art of improvisation, working with live musicians. They are the keepers of the flame and turn their attention and talents totally to the art of tap, refusing to be influenced or changed by other forms such as ballet, modern dance, or jazz. They have different motivations and goals from the contemporary dancer. Unfortunately, there are only a few of them left and with their passing goes their knowledge, for it has been little documented or recorded. The film *Tap* best explains their tap philosophy.

Waltz Clog

Executed in 3/4 time, this is both the dance and the step (leap, shuffle ball change) and is the original "5" because it contains five sounds. In the beginning it was performed in wooden clog shoes. Thus it took its name from the time signature of the music and the shoes in which it was first performed. Waltz music was brought to this country with the social dances of Austria and Germany and quickly went from the ballroom to the stage. The waltz clog was perhaps the best known and easiest of the performing dances, but it usually presents a challenge to younger students in a studio, who are more familiar with a 4/4 time signature.

PART III

A DICTIONARY OF TAP TERMINOLOGY

HOW TO USE THE DICTIONARY

The Dictionary section of *Tapworks* contains tap terminology, types of tap dances, broader headings such as turns, spotting, time steps, and breaks as well as the musical, stage, ballet, and jazz terminology that is especially pertinent to tap.

One of the main intentions of this section is to standardize, establish, and preserve any historical information relating to specific terminology and/or steps, for most information of this nature is not recorded but passed down verbally from dancer to dancer or teacher to teacher.

ORGANIZATION

In many cases, steps are known by more than one name. When this situation occurs, the term by which the step is most frequently referred to in the references researched is classified as the **MAJOR TERM**; in the example given below, the term **PICKUP** has been selected:

PICKUP (Pullback, Graboff, Snatch) [2 to many sounds] [& 1]

The other terms—**Pullback, Graboff, Snatch**—are given as **Secondary Terms**. Whenever possible, they are ranked in order of the number of references found, or if references are indecisive, they are listed in random order. Secondary Terms are alphabetically listed as "see" references to the MAJOR TERMS.

The first bracketed information in the example **[2 to many sounds]** tells the reader that the basic pickup contains 2 sounds, but, as explained in the dictionary, pickup variations may contain numerous sounds.

The second set of brackets **[& 1]** gives the usual, or normal, count when executing a single pickup.

Many terms are movements that, in themselves, do not contain sounds, such as over the tops; however **[w/wo sound]** indicates that tap sounds may be added to this step if desired.

Families of steps are quite frequent in the tap field, and many brothers and sisters have sprung up through the years. For the convenience of the teacher, who may presently be delving into the possibilities lying within a family, all the relatives have been placed under the major heading. Thus, under **CRAMPROLL** may be found all the different types of cramprolls and their definitions, plus variations. The teacher may then easily see at a glance the field of cramprolls, and choose the ones in which he or she is interested, keeping in mind the others that remain.

The ballerina icon represents a movement that is a ballet-based.

There is a list of abbreviations at the beginning of the dictionary to aid in reading the definitions and executions. For the most part, they are conventional, but to some they may be unknown, as terminology and abbreviations have never been formally standardized.

The dictionary is alphabetical, with cross-references between related terms. Note that although it is extensive, it is by no means complete. Many terms have never been recorded but are lying in the heads of the great performers and teachers of yesterday and today. The amount of reference material obtainable in the tap field is at a premium, and of the reference materials read by the author and tabulated, few referred to the era of tap in its vaudevillian or prevaudevillian form. Sad to say, much has probably already been lost in its original form. Anyone using this dictionary who has terms, definitions, printed matter, and so forth to contribute; please write to the publisher. The information will be gratefully received and registered for future publication.

ABBREVIATIONS

The following abbreviations may be used throughout the *DICTIONARY*. Please refer to them whenever necessary.

GENERAL

alt.	alternating
amt.	amount
ast	at the same time
beg.	begin, beginning
cont.	continue
cont'd.	continued
cor.	corner
ct., cts.	count, counts
d	double
dir	direction
e.g.	for example
etc.	and so forth, etcetera
i.e.	that is
lod	line of direction
M	measure
meas.	measure
mov.	movement
N.B.	note well
opp.	opposite
pos.	position
prep.	prepare, preparation
prev.	previous, previously
reg.	regular
rep.	repeat
rev.	reverse
s	single
str.	straight
t	triple
tog.	together
w/	with
w/o	without
w/w/o	with or without
wt.	weight
n/wt.	no weight
w/wt.	with weight
#	number
&	and
+	and

POSITIONS AND DIRECTIONS

ast	at same time
bk	back
bkwd	backward
cs	center stage
diag	diagonal
dir	direction
dnwd	downward
ds	downstage
ft	foot
frt	front
fwd	forward
inwd	inward
ip	in place
obl	oblique
otwd	outward
par	parallel
pt	point
R/P	relevé / plié
r/p	relevé / plié
sdwd	sideward
sl, sr	stage left, stage right
s/s	side by side
stip	step in place
tni	turn in
ti	turn in
tno	turn out
to	turn out
twd	toward
upwd	upward
us	upstage

FEET/LEGS

R	right
L	left
B	back
F	front
X	cross, crossed, crossing
Xing	crossing
xing	crossing
Xd	crossed
RXBL	right crossed back left
LXBR	left crossed back right
RXFL	right crossed front left
LXFR	left crossed front right

STEPS

bc	ball change
bc	ball change
Br	brush
Cr	cramproll
Drbk	drawback
Fl	flap
Hl	heel
HlDr	heeldrop
Pu	pickup
Sh	shuffle
Sp	spank
St	step

OUR COUNTING SYSTEM

Counting is a necessity in dance notation for it specifies the rhythms and communicates to the reader the exact timing of each section. Unfortunately in routines where there is extensive footwork, our system is inadequate. It has five divisions, here based upon 1 measure of 4/4 music:

(1) The quarter note or single time counts: **1 2 3 4**
(2) The eighth note couplet counts: **1&2&3&4**
(3) The eighth note triplet count: **1&a2&a3&a4&a**
(4) The sixteenth or quadruple count: **1e&a2e&a3e&a4e&a**
(5) The utterance **i** is used before the **e**, thus **1ie&a2ie&a3ie&a4ie&a**

Thus, we are capable of uttering **5** sounds within the beat itself. If the step requires more, for example, Shuffle Cramproll R Heel Drop R & L, Stomp R, and we start on **1** and end on **2,** we would have to express it as $\frac{9}{1\ 2}$ = nine sounds produced, beginning on **1** and ending on **2**.

THE DICTIONARY

ABE KABBIBLE (Scissors)
[4 movements] [a1a2] or [&1&2 counts]

Old vaudeville step, credited to performer Abe Kabbible. Also known as the scissors step (although the scissors step is slightly different) because of the way the legs open and close.

> **TO EXECUTE:**
> Leap R to R, leap L frt R, leap R to R, place L heel on floor to L [a1a2]

NOTE:
Step may be substituted for every leap in this execution.

ABOUT FACE See PIVOT

A CAPPELLA

To sing or dance without the accompaniment of music. To perform in silence. See TACET

ACCELERANDO

A gradual increase in the speed or the tempo of the music.

ACCENT

To put a special emphasis or loudness on a tap or sound, tone, or beat. See DYNAMICS: TAP SOUNDS

ACRO-TAP See STEPS AND STYLES OF TAP DANCE: STYLES AND DANCES

ACROSS THE FLOOR

To practice or perform tap steps or combinations from one side of the room to the other side of the room, or from one corner to the other corner.

AD-LIB

To improvise or to create on the spot with no previous planning.

ADAGE

French for the Italian word adagio. See ADAGIO

ADAGIO

- A series of slow controlled movements following center practice.
- The opening section of a classical pas de deux.

(THE) ADDAMS FAMILY

A 4-measure combination that rhythmically depicts the accents found in "The Addams Family" theme song. (From *The Tap Dance Dictionary* by Mark Knowles)

> **TO EXECUTE:**
> (A) Flap R, L, R, clap hold [a1 a2 a3 & hold 4], reverse (A) 1 M (B) flap R, clap, flap L, clap [&1& 2 &3], flap R, clap, flap L, clap [&4& 5&6], flap ball change R [&7&8]

(THE) ADVANCE
[8 sounds] [a1 a2 a3 a4]

Probably so named because the dancer travels forward or diagonally fwd, thus advancing the original position.

> **To execute:**
> While doing flap R, shuffle ball change L, ball change L bk-move diagonally fwd. [a1a2a3a4]

ADVANCED SOFT SHOE TIME STEP.
See TIME STEP: Advanced Soft Shoe

AERIAL ⚘ (Aerial Turn, Air Turn, Tour en l'air, Aerial Tour)
[w/wo sound]

Steps or movements performed when the body is off the floor and in the air. The following describes a stationary aerial turn. The principles are based on ballet.

> **To execute:**
> Place feet in opening position-parallel, tno, oblique etc., establish the plié, spring into the air, holding legs in desired position-open, crossed, posed, etc. Observe correct body placement and alignment at all times. Head remains frt as long as possible. At peak of elevation, body begins to revolve, head snaps and regains spot to the frt before body has completed the turn. The landing is then accomplished in plié.

Note:
- ✿ If a series of aerials is being executed, the ending of the first is the beginning of the second. Double preparations or double pliés are unnecessary.
- ✿ The landing may be done with tap sounds, such as regular or progressive cramprolls, steps, flaps, heel drops, etc.
- ✿ If double or triple aerials are executed (i.e., if two or three revolutions of the body are completed before landing) the head must snap an identical number of times.

AERIAL BARREL ROLL. See BARREL ROLL:
Aerial; AERIAL

AERIAL CRAMPROLL. See CRAMPROLL:
Aerial; AERIAL

AERIAL DOUBLE PICKUP. See PICKUP:
Double; AERIAL

AERIAL DRUMROLL. See CRAMPROLL:
Aerial; AERIAL

AERIAL HEEL CLICK. See BELLS

AERIAL HEEL ROLL. See CRAMPROLL:
Aerial; AERIAL

AERIAL MILITARY ROLL. See
CRAMPROLL: Aerial; AERIAL

AERIAL SPLIT. See SPLIT: Air

AERIAL SPLIT WING
[4 movements] [&a 1 2 3]

This is in the category of a flash step and is an expression of technique. Literally the name should be wing aerial split.

> **To execute:**
> Beginning in parallel first, plié, execute a double wing, landing in first position, plié, parallel or turned out. Spring into the air and execute a turned out straddle split, feet pointed or flexed (some dancers lean forward, flex the toes and touch them in the split position). Land in a closed plié position.

AERIAL STEP

A term, not a step. Steps or movements that take place in the air (e.g., splits, jumping over the leg, turns, etc.).

AERIAL TOUR. See AERIAL

AERIAL TURN. See AERIAL

AFRO

That which is traceable to having its origin in Africa. The later term became combined with other influences, such as Afro-Cuban, Afro-American, etc. Also pertains to a particular stylization of the hair.

AIR SHUFFLES

A movement that imitates shuffles, but the dancer does not strike the floor. Therefore, the correct action is present, but no sounds are made.

AIR STEP

A step or movement executed in the air. See AERIAL

AIR TAPS

When a step is executed but the taps never hit the floor; the action is present, but there are no sounds created.

AIR TURN. See AERIAL

AIRPLANE ARMS

A position of the arms: when the right arm is diagonally up, the left arm is diagonally down and vice versa.

AIRPLANE CHARLESTON
[1 2 3 4][5 6 7 8 counts]

TO EXECUTE:
Leap L R (foot passé position turned out or parallel),
hop L (AST, snap kick R fwd),
hop L R (foot passé position turned out or parallel),
jazz kick R to second position [1 M] reverse (1) thru (4) [1 M]

NOTE:
Use airplane arms: while one is straight up, the other is straight down, and reverse.

AIRPLANE TURNS. See BARREL ROLLS

AKIMBO. See KIMBO

ALAMO (The Lone Ranger)
[22 sounds] [&a1&a2&a3&4&a5&a6&a7&8]

TO EXECUTE:
Shuffle step, R L R [&a1&a2&a3]
ball change, L R [&4]
shuffle step, L R L [&a5&a6&a7]
scuff R, chug L [&a8]

ALEX'S RIFF
[7 sounds to fit from ct. 8 and end on ct. 1]

Named for dancer/choreographer Alex Romero.

TO EXECUTE:
Heel dig R, spank R, heel drop L [8ie]
heel dig R, spank R, heel drop L [a&a]
stomp R [1]

ALIGNMENT

The relationship of the body segments to each other. Correct vertical alignment occurs when the head is centered over the shoulders, the shoulders over the hips, and the rib cage and the pelvis are held in a neutral position. Finding and maintaining the proper alignment is not only a conscientious and constant procedure, but also a must for good technique and proper execution.

ALTERNATING (Changing)

A term, not a step. It means the act of changing from one foot, hand, etc. position to the other. Those steps that normally transfer wt. aren't usually labeled as alternating (e.g., shuffle step, toe heel, flap ball change, etc.). Those steps originally meant for repetition on one foot only, but that are now changing from foot to foot, are called alternating or changing (e.g., alternating wings, alternating pickups etc.). The term alternating shuffles is misleading as it is not really referring to shuffles but to shuffle steps.

ALTERNATING CRAMPROLLS. See
CRAMPROLL: Alternating

ALTERNATING DOUBLE PICKUPS. See
PICKUP: Alternating

ALTERNATING DRAWBACK. See
DRAWBACK: Alternating

ALTERNATING DRUMROLLS. See
CRAMPROLL: Alternating

ALTERNATING HEEL BEATS

Old term for alternating heel drops. Today, the term
beat connotes no transfer of weight. Theoretically,
one cannot alternate a heel beat, only a heel cramp.

ALTERNATING HEEL CRAMPS. See
ALTERNATING HEEL DROPS

**ALTERNATING HEEL DROPS
(Changing or Alternating Heel Beats, Heel
Cramps, Heel Rolls)
[2 or more sounds] [1 2] or [& 1 counts]**

Standing feet flat on floor, usually in a par position,
wt. fwd, in plié, lift first the R heel and forcibly
lower; then lift L heel and forcibly lower. Continue
in alternate fashion. When done in a continuous even
rhythm, a "rolling" sound is produced (See ROLL). If
the same level is to be maintained, remain in plié. If
a *bouncy* effect is desired, legs may straighten and then
bend with each sound. Alternating heel drops may be
done par, inverted, tno, from side to side, etc. See
HEEL DROPS

NOTE:
Heel beat is an old term and is now classified as not
carrying weight; therefore, one theoretically cannot
execute an alternating heel beat.

ALTERNATING HEEL ROLLS. See
ALTERNATING HEEL DROPS; HEEL DROPS

**ALTERNATING HEEL-TOE DROPS
(Alternating Heel-Toe Cramps,
Heel-Toe Beats)
[2-4 sounds] [a1a2 counts] or
[&1&2 counts]**

May be executed in two ways. Standing feet flat on
floor, usually in a par position, wt. centered.

> TO EXECUTE:
> Raise R heel and lower, then
> raise R toe and lower [&1]
> or [a1]
> Raise R heel and lower,
> raise L heel and lower; raise
> R toe and lower, raise L toe
> and lower [a1a2] or [&1&2]

ALTERNATING MILITARY ROLL. See
CRAMPROLL: Alternating

ALTERNATING PICKUP. See PICKUP:
Alternating

ALTERNATING PULLBACK. See PICKUP:
Alternating

ALTERNATING RATTLES. See
ALTERNATING SHUFFLES

ALTERNATING RIFF. See RIFF: Alternating

ALTERNATING ROLLING RIFFS. See
RIFF: Rolling.

**ALTERNATING SHUFFLES (Alternating
Shuffle Steps, Rattles, Threes, Triples,
Running Shuffles) [6 sounds] [&a1, &a2]**

Traceable to clog dancing.

Walking: The transfer of wt. from shuffle to shuffle
is done by stepping. Therefore, Sh St R & L. See
SHUFFLE: Walking

Running: The transfer of wt. from shuffle to shuffle
is done by leaping. Therefore, Sh R leap R, shuffle
L, leap L. Alternating shuffles can be done ip, fwd,
bkwd, sdwd, turning, etc. See SHUFFLE: Running

ALTERNATING SHUFFLE STEPS. See
ALTERNATING SHUFFLES; SHUFFLES: Running

ALTERNATING THREES (3's). See
ALTERNATING SHUFFLES

ALTERNATING TOE BEATS

Old term for alternating toe drops. Today, the term
beat connotes that there is no transfer of weight; one
theoretically cannot alternate a toe beat, only a toe
cramp.

ALTERNATING TOE CRAMPS. See
ALTERNATING TOE DROPS

**ALTERNATING TOE DROPS
(Alternating Toe Beats, Toe Cramps,
Toe Rolls)
[any number of sounds][a1a2] [&1&2]**

Stand with feet flat on floor, par usually in plié, wt.
centered. Lift and flex R toe, R heel remaining on
floor (wt. on L foot and/or R heel), forcibly lower R
toe. Repeat action on L. To maintain a level, remain
in plié, or if a *bouncy* effect is desired, legs may be

straightened and bent with each toe drop. Toe drop may be found in basic, elementary steps such as heel toe; but often it is involved in advanced work as a substitute for heel drop. Frequently, toe drops are used as an exercise to lengthen and strengthen the long cord or tendon that lies in the frt part of the leg. The control and loudness of toe drops is much more difficult than that of heel drops because the wt. is tipped slightly bkwd and the frt tendon is quite weak unless it is exercised often.

NOTE:
The term toe beat is no longer used in place of alternating toe drops, as beat connotes that no weight change takes place; therefore, alternating the toes is impossible.

ALTERNATING TOE-HEEL BEATS. See
ALTERNATING TOE-HEEL DROPS

ALTERNATING TOE-HEEL CRAMPS.
See ALTERNATING TOE-HEEL DROPS

ALTERNATING TOE-HEEL DROPS (ALTERNATING: TOE-HEEL CRAMPS, TOE-HEEL BEATS)
[2-4 sounds] [a1a2] OR [&1&2]

May be executed in 2 ways. Standing with the feet flat on floor, usually in par position, wt. centered. This step has the same components as a cramproll or a side travel.

TO EXECUTE:
• Lift R toe and lower, L toe and lower, R heel and lower, L heel and lower
[a1a2][&1&2]
    OR
• Lift R toe and lower, R heel and lower and reverse
[a1a2] [&1&2]

NOTE:
The term Toe Heel Beat is incorrectly used in this case, as Beat infers no weight transfer; but through constant usage it has remained in the tap vocabulary.

ALTERNATING TOE ROLLS

Drop R toe, then L toe in rapid succession and in a steady rhythm, thus creating a rolling sound.

ALTERNATING TRIPLES. See
ALTERNATING SHUFFLES

ALTERNATING WINGS. See WING:
Alternating

AMALGAMATED (Combined)

A term, not a step. Amalgamated, in dance, literally means the combining of one step with another step to form a third or new step, e.g., shuffle plus step = shuffle step.

In the very beginning of tap, the number of known steps was so few that they were listed numerically according to the number of sounds they contained.

One	= Step
Two	= Shuffle
Three	= Shuffle step
Four	= Shuffle ball change (or Hop Shuffle Step or Shuffle Hop Step)
Five	= Step shuffle ball change or hop shuffle step
Six	= Flap shuffle ball change or running shuffle R and L.

NOTE:
Some sources differ. The first term chosen is the one most referenced.

AMERICAN ROLL (Patricola)
[32 sounds] [8 &a1 a2 a3 4&a5 a6 a7 8&a1 a2 a3 a4 a5 a6 a7]

A short military combination.

TO EXECUTE:
(A) Hop shuffle, step R, X'd frt L, flap L to L (leaving R heel on floor), flip R toe up, spank step R to L [8 &a1 a2 a3]
reverse (A) [4&a5 a6 a7]
repeat (A) [8&a1 a2 a3]
(B) flap L to L, flap R frt L (two times) [a4 a5 a6 a7]

ANACRUSIS

In music, it refers to an unaccented beat, or the beginning of a movement.

ANN MILLER BREAK
[8 sounds] [1 2 3 &4&5 6 7]

TO EXECUTE:
Stamp R fwd [1], step L back [2], stamp R fwd [3], shuffle L ball change L R; (prep.) [&4&5], spot turn R to R [6], lunge L to L [7]

ANN MILLER STEP
[25 sounds] [1 2 3 &4& 5&6 &7 &8 & 1 2 3 &4& 5&6 7 8]

TO EXECUTE:
Stomp R (stomp) beside L [1], step R to R [2], step L X back R (back) [3], (brush heel step) brush R back, heel drop L, step R or drawback [&4&], (brush heel step) brush L back, heel drop R, step L or drawback [5&6], (back flap) back flap R [&7], (shuffle) shuffle L [&8], (heel) heel drop R [&], (step) step L back [1], (stamp) stamp R fwd [2], (stamp) stamp L in place [3], (brush heel step) brush R back, heel drop L, step R or drawback [&4&], (brush heel step) brush L back, heel drop R, step L or drawback [5&6], (stamp) stamp R fwd [7], (stamp) stamp L fwd [8]

(THE) APOLLO
[6 sounds] [1a2&a3]

TO EXECUTE:
Riffle R (brush R, scuffle, spank R), step R, heel drop R, toe drop R

APPLE JACK
A social and fad dance of the 1940s that involved the twisting of a knee inward then outward.

ARABESQUE ⚲
Considered one of the basic poses in ballet. While standing on one leg, which may be straight or in demi-plié, the other is extended backward at right angles to the body. One should adhere to the balletic principles as precisely as possible, unless the choreography or the execution of the tap sounds requires another solution. Arabesque turns may be done w/wo sound, in place, moving in a straight line or patterns, etc. and rendered on the R or the L as an inside or outside pirouette.

ARABESQUE TURN ⚲
While holding the arabesque position execute a turn or turns on the supporting leg. They maybe en dehors (outside) or en dedans (inside) and w/wo sounds. See ARABESQUE

ARCHED
A term, position, or movement; not a step. Literally means bent over. Arched could refer to the back, feet, the total curve of the body, etc.

ARCHED BARREL ROLL. See BARREL ROLL: Arched

ARCHED RENVERSÉ. See RENVERSÉ: Arched

ARMING
Two partners face each other: Run 2 steps toward each other, hook R arms and run 4 steps around clockwise, release arms and run 2 steps backward to their starting position.

AROUND THE WORLD. See COFFEE GRIND

ARSIS
The weak beat, the unaccented beat of a measure or the count of 2.

ASSEMBLÉ ⚲
[w/wo sound]
A joining together or assembling of the legs. Based on balletic principles, it was used extensively in classical tap, at which time sounds were added, primarily to the beginning, such as brush etc., or to the landing. Usually in the form of a progressive cramproll. See CRAMPROLL: Progressive

TO EXECUTE:
Slide working leg along the floor as far as it can go, as it lifts press off the floor with the supporting leg, both feet and legs return to the floor ast, landing in 5th position. Landing may be done with sounds such as cramproll, toe heel, etc.

ASSEMBLÉ CRAMPROLL. See CRAMPROLL: Assemblé

AT THE BARRE. See BARRE

À TERRE

A ballet term that literally means on the ground. Designates that the working foot is grounded and/or executes its movements or sounds on the ground, rather than being lifted in the air.

ATTITUDE
[w/wo sound]

A ballet pose in which one is standing on one leg with the other raised in the back at a 90-degree angle to the floor and usually in a turned out position. The knee of the working leg is raised higher than the foot. The supporting foot may be flat, in relevé, plié or r/p. Choreographically, the raised leg and knee may be inverted, tno, par to floor, behind body, to side or in frt of body. Attitude may be thought of as a *broken* line, and arabesque a *straight* line.

ATTITUDE TURN

- ✪ Turns that may be done in place, traveling in a straight line or patterns, with or without sound, inside or outside, inside/outside, R or L. See TURNS

- ✪ Being that attitude is a three dimensional position and has depth as well as length and width, many interesting and changing designs can be obtained (e.g., by tilting the axis to the R when the L is in the attitude position, with the L arm high, a spiral, off-center feeling is created). Many other designs can be found with a little experimentation.

- ✪ If there are tap sounds to be made then it is usually accomplished on the supporting foot as the turn is begun. Steps such as flap, toe heel, shuffle step, can be used.

B. S. CHORUS

A traditional chorus routine, usually executed as a background for tap soloists. This was a short routine, created in the 1920s and performed by the ladies of the chorus as a backup dance behind a star act. Many times the girls in the chorus were not very proficient dancers, so the steps were relatively simple, consisting of basic tap sounds and dance movements. The chorus girls were informed that the B.S. stood for boy scouts. In the 1920s and 1930s, chorus girls all over the U.S. had learned these movements and if they couldn't do them, they could certainly fake them. The routine consisted of a standard 32 measures, divided into 4 steps of 8 measures each: 8 M of a X step' 8 M of a cross over step, 8 M of buck and wing and 4 bars of over the tops, followed by 4 M of through the trenches, and a finish of a 2 M break of "shave and a hair cut—two bits."

The routine could be executed as sheer movement or include tap sounds depending on the proficiency of the dancers and/or the dance director. Thus, because each B. S. Chorus was based on a loose formula, it took on a different complexity and look. The basic structure is described in the following steps:

Step 1: 8 M of a stomp time step (not faked).

Step 2: A crossover step of 8M in which the legs crossed over each other in some fashion.

Step 3: 8 M of a buck and wing with pickups.

Step 4: 8 M of a flash step (trenches, over the tops, big movements . . .).

The traditional B. S. chorus often followed a chorus of shim sham. The following information was presented by Rosemarie DeLutis Boyden of Mansfield, Massachusetts, as taught to her by the late Leon Collins, jazz tap artist and musician.

TO EXECUTE:
Step 1: [32 counts]
6 buck (stomp) time steps, alternating feet, begin w/ R, stomp R, spank R, hop L, step R, flap L, step R [8 & 1 2 &3 &], 6 X's all tog. alternating [6 M], break: spank R, heel drop L, step R Heel [& 1 &], dig L, Spank L, hop R, step L, shuffle R [2 & 3 4 &5], leap R (w/wo a pickup) [6 &a], Step L, Hop L, Heel Dig R [7 & 8] [2 M]
Step 2: [32 counts]
(A) Spank R, heel drop L, shuffle step R [& 1 &a 2], spank step L, frt R, shuffle R, heel drop L [&3 &4 &], step R, Xd frt L, spank L, heel drop R [5 & 6], flap L, ball R, stomp L [&7 & 8], reverse (A) [2 M], repeat (A) through count 7, add heel drop L, heel dig R [& 8], repeat 2 M break of step I [2 M]

B. S. CHORUS (continued)

Step 3: [32 counts]
(A) Hop L, shuffle step R, brush L to 2, single pickup R [8 &a1 & hold 2 &3], spank step L, frt R, shuffle R, alternating pickup (land R) [&4 5& a6], step R, Xd frt L, spank L, heel drop R [5 & 6], shuffle L, alternating pickup (land R) [7&] [2 M], repeat (A) 2 more times [4 M], after last set of (A) add hop or heel dig R
(B) Repeat 2 M break of step I [2 M],
Step 4:
[32 counts] [Heading Home]
(A) Lunge fwd R, step L, shuffle ball change R [8 1 &2 &3], Repeat (A), Step fwd R [4 5 &6 &7 8] [2 M]
(B) Toe tap L bk R, step bk L, spank R, hop L, step R [1 2 & 3 &], spank L, hop R, step L, step R, step L [4 & 5 6 7] [2 M]
Repeat step IV but end with feet par 1st position, demi-plié

NOTE:
The B. S. Chorus also had a freeze chorus, usually the second chorus, where the dancers freeze on the breaks.

BACK A DOUBLE
[4 sounds] [1 2 3 4]

Old English term, originally derived from social dancing. It means to execute four even running steps to the rear as you move backward.

BACK BRUSH. See SPANK STEP

BACK BRUSH STEP. See SPANK STEP

BACK DROP/BACKDROP

Dance: Often referred to as a hinge: standing in a wide second position, tno, oblique, parallel, etc., slowly incline the body backward, hinging from the knees and supporting the weight in the thighs. The body remains in a straight line, from knees to head (choreographically, an arch or twisting may take place before the conclusion, but such a movement is a deviation from the normal).This is like the posture assumed when going beneath a limbo bar or pole. The back drop may end on the floor, supported by one or both hands or remain suspended in the air.

Theater: A scenic backdrop is a hanging unit of cloth, normally muslin or canvas, upon which is depicted a scene or atmospheric painting. After the drop design has been completed, battens of pipe or wood are sown into both ends to keep the cloth from wrinkling. In some cases, standing units may be used as well.

BACK ESSENCE. See ESSENCE

BACK FIVE
[5 sounds] [1 & 2 & 3]

Literally a step bkwd, followed by a back Irish crossing.

TO EXECUTE:
Step R to back, shuffle hop step L Xd bk R [1 & 2 & 3]

BACK FLAP. See SPANK STEP

BACK FLAP HEEL. See SPANK TOE HEEL

BACK FLAP HEEL HEEL. See SPANK STEP HEEL HEEL

BACK-FRONT
Old term for ball change. See BALL CHANGE

BACK HEEL BRUSH. See SCUFF

BACK HITCH KICK. See HITCH KICK: Back

BACK IRISH. See IRISH: Back

BACK KICK:
[1 2 3 4]

An eccentric movement, used in character and legomania dancing. Slightly misnamed as the kick is literally to the side, not to the back.

TO EXECUTE:
Step R frt L [1]
plié R and lift L leg to side and bend L [2]
turn L knee inwd to R and aim it dnwd twd floor [3]
kick L to L, straighten L leg, keeping L knee down twd floor, ast R leg may remain bent or be straightened [4]

BACK RALPH. See SPANK TOE HEEL

BACK RATTLE

Rattle is the old term for shuffle. A back rattle describes a shuffle placed in a bkwd pos. to the supporting leg. See SHUFFLE: Back Shuffle

BACK RIFF. See RIFF: Back Riff

BACK SCUFF. See SCUFF

BACK SCUFFLE
[2 sounds] [&1]

Raise working leg in fwd pos., swing leg bkwd, striking bk edge of heel in passing, brush R fwd.

BACK SLAP

Old term for bkwd slap or a spank step. Carries no weight.

BACK SLAP HEEL

Old term for spank step heel. See SLAP HEEL

BACK STEP
[17 sounds] [&a1 &2 &a3 &4 &5& hold 6 &7 &8]

TO EXECUTE:
Shuffle step R, ball change R bk L [&a1 &2], shuffle step L, ball change L bk R [&a3 &4], chug L 3 ball changes (R and L) [&5 hold 6], moving backward [&7 &8]

BACK STEPPING

Associated with Highland dancing, it consists of one foot starting in front in a passé position. The foot is then transferred to the back of the leg and with a springing movement, slides down the leg until it takes weight, while simultaneously lifting the other foot to a passé position in front.

BACK TAP

✺ A tap that is executed in a backward direction.

✺ A tap that is done in the back of the supporting foot.

✺ Tap may be considered a generalized term for a tap sound, but more specifically it deals with the ball or toe of the foot.

BACK TAP STEP

Old term for spank step.

BACK TO THE WOODS
[5 sounds] [&1&a2]

A very old term. This step later became a Cincinnati by changing the hop to a heel drop or chug.

TO EXECUTE:
Spank bk R, hop L, shuffle step bk R [&1&a2]

BACK TWO (2)

Old term for a back shuffle. See SHUFFLE: Back

BACKSTAGE. See DANCERS GUIDE TO THEATER TERMINOLOGY

BACKWARD BRUSH. See SPANK

BACKWARD RIFF. See RIFF: Back

BACKWARD TAP. See SPANK

BALANCÉ ⚹
[2 sounds] [1 2]

Tap uses the basic feeling and structure (Step R to R, L bk R, R to R) of the ballet balancé as a movement pattern for toe heels, flaps, flap heel, etc.

TO EXECUTE:
Step forward on the ball of one foot, then backward on the ball of the other

**BALL (Ball Tap, Ball Touch, Ball Step)
[w/wo sound] [1] or [&]**

The part of the foot and the shoe upon which the tap is placed. Ball is executed by:

- ✪ Placing the ball of the foot on the floor, the heel of that foot is raised, w/wo wt., w/wo sound.
- ✪ Striking the ball of the foot on the floor, w/wo wt., w/wo sound.
- ✪ Ball may be done in any direction or position, w/wo wt, w/wo sound.
- ✪ Some feel the term step is interchangeable with the term ball. This is correct only if there is a transfer of wt. and the step is on the ball of the foot.

BALL BEAT. See TOE DROP

BALL BEAT DOWN

Old term for toe drop. See TOE DROP

**BALL BEAT SWIVEL
[w/wo sound] [1 or 2 sounds]**

Using the heel of the working foot as a pivot point, lift the ball of the working foot and drop it toward the outside, then twd the inside. Usually done on the beat of the music.

BALL BRUSH. See BRUSH

**BALL CHANGE (Back- Front, Ball Stamp Change, Back- Front, Shift(s), Toe Change, Toe Down)
[2 sounds] [a1][&1]**

Commonly used step in tap dancing, done in many forms.

> TO EXECUTE:
> Step R bkwd; on ball of R. step fwd on L, either on the flat of the L or the ball of the L

Implies a quick transfer of wt., w/ accent on the last foot. May be done in any pos. of the feet: opened, xd., par, tno, tni, obl, in relevé, plié, r/p, flatfooted; done ip or traveling frt, sdwd, bkwd, or turning. Many times it was combined with other steps to form new steps such as shuffle ball change, flap ball change, step ball change, etc.

**BALL CHANGE DOUBLE (Pitter Patter)
[4 sounds] [a1a2]**

Execute two ball changes in succession; usually done lightly and on the balls of the feet. Often used in soft shoe routines.

BALL CRAMP. See TOE DROP

BALL DIG. See DIG

BALL DROP. See TOE DROP

BALL HEEL. See TOE HEEL

BALL HEEL HEEL. See TOE HEEL HEEL

BALL JAB. See DIG

**BALL LIFT
[1 sound] [&]**

Form of a toe drop. A ball lift is put after the toe drop and uses the heel as a pivot point while raising the sole of the working foot. See TOE DROP

BALL-OF-FOOT STRUT. See SUGARFOOT

BALL ROLLS

Fast toe drops done alternately and quickly.

BALL STAMP. See BALL CHANGE

BALL STAMP CHANGE

Old term for ball change. Very accurate physically, but rhythmically does not fit the action. See BALL CHANGE

BALL STEP. See TAP STEP

BALL TAP. See BALL

BALL TAP QUADRUPLE

Executing four toe drops alternately (e.g., R L R L). Ball tap is a step but the number of times it is executed depends on its usage and purpose.

BALL TOUCH. See BALL

BALLET TAP (Classical Tap)

Classical and ballet tap differ slightly: the former is always performed to classical music, and with a classical style, while the latter may be performed to lyrical and other styles of music. Both are combinations of ballet and tap. See *STEPS AND STYLES OF TAP DANCE.*

BALLIN' THE JACK (Georgia Grind, The Mess Around)

A popular social dance that originated in the south among the African-American population. In the basic movement the hands were placed on the knees as they swung from side to side; pelvic rotations were also used.

BALLON ⚊ (Elevation)

A descriptive ballet term, meaning to spring lightly, with bounce, from the floor, and pause a moment in the air before returning to the floor ending in plié.

BALTIMORE BUZZ

A movement.

> TO EXECUTE:
> Step on one foot; slide the other foot to it and relevé/plié; remain on the balls of the feet with knees bent and hips swinging to the side and direction of the first foot

BAMBALINA

Old term for traveling time step. A routine created by Eddie Rector, danced to a song called "bambalina," contained a traveling time step; thus, at that time,' "bambalina" became the name for all traveling time steps. Today, there are many different kinds of these time steps.

BAMBOULA

A fast, frenzied, flatfooted dance of African-American origin. Dancers tie bells or pieces of metal around their ankles and/or waists to produce sounds.

BANDY TURN
[2 movements] [1 2]

> TO EXECUTE:
> With weight on L, step frt of L (may be pigeon-toed or turned out [1], turn to L, executing 1/2 turn to L, end facing back [2]

BANDY TWIST (Denby)
[6 sounds] [1&2&34]

A step popularized by Jim Denby that included an upper-body twist. It is traceable to the banda, a form of the African shake dance.

> TO EXECUTE:
> Step R to R, shuffle ball change L bk R, arms to R, execute 1/2 turn to R, Step L to L (arms to L) [1 &2&3 4], repeat to face frt

BAR (Measure)

A unit of time in music contained between 2 vertical lines (bar lines) that intersect the 5 horizontal staff lines.

BARN DANCE

- ✿ Those dances that were held in barns for community recreation.
- ✿ A clog dance performed by a couple. Many times considered sinful because of the use of body contact.

BARNYARD SHUFFLE
[31 sounds] [1&a2 3&a4 5 &6 &a7 e&a8]

> TO EXECUTE:
> (A) Step L, shuffle step R [1&a2], step L, shuffle step R [3&a4], step L, 3 shuffle steps R, L [5 &6 &a7], flap R and L [e&a8]
> (B) Scrape outside edge of R [1], spank step R bk to L foot [&2]
> Reverse (B), Repeat (B), Reverse (B) [3&4 5&6 7&8]

BARRE

- ✿ The ballet or exercise barre (rail) in a dance studio or practice room where exercises are performed.
- ✿ The set of exercises done at the barre (i.e., barre work).

BARREL ROLLS (Windmill Turns, Airplane Turns)
[w/wo sound] [any number counts]

GENERAL DESCRIPTION

A particular type of pirouette, derived from a Spanish turn and characterized by using the arms in a *windmill* or *airplanelike* fashion. When one arm is up (palm out) the other arm is down (palm facing body). The *up* arm is by the ear and the *down* arm is by the thigh.

BARREL ROLLS (continued)

NOTE:

Both arms are never up or down together. The audience sees first one arm up, then the other. Barrel rolls may be executed inside or outside, R or L, single, double, triple, etc., with or without sounds, stationary or traveling or as an air turn.

The following is a basic description of the various body levels and position of the legs:

- **Upright:** Often referred to as a high barrel roll. Remaining upright is the usual manner of execution.

- **Arched:** The body starts in an inclined, flat back position and as the turn is executed, the head continues to spot frt, the back arches and the head drops backward to hold on to the spot. It is also possible to spot the floor, rather than frt, which creates a totally different look. As the body faces frt, it may remain inclined fwd or straight.

- **Inclined:** The body leans fwd in a flat-back position; the degree of the incline may vary. The body may retain the incline throughout, thereby maintaining the same relationship to the floor but with no arch, or the turn may begin on the incline and end in an upright position. *Regardless of the level chosen, the main motivation of the turn is, or appears to the audience to be, the arms.*

- **The Legs**
  (a) The raised leg is normally in a parallel Passé position, with the pointed foot held snugly against the side of the supporting leg. However, the passé may be turned out as well.
  (b) The toes of the working leg may also be hooked around the supporting leg.

GENERAL RULES FOR BARREL ROLLS

- When executing a traveling barrel roll, use a traveling spot (e.g., use an imaginary eye-level line in the frt), change the spot on each turn to a new spot further to one's L on R outside turns and when traveling to the left further to ones R on L outside. See SPOTTING: Traveling

- An outside R barrel roll (en dehors), turns bkwd to the R with the R foot being in passé, while the inside R barrel roll (en dedans) turns fwd and twd the R with the L leg in passé. rev. for L.

- Whether the barrel roll is inside R or outside R- the R arm goes up first. Reverse for L.

- The arms may be used in 2 different ways. It is assumed in this example that the ct. is 1&2.
  (a) R arm up on 1 (turn is begun), *R arm stays up* on & (turn in progress), L arm up, 2

(as turn is finishing). This will create a windmill effect.
  (b) R arm up on 1 (turn is begun), *arms go to second on & (turn in progress), L arm up on 2 (as turn is finishing). This will create an airplane effect.*

- The placement of the feet is crucial in the accuracy and finishing of a barrel roll: In an outside R traveling barrel roll, which begins on sr, upon the completion of the turn, as the first foot (R) is placed down, the second foot (L) *must step to the L and to 2nd, parallel and in line with the first (R) foot.* This keeps the line of travel straight and gets you there. However, if the barrel turn being executed is a R stationary turn, as the turn is being completed *the L then the R foot must step to a wide 2nd, in the exact place in which they started.*

STATIONARY BARREL ROLLS

Right Outside

[En dehors] [w/wo sound]
Turn will be executed on the L foot while turning backward to the R. Begin in 2nd position plié, with arms to 3rd, 2nd etc. As the turn begins, R arm swings up, palm out, L arm down, palm facing body; head spots frt, R knee to par Passé. As body turns and head snaps to regain spot, L arm goes up and R goes down, complete turn and step R to R in plié position or step R to R and L to L into plié position. The feet must always return to the exact spot in which they started. Reverse all of the above explanation if executing a L outside barrel roll.

BARREL ROLLS

Below are listed some tap sounds that might be added to the turn:

> **TO EXECUTE:**
> Tap R bk L, as the body turns backward to R; stamp R&L on ending plié [1&2] Spank R bk, drop L heel on turn back. End with toe heel R and step L to L [a1&a2]

OTHER STATIONARY BARREL ROLLS

Pump Barrel Roll

These are stationary turns and may be done inside or outside, following the rules as stated above. To execute, stand w/feet obl or to in 2nd. pos. plié. When beg. turn, relevé. Upon completion of turn, plié and sharply lower heel of supporting leg. Repeat. This is why it is called a pump turn, because the supporting leg pumps up and down. The arms and the plié relevé are the power for the turn.

Cramproll Barrel Rolls

May be done stationary or traveling. Execute a R outside pump barrel roll ending each turn in a fake cramproll, (i.e., ball R, heel drop R, heel drop L [1 &a2] or heel drop L, ball R, heel drop R and L [1 &a2]). The turn can also end in a regular cramproll (e.g., ball R, ball L, heel drop R, heel drop L. [1e&a2]). Supporting leg may remain in plié if desired. Arms are as above.

Riff Barrel Roll

[5] [a1&a2]

Refers to barrel rolls which begin, contain or end in a riff, for example, for R outside: spank R, heel drop L, R arm up, L arm down; snap head; as body faces frt, L arm up, R arm down, ast execute a 3-ct. riff R (ball R, scuff R, heel drop L). R foot ends in air. [&1a2] Repeat.

Right Inside

[En dedans] [w/wo sound]

Turn will be executed on the R foot while turning forward to the R. Begin in 2nd position plié, with the arms in 3rd, 2nd, etc. As the turn begins, R arm swings up, palm out, L arm down, palm facing body, head spots frt L knee to par passé. As body turns and head snaps to regain the spot, L arm goes up and R goes down, complete turn and step L to L in plié position or Step L to L and R to R into plié position. The feet must always return to the exact spot in which they started. Reverse all of the above information if executing a L inside barrel roll.

Below are listed some tap sounds that might be added to the turn.

> **To execute:**
> Tap L bk R, as body turns to R. End with stamp L and R in 2nd pos. plié [1&2]
> Turn on R, drop R heel, face frt and toe heel L to L and step R to R in 2nd pos. plié [1&a2]

Traveling Barrel Rolls

Right Outside

[En dehors] [w/wo sound]

If traveling in a straight line, begin at sr. Plié in 2nd position. Execute in the same manner as a R outside stationary barrel roll, but you must (1) step R and L into the ending plié and (2) on the step R, you must avoid stepping directly under yourself-Instead, step slightly to your L. ast step L to L, ending in 2nd

position plié with feet on a straight line with each other. You have now moved to the L and the feet are on a straight line with each other. The R foot ends the turn and keeps it facing the frt, while the L foots gains distance twd the L. Thus, after a series of turns, one will end on sl.

Note:

○ On all traveling outside barrel rolls, it is important to use a traveling spot, one which will remain on the same imaginary line, but will change continuously twd the line of travel. See SPOTTING: Traveling

○ Reverse the explanation for all L outside traveling barrel rolls

Below are some tap sounds that might be added to the turn.

> **To execute:**
> Spank bk R., toe tap bk R, stamp R and L on ending [&1&2]
> Heel drop L on turn bk R toe heel R and step L on ending [1&a2]

Note:

Barrel roll arms may be used with footwork used in any traveling turn.

Aerial Barrel Roll
[w/wo sound]

These are usually performed as an outside barrel roll (see general rules for barrel rolls) but may also be done as an inside turn. **See also Aerial**

> **To execute:**
> A R outside beg. at R side (for a str. line to L side). Arms prep. to L, body inclined fwd; swing arms down and through to R, raise R arm up as L arm goes down; ast raise R foot off floor, R knee high and par frt, snap head, turn, change arms and leap onto R foot, pulling L arm up, L knee high; leap L to L. Repeat. Spot is frt, ejection of knee in air, pull of arms and snapping of head, all motivate the turn.

BARREL ROLLS (continued)

NOTE:

As R leg is descending, lift L leg high in air, so that body remains airborne

Right Inside

[En dedans] [w/wo sounds]

If traveling in a straight line, begin on sl; Plié 2nd position. Execute in same manner as stationary R inside barrel roll, but you must (1) step L and R into the ending plié with feet on a straight line to each other and (2) see that each turn progresses twd sr, culminating in a straight line crossing of the stage from L to R.

Listed below are some tap sounds that might be added to the turn:

TO EXECUTE:

• Spank bk L, toe tap L bk on beg. of turn, turn ending with stamp L and R, turn to R [a1&2]
• Heel drop R as you turn R, toe heel L and step R in plié ending. [1e&a2]

NOTE:

✪ On all traveling inside barrel rolls, it is important to use a traveling spot. See SPOTTING: Traveling

✪ Reverse the explanation for all L inside traveling barrel rolls.

BARTLETT BREAK

[31 sounds] [&a1 e&a 2e &a3e &e4 e& a5e&a 6e& 7ea &a8]

Named for the dancer Bill Bartlett.
From The Tap Dance Dictionary by Mark Knowles, 1998.

TO EXECUTE:

(A) Heel dig R, spank R heel drop L [&a1], flap R, heel drop L [e&a], repeat (A) [2e &a3e]
(B) Heel drop R, spank bk L, heel drop R [&e4], toe tap R bk L heel drop R [e&], flap L, heel drop R and L, spank R [a5e&a], heel drop, tap R bk L, heel drop L [6e&], 6 count riff R [7ea&a8]

BASIC (STANDARD) BREAK. See BREAK: Standard

BASIC (STANDARD) TIME STEP. See TIME STEP: Standard

BATTEMENT ⚲ (Battement Kick) [w/wo sound]

Literally, "beating." There are two types of Battements, both derived from the ballet field, –grande (grands) and petits. The former infers a large beating of the leg originating from the hip. The later, which is inclusive of frappés, dégagé, etc. is a much smaller movement involving the calves. All may be used in conjunction with nerve brushes, taps, etc. on the outgoing movement where the foot disengages from the floor.

BATTEMENT KICK ⚲

Old term for battement.

BATTEMENT TENDU ⚲ [w/wo sound]

A term from ballet, is actually the beginning and end of a grand battement and literally means battement stretched. The working foot moves from a closed position to an open one without lifting the great toe from the floor. When the foot has reached its farthest point, it retraces its path to a closed position. Tap sounds are possible on both the beginning and the end of the movement.

BEAT

Dance:

✪ Any movement where one leg beats another or where both legs are beaten together.

✪ Old English term meaning to make a tap sound but with no weight transfer (e.g., execute a toe drop R with the weight remaining on the L foot). It was the opposite term from cramp, meaning when executing the toe drop R, the wt. remains on the R.

Music:

A steady rhythmic pulsation much like the beating of a heart or the ticking of a clock that in music is a unit of measure.

BEES KNEES

A favorite movement of the Charleston, derived from a version of the patting juba. Knees are bent, body is bent over the knees and both are open to the sides. With body leaning front, put R hand on R knee and L hand on L knee. Draw knees together and switch hands, R hand on L knee and L hand on R knee. Hands are crossed. Then open knee and switch R hand on R knee and L on L knee. Now back to original position.

BELL CRAMPROLL
[6 sounds] [1 2 a & a3]

Usually done in waltz rhythm, often used in eccentric routines or waltz clogs.

> TO EXECUTE:
>
> Step R frt L, plié, ast raise L to L with leg bent, while in the air, bend both legs and click heels tog. Body inclines to the R, L foot flicks off and L leg reaches up higher, land on R in plié, ip or R Xd frt L, ball L to L drop R and L heels to repeat or L and R heels to reverse.

BELL CUT. See BELLS

BELL KICK. See BELLS

BELLS (Aerial Heel Click, Bell Cut, Bell Kick, Bell Step)
[w/wo sound]

Traceable to prevaudeville. Often used in eccentric routines. Bells are a character form of cabriole. See CABRIOLE

> TO EXECUTE:
>
> Step R frt L, plié, raise L to L, with L knee bent, spring into the air, and click heels tog. in air. Body describes a slanted line, knees are well bent and tno, feet may be flexed. L foot flicks off and L leg reaches up higher; land on R in plié IP or R X'd. frt L [1&a2]. Reverse

The step, when alternated from side to side, resembles the tolling of a bell, whence it receives its name.

BELL STEP. See BELLS

BELLY ROLL

Rippling movements of the body from the chest to the pelvis; used in many forms of dance, of primitive origin. Used much later in burlesque.

BICYCLE
[13 sounds] [&a1 &2 &a3 &4 5 &6]

> TO EXECUTE:
>
> Shuffle step R, ball change L bk R [&a1 &2], shuffle step L, ball change R bk L [&a3 &4], leap flatfooted onto R, with leg to toe bk and straight (lean fwd) [5], scuff L, swing L leg fwd and extended frt [&], chug R, bend L leg par with shin perpendicular to the floor [6]

BIG APPLE

Popular dance craze of the 1930s, a combination of several fad dances of the era such as truckin', the Suzi-Q, etc.

BIG CIRCLE DANCE

A clog dance where the dancers begin in a circle, break off into couples, then come back to the circle.

BIG FINISH (Flash Ending, Flash Finish)

The last portion of a tap routine, usually the final 4 to 8 M, filled with flashy steps or tricks to bring the routine to a conclusion, hoping for a huge ovation.

(THE) BILL
[20 sounds] [&a1 &2 &a3 &4 &a5 &6&a 7&8]

(From *The Tap Dance Dictionary* by Mark Knowles)

> TO EXECUTE:
>
> (A) Shuffle step R, ball change L bk R [&a1 &2], reverse (A) [&a3 &4]
>
> (B) shuffle R, (swing L bk), chug fwd L [&a5], toe jab R bk L, step R, shuffle L [&6&a], chug R, toe jab L bk R, step L [7&8]

BILL ROBINSON BREAK. See BREAKS: Bill Robinson

BILL ROBINSON STEP
[10 sounds] [1&a2&a3&a4]

TO EXECUTE:

With hands on the hips, feet
slightly turned out and on
the balls of the feet:
St R to R, ast twist lower
body to R, click L heel to R
heel, drop R heel [1&a]
St L to L, ast twist lower
body to L, click R heel to L
heel, drop L heel [2&a]
St R to R, ast twist lower
body to R, click L heel to R
heel, drop R heel [3&a]
St L to L [4]

BILL ROBINSON CROSSING STEP
[14 sounds] [8& 1 &a2 &3 &4 &5 6 7]

Usually stylized with both hands on hips and elbows
out. Executed while high on the balls of the feet.

TO EXECUTE:

Shuffle R [8&], hop L [1],
shuffle R, step R back L
[&a2], flap L to L [&3],
shuffle R, hop L, step R X
frt R or front irish [&4&5],
heel drop R [6], toe tap L to
L and look over L shoulder
[7], reverse 8-7 [8-7]

BING'S DRUM RIFF
[20 sounds] [&a1 &2 &a3 &4 &a5 &6 &a7&8]

TO EXECUTE:

(A) Shuffle step R, ball
change L bk R [&a1
&2], reverse (A) [&a3
&4]

(B) shuffle R, (swing R bk),
chug L [&a5], toe tap R
bk L, step R [&6],
reverse (B) [&a7&8]

BIRDIE IN THE CAGE

A section of the Kentucky running set in which the
dancers run in a circle to the left while the woman in
the center spins to the right. Then the caller shouts
"bird hop out, crow (or owl) hop in." The woman
joins the circle, which is running to the left while the
male is in the center spinning to the right.

BIRMINGHAM BREAKDOWN
(Cincinnati Breakdown)

Standing in 2nd position, Spring into the air and land
on one or both knees. Rise from the knees with a
series of short, jerky movements.

BLACK BOTTOM

Dance craze of 1926 that quickly replaced the
Charleston and became a popular stage dance. See
STEPS AND STYLES OF TAP DANCE: *Styles and Dances*

BLACK-FACED

White minstrels who used burnt cork to blacken their
faces; thus, white minstrelsy was sometimes referred
to as black-faced minstrelsy.

BLEKING STEP
**[10 sounds] [a1 hold 2 a3 hold 4 a5 a6 a7
hold 8]**

TO EXECUTE:

Hop R-heel dig L-hold [a1
hold 2], leap L-heel dig R-
hold [a3 hold 4], leap R-heel
dig L [a5], leap L-heel dig R
[a6], leap R-heel dig L [a7
hold 8]

BLUES

A style of music made popular among plantation
slaves of the south, expressing their melancholy life
and work. Originally used to send messages to each
other through song.

BODY MUSIC

Patting and slapping the body, clapping or making
rhythms with the feet.

BODY PLACEMENT. See PLACEMENT

BODY ROLLS

Borrowed from the modern dance and jazz worlds.
An isolated, but smooth, rolling movement that starts
at the knees and continues through the thighs, pelvis,
rib cage, and head, or it may begin from the top and
move downward. It demands control of each body
section individually with a visual look of a smooth
wave or roll.

BOJANGLES

Bill Robinson received the name Bojangles in the 1920s because of his wonderfully clear and controlled sounds and marvelous rhythms. Literally, a "Bojangle" is one who creates rhythms while playing the bones. See BONE JANGLER

BOJANGLES BREAK. See TIME STEP: Bojangles Break

BOJANGLES TIME STEP. See TIME STEP: Bojangles Time Step

BOLERO SHUFFLES
[18 sounds] [1 &a2 3 &a4 5 &a6 &a 7& a8]

Usually stylized with both hands on hips and elbows out. Executed while high on the balls of the feet.

> TO EXECUTE:
> Double shuffle R [1&a2], double shuffle R [3&a4], 5 shuffles w/ R [5 &a6 &a 7& a8]

BOMBERSHAY (Bumbishay, Bomborshay)
[3 -4 sounds] [&1 &2]

The bombershay has many spellings and many variations. It rose from social dance and its roots are probably the Suzi-Q, a step of the 1930s. The movement became a jazz step. Later, tap sounds were added.

> TO EXECUTE:
> Step or flap L to L, ast, lift R toe and turn it to R, while using the R heel as a pivot point, spank step R frt L (turn R toe twd L) step or flap L to L, ast, lift R toe, twist toe, to R [1] or [&1]

BOMBORSHAY. See BOMBERSHAY

BONE JANGLER

A musician who plays the bones (or sticks) and creates rhythm. The source of Bill Robinson's nickname, Bojangles.

BOOGIE BACK
[1 hold 2]

A favorite movement from boogie woogie and one in which partners face and back away from each other.

> TO EXECUTE:
> Step diagonally bk R, ast Lift L toe up, twist toe twd L; R heel remains on the floor. Reverse

BOOGIE WOOGIE

- ✪ A style of jazz music, in which musical patters have 8 beats to the bar.
- ✪ A dance movement in which the legs and knees are kept bent close together. The hips are swayed to the same side as the working foot.
- ✪ The music is expressed in 12M phrases.

BOP

A musical style in which the off-beat is accented.

BOSTON TIME STEP

Old name for a traveling time step. See TIME STEP: Traveling

BOUNCE

A musical tempo, usually played in 4/4 rhythm at a medium rate of speed with the accents on the second and the fourth beats.

BOW

A measure of respect and thanks to the audience, then to a partner or master of ceremonies, and the musical conductor before an exit is made. Also called RÉVÉRENCE

BOX STEP (Going No Place)
[8 movements] [1 2 3 4 5 6 7 8]

> TO EXECUTE:
> Step R fwd, dig L beside R [1 2], step L to R beside R [3 4], step L bkwd, dig R beside L [5 6], step R to R, close L beside R [7 8]

BREAK(S)
Music

- ✪ A place in the range of a voice or an instrument in which the quality of the tone changes very noticeably.
- ✪ A break, change, or complete stopping of the music for dramatic effect, or one in which the artist(s) may be featured.

BREAK(S) (continued)

- ✪ In jazz music, a pause in the music, which is often left unfilled or may be filled with a single instrument as a solo.
- ✪ In standard music, the last 2M of an 8M phrase.

Dance: Rehearsal

A period during a rehearsal when everyone has a designated amount of free time.

Dance: Break

In the score of a musical comedy, a part of the music written purposely for the dancer(s).

Tap Break:

- ✪ Music that is left open, with little accompaniment, in which the tap dancer allows his taps to become the focal point
- ✪ In vaudeville, usually the last 2M of an 8M phrase, reserved for the break of a time step. In the early days, this 2M break was a moment for improvisation to show one's talents and creativity. In many ways, the break was the high point of the step

NOTE:
Through the years, time steps took on certain characteristics and so did their breaks. The shuffle hop time step became known as the standard or basic time step, while the stomp or scuff time step was known as the buck or rhythm time step. See TIME STEPS

To add to the confusion, for many years the term rhythm was linked to the Standard time step as well as to the buck time step.

The following criteria are pertinent to both the break and the time step:

- ✪ If the time step is single, double, or triple, the break is also capable of being singled, doubled, or tripled.

NOTE:
The term single, double or triple connotes the number of sounds that occur after the `hop' of the time step. Therefore, A single = 1 sound (step); A double = 2 sounds (flap) and A triple = 3 sounds (shuffle step).

- ✪ The standard and buck breaks, although they have the same format, differ in their beginnings: the standard = shuffle R, hop L, step R [8&12], while the buck = stomp R, spank R, hop L, step R [8&12]
- ✪ The standard and buck breaks, although they have the same format, differ in their endings: the standard = shuffle step R, shuffle bc L [4&5&6&7], while the buck = shuffle R, hop L, flap bc R[4&5&6&7].
- ✪ The half break for both is the first measure of a 2M break:

TO EXECUTE:
Standard Half Break
Sh hop St R, Sh St L
[8&12&3&]
Buck Half Break
Stomp R Sp R hop St R Sh St L [8&12&3&]

NOTE:
- ✪ To create a double half break, change`the step to flap.[&2].
- ✪ To create a triple half break, change the flap to Sh St [&a2].
- ✪ The standard, single half break was also known as one-step rhythm.
- ✪ A full break is the whole 2 measures of the break.

TO EXECUTE:
Standard Full Break
Sh Hop St R, Sh St L, Sh St R, Sh bc L
[8&12&3&4&5&6&7]
Buck Full Break
Stomp R, Sp, hop St R, Sh St L, Sh R, hop L, Fl bc R [8&12&3&4&5&6&7]

NOTE:
- ✪ To create a double full break, change the step to flap [2].
- ✪ To create a triple full break, change the step to Sh St [&a2].
- ✪ The term round break is an old term meaning a full 2 measure break. It is unclear whether this pertained to the buck or the standard break, or to both.

OTHER BREAKS

Below are listed in alphabetical order other breaks that have been created. Some were attached to time steps, some were not. Some were a favorite combination of a famous dancer and became attached to the ends of their step. Others were hardly breaks at all, but through their usage have been classified as such. (The Ann Miller, Bill Robinson, and Louie DaPron are courtesy of Tom Ralabate of Williamsville, New York, as taught by Ann Marie Garvin.)

Ann Miller Break

[16 sounds] [&1&2&3&4&5&6&7&8]

TO EXECUTE:
Flap R to R, drop L and R heels (feet in second) [&1&2], toe drop L and R (pt. toes to R), drop L and

R heels (pt. heels to R) [&3&4], flap L to L, ast lift R toe, using edge of R heel as a pivot pt. [&5], toe drop R to R, drop R and L heels (feet in second) [&6&], Sp. bk R, drop L heel, tap R bk L [7&8]

Bill Robinson Break

[14 sounds] [8&12&3&4&5&6&7]

TO EXECUTE:
Sh hop St R, flap L fwd, St R ip [8&12&3&], Sh L, hop R, flap L and R [4&5&6&7]

Louie DaPron's Breaks (Standard Cramp Breaks):

The following breaks were created by Louie DaPron for his students. The word cramp was the old term for a heel drop (or a toe drop) which carried weight. Although they may not be breaks as we know them—they are well conceived and of true historical significance:

NOTE:
A Cramp consists of 5 sounds-Sh toe heel R, heel dig L [a1&a2].

TO EXECUTE:
cramp #1
flap R and L [a1a2], cramp R [a3&a4], reverse
cramp #2
cramp R [&1&a2], Sp bk L, drop R heel [&3], tap L bk R, clap [&4], reverse
cramp #3
cramp R [&1&a2], Sp L, heel drop R, toe L bk R [&a3], heel drop R, toe tap L bk R [&a], heel drop R [4], reverse
cramp #4
cramp R [&1&a2], drawback L bk R [&a3], flap R to R [a4], reverse
cramp #5
cramp R [ie & a1], drawback L, heel drop L [& a2 &], toe

heel R to R, toe heel L frt R [3&4&], spank toe heel R, heel dig L [5&a6], Sp heel tap L BR, clap [&a78], reverse

Maxie Ford Breaks

The Maxie Ford is a well-known step and break, credited to a fine wing dancer in vaudeville—Max Ford.

TO EXECUTE:
Maxie Ford step
leap R to R, Sh leap L, toe R bk L [1&2&3]
Maxie Ford Break
leap R to R, Sh leap L, toe R bk L [1&2&3], leap R to R, Sh leap L, toe R bk L [4&5&6], leap R to R [7]
Maxie Ford with Graboff
leap R to R, Sh alternating pickup R to L, tap R bk L [1&2&a3], leap R to R, Sh alternating pickup R to L, tap R bk L [4&5&a6], leap R [7]
Advanced Maxie Ford
Leap R to R, Sh alternating pickup L, heel drop L, tap R bk L [1a2e&a3], leap R to R, Sh alternating pickup L, heel drop L, tap R bk L [4&5e&a6], leap R [7]

Shim Sham Breaks

To execute:
Shim Sham Half Break
leap R fwd step L bk [8 1], Sh BC R [&2&3], repeat [4 5 &6&7]
Shim Sham Break:
dig L to R step L to L [12], drop L heel, St R bk L [3&], Hold 4 drop R heel, St L bk R [&5], stamp R and L in 2nd [67]

BREAK(S) (continued)

There are a number of Soft Shoe Breaks:

TO EXECUTE:

Soft Shoe #1
step L to L, brush BC R frt L [1&a2], Sh hop Sh St R bk [&a3&a4], Sh hop St L bk R [a&a5], flap R and L fwd [a6a7], stamp R and L in 2nd [&8]

Soft Shoe #2
step L to L, brush BC R frt L [1&a2], Sh hop Sh St R bk [&a3&a4], Sp St bk L and R [a5a6], flap L fwd [a7], step RLR fwd [&a8]

Soft Shoe #3
step L to L, brush BC R frt L [1&a2], hop step bk R and L [3& hold 4 &5], flap fwd R, flap BC L [a6a7a8]

Soft Shoe #4
flap L and R fwd, step fwd L [&1&a2], Sh hop Sh St R bk, brush L fwd [a&a3&a4], hop R, walk LRL in circle to L [&567], brush R fwd hop L [&8]

Soft Shoe #5 (Swannee Break)
spank R bk, hop L (both arms swing bkwd) [&1], brush fwd R, hop L (both arms swing fwd) [&2], spank R frt L, hop L (both arms cross) [&3], slide R foot to R (arms on diag to R) [4], step L bk R leap R to R (arms bk) [5&], step L frt R, leap R to R (arms bk) [6&], step L bk R, slide R to R (arms diag R) [7 8]

Soft Shoe #6 (Syncopated Swannee Break)
spank R bk, hop L [&1], brush fwd R, hop L [&2], spank R frt L, hop L [&3], slide R foot to R [4], brush fwd L, hop R [&5], spank L bk, hop R [&6], fast Sh hop St L frt R [e &a7], slide R to R [8]

Soft Shoe #7 (Off-beat Break)
flap fwd L and R [&1&a], step L [2], Frt Sh R, hop L [&a3], side Sh R [e&], hop L, St R [a4], brush hop St L fwd [&a5], step R (1/2 turn R, face bk) [6], step L (1/2 turn R to A2) [7], Fl R frt, St L ip (to A2) [&a8]

Soft Shoe A8 (The Common Break)
flap L fwd [a1], brush R fwd, brush R frt L [&a], brush R fwd, brush R bk [2&], ball change R-L [a3], flap R fwd [&4]

Traveling Time Step Break
There are very few traveling time step breaks. This one is of very early vintage.

TO EXECUTE:
Sh L, hop R, hop R, Br St fwd L, St R ip [8&12&3&], Sh L, hop R, flap L, Sh St R [4&5&6&7&]

BREAK A LEG

This is a phrase often said to dancers before they enter the stage; It does not literally mean to break your leg, but intimates that if the audience likes you and applauds for a long time, the lady must curtsey over and over, therefore, bending her leg to bow, and the gentleman with feet together must bow forward to show his appreciation.

BREAK OUT
[6 sounds][&1&2&3]

TO EXECUTE:
Flap R fwd St bk L, shuffle R, hop L

NOTE:

Actually the end of a time step; good way to teach one also.

BREAKAWAY

Used often in the big apple and the Lindy. It consisted of either partner performing an impromptu solo or the two partners separating briefly while holding with one or no hands.

BREAKDOWN

A lively country, shuffling kind of dance similar to the hoe down.

BRIDGE

The 3rd 8 measures of a 32M standard chorus, sometimes referred to as the release. It is the different melody, the other three 8-measure strains being of the same melody. Some musical pieces have no bridge.

BRIGHT

A fairly fast tempo, usually 4/4.

BRIGHT TEMPO

A tempo that is faster than a medium tempo.

BRISÉ ⃟

Literally, "broken," A ballet term used often in classical tap. It may begin on one or both feet and end the same way. It may be described as an assemblé that is beaten and travels. Starting in a closed position, the working leg brushes off the floor and beats in front of or in back of the other leg which has come to meet it. Both feet descend at the same time to end in a closed position, usually 5th in demi-plié.

BRISÉ CRAMPROLL. See CRAMPROLL: Brisé

BROADWAY DANCER

The Broadway dancer studies a number of different styles within the dance field—jazz, tap, ballet, acrobatics. He or she is interested in blending these techniques together as well as being proficient in each of them individually. It is, presently, what auditioners expect from a dancer unless the particular production is of a different nature.

BROADWAY SQUARE (Time Square)
[32 sounds][&1&2&3&4&5&6&7&8] [32 cts]

This is an often–performed exercise that has been formatted and named by Al Gilbert, well–known and respected teacher.

TO EXECUTE:

face frt. flap R to R heel drops L-R [&1&2], back brush L (or spank), heel drop R, toe back L, heel drop R (or Broadway) [&3&4], reverse 1- 4 facing stage L [5- 8], repeat 1- 4 facing up stage [1- 4], reverse 1- 4 facing stage R [5- 8]

BROKEN RHYTHM

Broken rhythm refers to the interspersing of eighth, sixteenth, etc. notes, creating a combination of 2 or more rhythms within one measure of music (e.g., **[1&2&a34]**).

BRUSH (Ball Brush, Toe Brush)
[1 sound] [1] or [&] or [a]

Brush is one of the main steps in tap. It combines with many other steps to form new steps. It implies that the working leg is creating the sound as it moves *away from the body,* while the term spank implies that the working leg is creating the sound as it moves *twd the body.* However, this difference is not standardized throughout the dance field. Many times the term back brush or backward brush is used in place of the word spank. Below are some of the different ways the term brush is used.

BRUSH

Forward

A forward brush implies that the striking of the ball of the foot is in an outward direction away from the body. This movement could take place with the working leg crossed over the supporting one and continue all the way to a center back position, at which time the working leg would have to be well turned out to accomplish the sound.

Backward

A backward brush is called spank. See SPANK

Short

A short quick brushing sound in any direction.

Long

A slower, prolonged brushing sound in any direction.

BRUSH BACK. See BRUSH; SPANK STEP

BRUSH BACK STEP. See SPANK STEP

BRUSH BALL

If slap (no wt.); if flap (with wt.).

BRUSH BALL CHANGE
[3 sounds] [&a1] or [1&2 counts]

Brush or spank R in any dir. Away from body or twd body, and add BC R–L, feet in any pos., Xd, open, closed, in relevé, plié or r/p. Feet can cross frt, bk or remain par; travel fwd, bkwd, sdwd, turn or stay ip.

BRUSH BALL HEEL. See Flap Heel

BRUSH BALL HEEL HEEL. See Flap Heel Heel

BRUSH CRAMPROLL. See Cramproll: Brush

BRUSH DIG STEP
[3 sounds][&1 2]

Not classifiable as a step, rather a well-known short combination and/or movement.

> To execute:
> stand on L, brush R to L, dig R beside L, step R to R, reverse.

BRUSH DOWN. See Brush Step

BRUSH KICK. See Kick: Brush kick

BRUSH STEP
[2 sounds] [&1]

A brush fwd R followed by step R. Both the brush and the step have the same rhythmic value, that of an eighth note. Although the execution of brush step is the same as flap, the rhythmic value is not; flap is sixteenth notes **[a1]**.

BRUSH STEP BACK. See Spank Step

BRUSH STEP BALL CHANGE. See Flap Ball Change

BRUSH STEP FORWARD. See Flap

BRUSH STEP HEEL. See Flap Heel

BRUSH STEP HEEL HEEL. See Flap Heel Heel

BRUSH TOE HEEL. See Flap Heel

BRUSH TOE HEEL HEEL. See Flap Heel Heel

BUCK
[1 sound] [1]

Slide fwd on balls of both feet and drop both heels simultaneously at end of slide.

BUCK AND CATCH
[2 sounds] [1 2]

Standing with feet close together and legs straight, slide both feet forward ast. Feet remain in contact with the floor. Both heels are dropped simultaneously to emphasize the end sound. Knees are now bent. Return to opening position by pulling legs straight and sliding bkwd to starting position. Again feet remain in contact with the floor, throughout.

BUCK AND WING

The buck and wing used the buck dance as its basis and added to it a newly found movement, the wing. See Steps and Styles of Tap Dance

BUCK BREAK. See Breaks: Buck

BUCK DANCING

A flat footed type of dancing that was a mixture of the jig and the clog. It was characterized by great strength and vigor, thus named after the male of most animal species, the buck. Its main step was the time step. Later it became the basis for the buck and wing. See Steps and Styles of Tap Dance

BUCK TIME STEPS

Also known as off-beat, negro, rhythm, and stomp time step. See Time Step: Buck

BUCK WALK

A stylized walk, placing first the heel on the floor and then lowering the toe.

BUFFALO STEP
(Shuffle Off to Buffalo)
[4-6 sounds] [1&a2] or [&1&a2] or [&a1 &a2]

The Buffalo step is very old, having its origin in Shea's Buffalo theater in Buffalo, N.Y., created by a choreographer to exit a tiller line. See An Historical Look at Tap. Its characteristic action is the sharp bending of the working leg in frt of the supporting leg in the figure 4. This step was popularized in the 1880s by Pat Rooney.

TO EXECUTE:

single: leap R to R, shuffle L to L, leap L X bk, ast, bend R frt L knee [1&a2] double: flap R to R, shuffle L to L, leap L X bk, ast, bend R frt L knee [&1&2] triple: Sh St R to R, shuffle L to L, leap L X bk, ast, bend R frt L knee [&a1&a2]

BUGGY RIDE TIME STEP. See TIME STEP: Buggy Ride

BUMBISHAY. See BOMBERSHAY

BUMP

A thrust of the hips or pelvis in a frontward direction.

BUMP AND GRIND

Bumping occurs when the pelvic area is thrust forward, while grinding connotes using the pelvic area in a circular manner. Both are affiliated with burlesque and are used in a more controlled manner in jazz.

BUNNY HOPS

Jumps with the feet together fwd, bkwd, sdwd or ip.

BURPEE (Squatthrust)

A burpee is meant to draw applause and show agility. It is classified as a flash or trick step.

TO EXECUTE:

Stand with legs straight and feet together. Squat with legs still together and place both hands on floor in front to support the weight. Thrust both legs bkwd, with feet together and legs straight, retract feet together to a squat position, hands still on floor and return to standing position.

OPEN BURPEE

Executed in the same fashion as a regular burpee; however, when the body reaches the squat position and the legs are thrown backward, separate both legs, keeping them straight. Some dancers arch the back at this point and raise one arm straight up for a more vivid picture, then recover by pulling up the legs and feet together in a squat position and stand up. See BURPEE

BUZZ STEP
[7 sounds] [1&2&3&4]

Literally, a paddle step. Usually travels to side or turns in place.

TO EXECUTE:

step R to R, execute 3 bc's, L-R, L-R, L-R [1&2&3&4]

BUZZ TURN
[7 sounds] [1&2&3&4]

A paddle step turning. The turn is normally done to the R on the R foot and to the L on the L foot, thus an inside turn. See BUZZ STEP

C

CABRIOLE

A step of elevation in which the legs are beaten together in the air. The working leg is extended and moves into the air; the underneath leg follows and beats against it, lifting the first leg higher. The landing is made by the underneath leg. The term cabriole comes from ballet.

CAKEWALK

A highly stylized, strutting routine, created by southern plantation blacks in mockery of their white family and their European dances. Eventually, competitions were held in the public square and winners would win a very large decorated cake. The dance theoretically was introduced on Broadway in 1885 by Charles Johnson, where it gained instant popularity. However, it was never popular in the ballrooms of the U.S. See STEPS AND STYLES OF TAP DANCE

CAMEL WALK

The basic walk tilts slightly fwd; as you step forward on a straight leg R, allow the L knee to bend in a popping fashion and the left heel to leave the floor, then reverse.

CANCAN

Developed in Europe in the 1830s, the cancan became the outlandish dance of the period, with the skirts being lifted and daringly showing the girls

CANCAN (continued)

ruffled panties and gartered stockings. It usually concluded with a multitude of high kicks and then contagiously (See CONTAGIOUS) falling into a final front and back split, accompanied by vocalization.

CANON. See CONTAGIOUS

CAR CHECK TAP

Theoretically, this was a trolley car token, placed at the instep of the shoe, thus creating a clinking sound, much like a jingle tap.

CARRYBACK. See IRISH: Back

CARRYBACK IRISH. See IRISH: Back

CARRYOVER. See IRISH: Front

CARRYOVER IRISH. See IRISH: Front

CASTLE ROLL
[5 or 6 sounds] [&1&a2]

2 fast shuffles R, followed by heel drop L.

(THE) CASTLE WALK

A social ballroom dance introduced by Vernon and Irene Castle. The man was tipped backwards in a straight line and the woman at a forward angle. The walks were stiff-legged and in relevé and the attitude was stately with broad movements.

CATCH. See HITCH; CLIP

CATCH AND HITCH
[w/wo sound] [1 2] or [1&]

Execute in the same manner as buck and catch but the return backward is made on one foot, not two. Catch is sometimes referred to as a chug fwd on one foot. See BUCK AND CATCH

CATCH STEP (Hitch Step)
[w/wo sound] [1 2]

Leap onto R foot, bkwd or ip, ast release L foot fwd in low or high battement; step bk with L. Step resembles an exaggerated bc.

CENTER(ING)

Centering, or to be centered, has numerous meanings, all of which lead to good dancing. Some of the most apparent ones are: (1) The body is in proper alignment and placement. (2) The weight is properly and equally distributed over the feet and

toes. (3) The dancer is completely focused and concentrated on the work and (4) knows where his center is at all times.

CENTER STAGE

1   The exact center of the stage, where all the sight and stage lines intersect. See PERFORMING: The Stage Area

2   Part of regular class procedure. Once warmup is completed, the class is called to the center of the floor to continue without the aid of a support or barre. Here port de bras, short steps, pirouettes, etc. can be practiced.

CHA CHA
[1 hold 2 3 hold 4 5 6 hold 8].

A Latin ballroom dance where the rhythm is slow, slow, quick, quick.

The hips sway with each walk in the direction of the weight bearing feet.

CHAÎNÉ ⚲
[w/wo sounds]

Literally, "chained." Chaîné turns are the backbone for most traveling tap turns, so called because each turn acts as a link in the chain to the next turn. This type of turn lends itself well to tap sounds as it may be done in Relevé, Plié, r/p, etc. See also TURNS; SPOTTING

General Direction: For a right chaîné turn, progressing in a straight line from SL to SR, Step R to R (flat, in relevé, r/p, ¾ foot, etc.) , R leg str., bent, tno, tni, par, etc. Arms open to 2nd, body faces frt, head spots over R shoulder [ct. 1]. Executing ½ a turn to R, step L to beside R, (the degree of closeness of feet depends on distance to be covered, the sounds to be executed, the look desired, etc.); arms are now in closed pos., body faces bkwd, head is over L shoulder, concentrating on same focal point [ct. 2]. W/a rapid motion, snap the head to the R, returning it to the focal point [&].

NOTE:
The head snaps and finds the focal point previously to the body returning to the frt. The chaîné turn is a series of ½ turns or *face frt, face bk* and when done in succession, produces a chain of turns.

Variations: Many different sounds or steps may be executed during the chaîné turn. See TURNS: *Traveling:* Chaîné

Inside: A R chaîné turn may be classified as being inside if the R foot steps to the R and the turn rotates forward and inward to the R. Reverse the process for L inside Chaînés. See TURNS: Inside and Outside

Outside: A R chaîné turn may be classified as being outside if the R foot steps to the R and the turn rotates backward and outward to the L. Reverse the process for L outside chaînés. See TURNS: Inside and Outside

CHAÎNÉ CRAMPROLL. See TURNS: Traveling; STAMP CRAMPROLL TURN

CHALLENGE

- ✪ The challenge, usually friendly, takes place between two dancers to see who can produce the most intricate and exciting footwork, rhythms and flash steps. It's what traditional tap dancers revel in and enjoy. It involves improvisation and creativity and began the expressions trading fours and trading eights-give me your best 4 or 8 M. It is the lifeblood of learning. Sometimes it is done by a group, but with only one person at a time meeting the challenge. Our present-day competitions are not challenges in this respect as the work is well rehearsed and not improvised.

- ✪ A dance in which the competing performers tried to outdance each other. Usually, the judging panel consisted of three judges, one for execution, who sat underneath the stage and listened to the sounds, accents, and quality of the performer; a style judge who sat in or near the orchestra pit, and a timing judge, who made sure that each contestant had the same amount of performance time. At the end of the challenge, the three judges added their scores and a winner was announced. Often the challenge began with the first competitor setting the tempo by stamping and clapping four times and doing time steps and a break, which would lead directly into the first competition step.
(From *The Tap Dance Dictionary* by Mark Knowles)

CHANGEOVER

An old term equivalent to alternating. To change over from one foot to the other, used in connection with cramprolls, wings, pickups, and other movements.

CHANGEOVER CRAMPROLL. See CRAMPROLL: Alternating

CHANGING CRAMPS. See CRAMPROLL: Alternating

CHANGING CRAMPROLLS. See CRAMPROLL: Alternating.

CHANGING DRUMROLLS. See CRAMPROLL: Alternating.

CHANGING GRABOFF. See PICKUP: Alternating.

CHANGING PICKUP. See PICKUP: Alternating.

CHANGING PULLBACK. See PICKUP: Alternating.

CHANGING RIFF. See RIFF: Alternating.

CHANGING WING. See WING: Alternating.

CHARACTER TAP

A tap routine that utilizes the costume, wardrobe, music, or steps of a certain ethnic group, such as the Dutch, French, etc., or well-known figures such as a soldier or a sailor; or characters such as Kermit the Frog and Popeye, and through their dancing characterization and actions make the audience feel that the characters are alive and present.

CHARLESTON

A dance craze of the 1920s. The first American dance to cross a dance to watch with a dance to perform; born in Charleston, South Carolina, it had its basis in African dance. It was characterized by a twisting in and out of the knees and feet—and was a social dance performed by both men and women. See STEPS AND STYLES OF TAP DANCE.

> TO EXECUTE:
> Step fwd R, snap kick L fwd, tilt bkwd [1, hold 2, 3 hold 4], step bkwd L, [5, hold 6], ball change R bk, lean fwd [7, 8]

CHASSÉ (Sashay)
[w/wo sound]

Literally, "chased." A ballet term, traceable to folk and character dancing. A step in which one foot displaces the other in a chasing or sliding motion. May be done in any direction. Level may remain even or be of a bouncy nature.

> TO EXECUTE:
> Step, slide or glide R to desired position (fwd, Xd etc.). As L comes to replace R there is a small lifting into the air. The landing is on the L and in plié.

CHASSÉ TURN ☥

Literally this is a three-step turn, footwise THREE-STEP TURN, but on the second movement, where the feet come together, there is a little lift in the air, returning to do the last step out. Traceable to folk dancing. See CHASSÉ.

CHOP

[w/wo sound] [1 sound]

Traceable to country and character dancing.

> TO EXECUTE:
>
> Step to floor in backward direction while keeping supporting knee straight. Takes the body weight. Resembles the goose step of the German army.

CHOREOGRAPHER

The word choreographer, originated by Doris Humphrey, is the combination of the two Greek words—*khoreia* and *graphe*—one who plans dances. The choreographer was formerly known as the dance director and rightly so, for many of them were not dancers, but directors who moved the dancers, while others, including the performers themselves, created the steps. Busby Berkeley fell into that category. Today, the choreographer's job is far more extensive than creating actual dance pieces, especially in the field of musical theater. See AN HISTORICAL LOOK AT TAP: DANCE DIRECTORS AND CHOREOGRAPHERS; *THE ART OF MAKING DANCES* by Doris Humphrey.

CHOREOGRAPHY

The dances, movements, and steps that are created and arranged for dancers by the choreographer. The term originally pertained to ballet and modern dances.

CHORUS

Usually connotes a group of people such as a chorus of dancers and/or singers who interpret the content and sentiment of the work. Musically, it could be made in reference to the standard chorus which consists of 32 measures of music See STANDARD MUSIC

CHORUS KICK

[w/wo sound]

General Information: Has its background in the vaudeville chorus lines of the country, where kicks were used for the ending of a routine. Later, because of their mounting popularity, they became the major focus of the entire dance. John Tiller, an English dance director, created and brought to this country the famous Tiller kick line, while Ned Wayburn, an American dance director, classified and defined dozens of chorus kicks and routine patterns. One of the last of the precision, high kicking groups today is The Radio City Music Hall Rockettes. The term chorus kick refers to a large and overlapping range of movement, as explained below:

Straight Kick: Also known as a battement kick. The working leg remains str. from hip bone to toe. with back of the knee being fully stretched.

> TO EXECUTE:
>
> While standing on the L, battement R to the desired height. May be done tno, par, tni, croisé oblique etc. w/wo sound.

Knee Kick: Also known as flip kick, flex kick, and flick kick. See JAZZ KICK Done by first raising the knee of the working leg and then extending the lower leg into the desired position and direction. Leg may be returned to floor by rebending at the knee or by lowering it while it is straight. Knee kick may also refer to lifting the knee to a desired height without straightening the leg.

Stationary or moving: All the above types of kicks may be done on the spot (stationary) or moving (traveling) or turning, depending on the choreographic content of the routine.

CHORUS LINE

- The old chorus line received its name from the fact that dancers (usually women) danced in one straight line. The work consisted of steps and kicks performed in precision.

- Today's chorus lines are an integral part of the production, contributing to the plot by singing, dancing and acting. They are no longer a mere entertainment appendage.

(A) CHORUS LINE TAP

The old chorus line look was a precision line of female dancers, who remained in a straight line and performed precision kicks and steps, such as The Tiller line, The Rockettes, Busby Berkeley Dancers, etc. The strength and beauty lay in the precision. With more modern music being created, the lines began to vanish, and a more individual movement took its place. Then, A CHORUS LINE was created by Michael Bennett, and in a more innovative way, the chorus line was back.

CHUG (chut, heel thump, shoot)
[1 sound] [1]

While standing on one foot, the other held in posed pos. in air (usually with leg bent at knee) slide fwd on ball of the supporting leg, remaining in contact with the floor throughout, and, at end of slide, sharply drop the heel, making a sharp, clear sound. Supporting leg ends in plié. Accent is on heel drop.

NOTE:

If both feet perform chug simultaneously, the step is called buck.

CHUG BREAK
[16 sounds] [&1&2&3&4&5&6&7&8]

TO EXECUTE:

(a) brush R fwd, chug L bk [&1], spank R bk, chug L fwd [&2], repeat (a) one more time [&3&4], (b) brush hop step fwd R and L [&5&6&7], stamp R and L [&8]

CHUT. See CHUG

CIGARETTE TWIST. See FRENCH TWIST

CINCINNATI (Back to the Woods)
[5-7 sounds] [&1&a2, &a1&a2] or [e&a1&a2]

This step usually travels bkwd, but it may also be executed fwd; sdwd or ip. The Cincinnati is derived from a much older step called back to the woods. The two are identical in their singular form, the difference lying in changing the hop of the back to the woods into a heel drop for the Cincinnati.

TO EXECUTE:

Single: spank bk R, drop L heel, Sh St bk R [&1&a2], double: spank bk R, drop L heel, Sh bk R, drop L heel, St bk R [&a1&a2], triple: Sh R, drop L heel, Sh bk R, drop L heel, St bk R [e&a1&a2]

NOTE:

A Double Cincinnati is executed in the same manner as a Triple Drawback.

A Front Cincinnati is performed by substituting a frt shuffle for the normal shuffle and by stepping the working leg fwd each time.

CINCINNATI: WITH PICKUP

TO EXECUTE:

Sp R, Heel drop L, Sh R, Heel drop L, St bk R, alternating pickup from R to L, Sh R, Heel drop L, St bk R [&a1&a2&a3&a4].

CINCINNATI BREAKDOWN. See

BIRMINGHAM BREAKDOWN

CIRCULAR KICK. See FAN KICK

CLAP

Literally, to strike the palms of the hand tog., thus creating a loud noise. One hand may be clapped into the other or both beaten tog., simultaneously.

CLASS ACT

Two or three dancers, usually male, impeccably dressed in full evening attire, who perform an elegant soft shoe routine with great precision while dancing to a very slow tempo. See STEPS AND STYLES OF TAP DANCE: Styles and Dances.

CLASSICAL TAP

A combining of the fields of ballet and tap, often using classical music as its accompaniment. See STEPS AND STYLES OF TAP DANCE.

CLICK
[w/wo sound] [1]

The term click has never been satisfactorily defined. It is often used interchangeably with Clip, Catch, Stub, Hit, Stub Hit, and Strike or left up to the teacher, choreographer or dancer as to which term to choose. Perhaps the most accurate description for clicking is, when both parts of the body share the action and the force equally (e.g., when balancing on both heels simultaneously strike the toes together ast a clicking occurs, for each foot has contributed an equal force). But in the case where one foot is passing the other, such as when balancing on the both heels simultaneously and the heel of one foot, in passing strikes the toe of the other, then the term clip, catch, or stub is used.

CLICK HEEL(S). See HEEL CLICK

CLIP (Catch, Stub) [w/wo sound]

The term clip implies that one part of the body passes another, and in doing so, touches and/or makes a sound in passing (e.g., my hand passes from frt to back and clips my thigh in the passing, or while suspended on the R heel, with the toes up, my L heel, in passing from L to R, hits or clips the toes of my R foot). This would be considered a heel-toe catch, the part of the body initiating the movement is named first.

NOTE:
Two sources differed with this explanation claiming that the first term is part of the body receiving the action. Thus, the above would be a toe-heel clip.

CLIP WALK

Any walk in which a toe or a foot, clips, in passing the heel of the weight-bearing foot or that the heel of the working foot clips the toe of the weight bearing foot.

NOTE:
The toe or heel of the foot to be clipped must be in a raised position.

CLOCHE WING. See WINGS: Pendulum

(THE) CLOCK

Considered a Flash trick.

> TO EXECUTE:
> Begin in a squat position, facing frt, quickly thrust both feet to the L, ast, R hand on floor which supports the weight, L arm usually u; both legs are thrust up to the L, they may be crossed, or remain par, while supporting lifted body on R hand, with R arm straight and L arm held diagonally up, Step L frt R, Step R to R, keeping legs straight; slowly revolve on R and palm to the R hand until the body turns in a complete circle and ends facing the front in the starting position. Legs remain straight throughout.

CLOCKWISE

Progressing in the same direction as the motion of the hands on a clock, as seen from the frt.

CLOG (DANCE)

The clog dance existed in England, Ireland and Wales. It was a recreational and performing dance using wooden clog shoes, from which it took its name. The most famous of the cloggers were from Lancashire, England, where, weather permitting, factory workers held competitions during their lunch hour on the cobblestone streets. See AN HISTORICAL LOOK AT TAP

CLOG (SHOES)

Clog shoes were made from one solid piece of wood and seldom wore out. They were known as sabots (pronounced sah-BO) and were used for work as well as play. At a certain point, the sole was split into three sections, which allowed better foot control and clearer sounds. With the advent of leather, the shoe became soft, but in many cases the sole and heel remained of wood, maple being the best sounding and sturdiest. Through the minstrelsy and most of vaudeville, all true clog dancers wore wooden shoes. See AN HISTORICAL LOOK AT TAP

CLOG STEP. See WALTZ CLOG

CLOSE
[w/wo sound]

To place together or side by side.

CLOSE TO THE FLOOR

This is a style of tapping, popularized by John Bubbles around 1922, in which the feet remain very close to the floor, usually with double rhythm being frequently used. It was initially known as rhythm tap and included paradiddles, cramprolls, riffs, etc. See STEPS AND STYLES OF TAP DANCE

CLOSED THIRD
[3 sounds] [&a1]

> TO EXECUTE:
> Execute a flap fwd R, but allow R heel to tap before the step R

CLUSTER

Associated with and probably coined by Beale Fletcher, a well-known and highly respected teacher, author, and choreographer. It presents the theory that each step has an internal rhythm of its own and when steps are combined with other steps, one must cluster all the sounds together and through accents and shading find understandable and workable rhythms that will display the new step as a whole, not a combination of separate steps placed together.

COFFEE GRIND(ER) (Around the World, Over the Tops)
[w/wo sound]

Traceable to vaudeville and Russian folk dancing. This was a very popular movement in the 1920s and falls in the category of a flash step—one expressly used for the purpose of gaining applause.

TO EXECUTE:
Place both hands on the floor and assume a squatting position. While balancing on one leg, extend the other to 2nd. The extended leg subscribes a large circle on the floor by traveling fwd, then twd the opposite side, around bk and returns to its original position; both the hands then the standing leg must jump the circling leg on its approach.

NOTE:
Dancer Willie Covan performed a double coffee grind using no hands. The coffee grind is a form of over the tops.

COHAN WALK

A stylized walk introduced by George M. Cohan, a headliner on the vaudeville circuit. Cohan would lift the upper body out of the hips, and, with a very straight back, tilt slightly forward. With straight legs, he would proceed to lift each leg up, almost like a parallel goose step and march straight down center stage toward the audience.

COMBINATION

A series of separate steps placed together to form a longer one.

COMMON BREAK. See BREAK: Other Breaks, Soft Shoe 8

COMMON TIME

Denotes 4/4 time with 4 quarter notes to the measure.

COMPASS TURN
[w/wo sound]

A stationary turn performed on one foot while the other leg and foot in an affixed position subscribes a full circle on the floor. They are generally performed as an inside turn.

TO EXECUTE:
Begin turn by stepping onto the R foot with L extended to 2nd or 4th position. Continue to turn to the R (R inside turn). The working leg is tno and may be slightly bent or straight. The supporting leg may be either straight or bent or may switch between the two levels. Once the opening pose is established, the relationship between the body and the extended leg does not change during the turn. The inside edge of the great toe of the supporting leg lightly grazes the floor for the full revolution, thus subscribing an imaginary circle on the floor. To perform as an outside turn: proceed as above but after stepping on the R foot, turn bkwd rather than fwd.

COMPOUND TIME

More complicated musical time signatures used by progressive jazz musicians like Dave Bruebeck, etc. (e.g., 5/4, 7/8, 12/8, etc.).

CONTAGIOUS (Follow up, Canon)
[w/wo sound]

The spreading of a pose, a movement, a movement phrase, or a sound from one person or a group to others. It may be done fluidly or percussively, overlapping each other's moves or ending each movement before the next begins. It may proceed in logical order from L to R or in random order. It may not even be identical movement. Its sole purpose is for the choreographic effect.

CONTAGIOUS (continued)

NOTE:
The term canon is used when this overlap is created by a musical or movement phrase. It seldom denotes individual pose positions or sporadic movement.

CONTRACTION

The contraction was born in modern dance and has found its way into the jazz and tap fields. When executed the abdominal muscles are contracted, thus, hollowing out the front of the body and causing the lumbar muscles to elongate. Contractions facilitate the finding of one's center and build great strength and control. Contractions may also occur in the shoulder, chest, etc.

CONTRAST

Loud sounds against soft ones, fluidity against percussiveness, relevé against plié, etc. It explores differences rather than sameness and its interest is in bringing new life to movements and sounds, thus not allowing monotony to set in.

CORKSCREW
[4 sounds][&1&2]

A very early step which involved the twisting of the foot. It was often referred to as a tanglefoot. See TANGLEFOOT

> TO EXECUTE:
> Hop L, step fwd on R heel with toes raised and turned inward. Step L to L ast twist toes outward, using the R heel as a pivot point. Step R to R. Reverse.

CORKSCREW TURN (Spiral)
[w/wo sound]

Often used in eccentric or comedy routines in vaudeville and in the musicals of the 1930s. This movement received its name from the barber pole or corkscrew effect it created. May be done half way to floor or fully to floor. Ray Bolger perfected and popularized this particular turn as the Scarecrow in *The Wizard of Oz*.

> TO EXECUTE:
> Cross L frt R, leaving feet in that position, slowly turn to R and begin to plié, until you can sit on the floor. Leaving feet in same pos. turn bk L, slowly straighten legs and return to standing.

66

CORNER DIRECTIONS. See REFERENCE
MANUAL: Performing, The Stage Area

COUNTERCLOCKWISE

Moving in the opposite direction from that of hands of a clock.

COUNTERPOINT

In music refers to a note playing against another note or a voice against another voice. In dance, it refers to a soloist dancing rhythms against another dancer or two different groups or melodies performing at the same time, with contrasting yet harmonious steps, rhythms and styles. It may also refer to the dancer, dancing in contrast to the rhythmic qualities or textures present in the accompanying music.

COUNTRY WESTERN

A type of music that is rural in sound and quality. Played for country square and round dances.

COUPÉ

Literally, "cut." A small secondary step that acts as an impetus for the step to be performed.

COUPLET

A 2-sounded rhythm, usually eighth note combinations (e.g., **[1&2&3&4]**).

CRAMP

The old term meaning to place weight upon the movement being performed (e.g., when executing a heel drop R, wt. is placed on the R). It is the opposite in meaning from the term beat, in which no weight would be placed on the heel drop.

CRAMP BARREL ROLL

The term cramp implies that there is a heel drop or drops involved in the execution of the barrel roll. See BARREL ROLL: Cramproll

CRAMP CROSS
[6 Sounds] [&a1&a2]

A type of heel-toe, toe-heel clip.

> TO EXECUTE:
> Stand on L, point R to R. Using L heel as a pivot point, raise L toes. Move R frt L with toes flexed and in passing, clip L toes with R heel. Toe drop L. Step on ball of R frt L, clip R heel with L toes in passing. Drop R heel and step, L to L.

CRAMP HEEL. See Heel Drop

CRAMPROLL (Crunch, Drumroll, Heel Roll, Military Roll)
[4 sounds] [a&a1] or [1&a2]

General: There are many types of cramprolls, progressive, regular, alternating and fake. Except for the names by which they are called, the work presented below seems to have a general acceptance.

Note:
A 4-point and a 4-count cramproll are interchangeable terms. Both connote that 4 sounds are being executed in that particular cramproll.

Regular (Full) Cramproll: Contains 4 sounds. May be counted [a&a1] or [1&a2].

1 The order of these sounds must be: ball (of one foot), ball (of the other foot), heel (of one foot), heel (of the other). If these sounds are executed in any other order, then it is not a regular cramproll.

2 If the cramproll is a R cramproll, it must begin with the R foot.

To execute:
Ball R, ball L, heel drop R, heel drop L [4 sounds] [a&a1][1&a2]

3 If the cramproll is a L cramproll, it must begin with the L foot.

To execute:
Ball L, ball R, heel drop L, heel drop R [4 sounds] [a&a1][1&a2]

Alternating Cramproll (Changing or Changeover Cramprolls, Cramproll Changes, Changing Cramps, Changing Drumrolls, Cut Out Cramproll, Pass Cramproll, Reverse Cramproll)

The word alternating connotes that the cramproll can be done first with one foot, then with the other.

To execute:
R alternating: ball R, ball L, heel drop L, heel drop R [4 sounds][a&a1][1&a2]
L alternating: ball L, ball R, heel drop R, heel drop L [4 sounds][a&a1][1&a2]

Variations: Cramprolls have many variations, some of which are listed below.

Aerial Cramproll (Heel Roll, Drumroll, Military Roll)

[4 sounds][1a&a2] or [&1&a2]

Execute a R aerial (See Aerial) and end in a progressive R cramproll (e.g., toe heel R and toe heel L). See Cramproll: Progressive

Alex Cramproll. See Press Cramproll, Cramproll: Fake Cramproll, Example (3)

Assemblé Cramproll

[4 sounds] [1a&a2]

Execute an assemblé and end in a R progressive cramproll (e.g., toe heel R and toe heel L). See Cramproll: Progressive; Assemblé

Bell Cramproll

[6 sounds] [1 2 3 &a4]

To execute:
For a R bell cramproll : Stand on R, tendu L to second position. Step L frt. R, execute a bell to R. After legs are bent to R and heels are clicked, land in either a R cramproll to reverse or a L cramproll to repeat.

Brisé Cramproll

[5 sounds] [1a&a2]

1 Execute a R brisé (See Brisé) and end in a progressive cramproll.

To execute:
Toe heel R and toe heel L.

See Cramproll: Progressive

2 Execute a R brisé and end in a regular or alternating cramproll. See Brisé

To execute:
Brush R, land ball R and L, heel drop R and L
OR
Brush R, land ball R and L, heel drop L and R

Brush Cramproll (5-pt. Cramproll, Flap Cramproll)
[5 sounds][1a&a2]

Execute a brush followed by any kind of cramproll.

67

CRAMPROLL (continued)

Clickout Cramproll

[5 sounds] [1a&a2]

Based on an alternating cramproll. Stand on L, swing R foot twd L, ast clicking R heel to L heel, ball R, ball L, to L, drop L and R heels.

Cut Out Cramproll

[4 sounds] [1&a2]

An alternating cramproll, but with the legs swung under the body line and to the side resembling the swaying action of a bell.

> TO EXECUTE:
> Do a R alternating or regular cramproll, and end with the legs to the L side of the body

Double Cramproll

[6 sounds][a1a&a2]

> TO EXECUTE:
> Do flap R and L and heel drop R and L (to remain on the R) or heel drop L and R to change to the L

Drop Cramproll (Flat Cramproll)

[4 sounds] [1&a2]

Toe drop R then L, heel drop R then L. Fills all the requirements of a regular cramproll, even though toe drops are substituted for ball-ball. May be done ip or traveling fwd, sdwd or bkwd. This form of cramproll is also a form of a parallel travel, if during the execution it travels to the side.

Fake Cramproll (Alex Cramproll, Press Cramproll)

[5 sounds] [1a&a2]

Exactly as the name implies, it closely resembles a true cramproll, but doesn't quite fulfill the requisites. Below are listed some examples of fake cramprolls.

> TO EXECUTE:
> 1 Ball R to R. Heel drop R and L [3 sounds][&a1]-(short 1 sound).
> 2 Stomp R fwd, ball R beside L, heel drop R and L [4 sounds][1&a2] (overuses R foot)
> 3 Heel drop L, ball R, heel drop R and L [4 sounds][1&a2] (too many heel drops)
> 4 Hop R, heel drop R, toe heel [8&a1] (can repeat or reverse by putting wt. on last heel drop)
> 5 Flap R to R, toe drop L, drop R and L or land R heels

Flap Cramproll

[5 sounds] [1e&a2]

Execute a flap R, then ball L, drop R then L heels (to remain on R) or drop L then R heels to alternate.

Heel Cramproll (Reverse Cramproll) [1&a2]

Begin with feet in parallel 1st position and drop R and L heels, then toe drop R and L [1&a2].

Hop Cramproll

[4 or 5 sounds] [1&a2] or [1e&a2]

This cramproll may be executing in two ways:

> TO EXECUTE:
> • Hop L. Execute a fake cramproll R (ball R, heel drop R then L) [1&a2] May be done alternating as well
> • Hop L and execute a full cramproll R. May be done alternating as well [1e&a2]

Leaping Cramproll

Any cramproll that begins with a leap [1e&a2].

Press Cramproll (Alex Cramproll)

[4 sounds][1 &a2]

See CRAMPROLL: Fake Cramproll, Example (3)

> TO EXECUTE:
> Drop L heel (wt. remains on L) [1], ball R, drop R and L heels [&a2], remains on the same foot throughout

Progressive Cramproll

Contains 4 sounds, but in a slightly different order:

Toe heel (with one foot), **toe heel** (with the other foot) [4 sounds][a&a1][1&a2]. Progressive cramprolls are used when landing from the air after executing a step such as brisé or assemblé. The ballet principle being: when performing this landing from such a step, one should not linger in a relevé position, but go through the feet to plié. The use of a progressive cramproll accomplishes this a little sooner.

Reverse Cramproll. See ALTERNATING CRAMPROLL

Scuff Cramproll

[5 sounds] [1e&2]

Scuff R, leap R, ball L, drop R, then L heel [1e&2]. May be done alternating as well.

Shuffle Cramproll

[6 sounds] [&1e&a2]

May be done two ways:

> ### TO EXECUTE:
> - **Remaining on same foot: shuffle R, ball R then L, heel drop R then L [&1e&a2]**
> - **Shuffle Alternating: shuffle R, ball R then L, heel drop L then R [&1e&a2]**

Side Cramproll

Any cramproll that is executed to one side or the other or from side to side.

Spank Cramproll (5-pt. Cramproll, Spank Step Cramproll) [5 sounds] [1e&a2]

Stand on L and execute a spank on the R, ball R, ball L, heel drop R and L (regular) or heel drop L and R (alternating) cramproll.

Standing Cramproll

[6 sounds] [a1e&a2]

Shuffle R, ball R, heel drop R and L, dig R beside L. (ball or heel dig or stomp)

Toe Click Cramproll

[5 sounds] [ie&a2]

This step can remain ip or travel to the side.

1. To stay ip, begin w/ toes tno and heels tni. Leave a little space between the heels

> ### TO EXECUTE:
> **Lift toes, inverted and pigeon toed and strike them tog. [1],**

Toe drop R to R, toe drop L to L, now in tno pos. [e&], Stay tno and drop R and L heels [a2], Repeat over and over, stay ip

2. To travel fwd, repeat (1) above, over and over and by slightly chugging fwd on each heel drop, the step will progress fwd.

3. To travel to R, start L side in tno 1st position

> ### TO EXECUTE:
> **Click toes tog. in frt [&]**
> **Toe drop R & L to R [1&]**
> **heel drop R and L to R, stay tno [a2]**

NOTE:
You must gain distance on the Toe Drops.

Traveling Cramproll

[4 sounds] [1&a2]

There are several kinds of traveling cramprolls; a few are listed below:

> - ✪ Toe drop R and L to R (toes pt R), heel drop R and L to R (heels pt R). Repeat and traveling will take place to the R. This is a drop or flat cramproll and a form of a parallel travel.
>
> - ✪ Stand on L with R raised. Toe drop L twd and pt. to R, ball R to R (both toes are pt to R), drop R and L heels twd R.

Turning Cramprolls

Two distinctions should be made:

> - ✪ A turn which is entirely motivated by, and makes use of cramprolls (e.g., heel drop L, ball R, drop R & L heels).
>
> - ✪ A turn which uses cramproll as an element contained in the structure of the turn itself (e.g., stamp cramproll turns, cramp barrel roll turns).

Cramproll Turning on the Spot

[4 sounds] [1&a2]

Heel drop L, ball R. heel drop R and L. Execute as a R outside stationary turn. The L ball acts as a pivot point while the R foot helps accomplish the turn. Spot is dir. frt

NOTE:
The last heel dropped (L) is also the first heel to beg. the next turn, thus, a double L heel drop is performed. Execute as many turns as possible to each set of cramprolls.

CRAMPROLL (continued)

Cramproll Turns Traveling in a Straight Line

[4 sounds] [&1&2]

Beg. sl execute the following as outside L turns progressing from sl to R. Leap R to R, leap L Xd bk R w/body facing frt. Using balls of feet as pivot pts., turn bk to L and execute heel drops R and L, ending w/ body facing frt and L Xd frt R. Spot can be dir. frt or to R. Steps can replace the leaps and the turn can change level from relevé to plié.

CRAMPROLL CHANGES. See CRAMPROLL: Alternating

CRAMPROLL TIME STEP. See TIME STEP: Cramproll

CRAMPROLL TURN. See TURN: Cramproll

CRAWLING SPLIT. See SPLIT: Crawling

CRISSCROSS

Crisscross describes the pattern of a movement or a step, such as alternating drawbacks. The usual pattern is back on the right, cross L frt R, back on the R, back on the L, cross R frt L etc.

CROISÉ (Crossed, Crossed Over)

A ballet position in which the legs are crossed and/or the body is facing at an oblique angle from the audience.

CROSS:

- ✪ Crossing the feet, hands, arms etc.
- ✪ Old term: St L, Sh bc R Xd frt L [1&2&3]

(THE) CROSS

[8 sounds] [1 &a2 &3 &4]

> TO EXECUTE:
> Step L, tap R bk L, hop L, step R frt L [&1 &2] click L, toe to R heel, hop R, tap L, step L [&3 &4]

Cross and Hop

[w/wo sound]

(From *The Tap Dance Dictionary* by Mark Knowles).

> TO EXECUTE:
> 1 Step L Xd frt R ast slap L knee w L hand [1], hop L [2], reverse (A), repeat (A), reverse (A) [3 4 5 6 7 8]
> 2 While feet remain Xd, leap bk on L, fwd on R, bk on L, fwd on R [1 2 3 4]
> 3 Plié R ast touch L to L, step L [5&], reverse (C), repeat (C), reverse (C) [6& 7 &8]

Cross Bar

[18 sounds] [8 &a1 2 &3 &a4 &a5 &6 &a 7 hold 8]

A very old step which crosses the feet and moves from side to side.

> TO EXECUTE:
> Hop L (or heel change), shuffle R [8 &a1], hop L, shuffle R frt [1 2&], hop L, shuffle step R to R [3 &a4], shuffle step L X R frt R [&a5], shuffle R, alt. pick up from L foot to R foot [&6 &a], toe tap L bk R, hold [7 hold 8]

Cross Leg Walk

[4 sounds] [1 2 3 4]

> TO EXECUTE:
> Toe heel L to L, toe heel R frt L [1 2 3 4]

Cross Over

Any step in which one foot or leg crosses over the other. (e.g,. alternating drawbacks, grapevine, falling off a log, etc.).

Cross Rhythm. See SYNCOPATION

Cross the Bugle

[9 sounds] [1&2&a 4&a]

> TO EXECUTE:
> Step L to L, shuffle toe heel R frt R [1&2&a] step L, hop L, shuffle R [3 4 &a]

CROSS WALK. See WALKING GRAPEVINE

CROSSED. See CROISÉ.

70

CROSSED OVER

Old term. A step where one foot crossed the other. See Croisé.

(THE) CROSSOVER

The second step of the shim sham shimmy.

> TO EXECUTE:
> Ball R to R, St L ip 2 Xs, St R to R, scuff L, L frt R heel drop R, St L frt R, St R to R [12345&hold 6&78]. Reverse & repeat (6M) and add shim sham break. See shim sham break

CROSSOVER RIFF

A riff in which one foot crosses over the other. See RIFF: Pendulum

CRUMP

A poorly executed or muffled cramproll.

CRUNCH. See CRAMPROLL

CUBAN WALK (Latin Walk)
[w/wo sounds]

Derived from ballroom dancing.

> TO EXECUTE:
> Walk fwd on R. R knee bent, L straight [1], L hip to L, both feet on floor ast. Reverse and progress fwd.

CUBANOLA GLIDE. See TIME STEP: Traveling

CURTAIN TIME (Show Time)

The time when the performance is scheduled to begin.

CUT

Dance: To cut legs from side to side or take a certain section of the dance out.

Music: To omit a certain section, phrase, or bar from the music.

CUT OUT

- ✿ Traceable to character dancing. Swing legs from side to side, alternating supporting feet, usually done by leaping or sliding; was performed often in soft shoe or as a flash step by leaning fwd. Heel clicks may be added as legs go to 2nd.
- ✿ A swinging of the legs from side to side, w/wo sound; implies that the free leg is lifted directly to the 2nd position and that each supporting leg lands in the exact spot as the previous leg. (e.g,. directly under the center of the body).

CUT TIME

4/4 time cut in half: 2/4 time with 2 beats to 1 measure of music.

CUTAWAY
[w/wo sounds]

An action or movement where the second foot replaces the first foot in the exact spot where the first foot was located.

- ✿ Example: In a trench, the second trench takes place in the exact spot where the first foot was located.
- ✿ Example: leap R, landing on R directly under the center of the body line, and in the exact spot where the first foot was placed.

DANCE DIRECTOR

Old term for a choreographer. Many dance directors were not dancers, but directors of movement. Many were visionaries with camera angles and large groups of people. Such a person was Busby Berkeley.

DANCE DOWN

At one time, when tap dance marathons were prevalent, tap dancers were notified by a judge or monitor to leave the floor, as they had been out danced, and were no longer in the competition.

DANCE NOTATION

A method of recording, through symbols or writing, the movements, steps, counts, and style of dance works. Labanotation and Benesh are two of these systems.

DANNY DANIELS TOE STAND
[6 sounds] [a12a 3 4]

> TO EXECUTE:
> Flap L, toe stand R and L [a12a] stamp R and L [3 4]

DANNY DANIELS TRAVELING STEP
[18 sounds] [a1 a2 a3 &a4 a5a6a7&8]

> TO EXECUTE:
> Flap R, L, R, L, stamp R
> [a1a2a3&a4], reverse the
> above [a5a6a7&a8]

DEBBIE
[18 sounds] [&a1 &2 &a3 &4 &5 &6 &7&8]

(From *The Tap Dance Dictionary* by Mark Knowles)

> TO EXECUTE:
> (A) shuffle step R, ball change L
> [&a1&2], reverse (A)
> [&a3&4],
> (B) heel toe R, step L [5 &6],
> heel toe R, step L [7 &8]

DELAYED "4". See PICKUP: Double

DELAYED WINGS. See WINGS

DEMI PLIÉ ⍓ (Half Plié, Half Bend)

A ballet term. Literally, half a plié; inherent in all dance mov.; used to soften mov.; to prep. for steps of elevation and to complete them. See PLIÉ

> TO EXECUTE:
> Stand w/ feet in 1st pos.(or
> any two or par pos.) bend
> knees, maintain proper
> placement, keep back erect,
> knees over toes and heels on
> floor. Demi plié is reached
> when the knees can be no
> further bent w/o destroying
> the body line.

DENBY. See BANDY TWIST

DIAGONAL (Oblique)

- ✿ An imaginary or actual str. line extending from cor. to cor.
- ✿ May refer to placing the body itself on a diag. line from cor. to cor.
- ✿ Usually refers to the line of travel or movement.

DIG (Ball Dig, Ball Jab, Heel Dig, Heel Jab, Toe Dig, Toe Jab, Side Dig)
[w/wo sound] [1 count]

A forceful mov. of one foot, executed by striking or placing the ball, toe or heel of the working foot close to the supporting foot.

NOTE:
Because many terms have never been standardized, they carry a multitude of names, such as this one. For our purposes, we will assume that dig carries no wt. and that after the sound has been made, the foot [ball] etc. remains grounded, (i.e., not lifted). It may also, be considered as a pose.

DIGFLE
[2 sounds] [&1] or [a1]

> TO EXECUTE:
> Heel dig R followed by a bk
> brush R

DIRECTION

May apply to the direction in which a dance moves on the stage—upstage, downstage, etc.—or the instructions a dancer receives from the choreographer or director.

DISCO

A dance and musical form of the 1970s, popularized by the psychological theories of the day—individuality, the ability to explore the body, and the "do one's own thing" attitude; it also dispensed with the idea that couples had to hold hands throughout the dance or that they had to do the same step at the same time.

DIVERTISSEMENT ⍓

Literally, "diversion." In music, a light, amusing piece; in dance, it is much the same thing, but could also pertain to small numbers inserted into a classical ballet.

DIXIELAND

A type of music, born in the South, that uses 12-M phrasing and shares lineage with the blues.

(THE) DOROTHY

Named for the character Dorothy in the *Wizard of Oz* clicking her heels together twice when making a wish. See DOUBLE HEEL CLICK

DOUBLE

A term of many meanings. It could infer, do twice as many of something, do it twice as fast such as in double time, use both feet as in a double toe stand, do twice as many sounds, but in a different order, such as, a double pickup as compared to a single pickup. It was an old term for shuffle, because it created 2 sounds.

DOUBLE BALL
[2 sounds] [a&] or [e&]

To strike the ball of the same foot 2 times in rapid succession.

DOUBLE BALL CHANGE
[4 sounds] [&1&2] or [a1a2]

Old term for shuffle bc because a double was a shuffle and a bc had two sounds. Could also connote doing 2 bcs.

DOUBLE BREAK

Changing the step that follows the hop of the break into flap, which has two sounds. See BREAKS: Single, Double, Triple

DOUBLE BUCK
[8 sounds] [1 2 &3 a&a4]

An old term and short combination.

> **TO EXECUTE:**
> Slow shuffle R, chug fwd L 2 X's [1 2 &3], shuffle ball change R [a&a4]

DOUBLE CHANGE
[4 sounds] [a1a2]

A very old term for flap ball change, as the flap was known as two and the ball change implied that the ball of the foot was used, and then you change feet.

DOUBLE CLICK

- ✿ When executing a bell, click heels together twice.
- ✿ When executing a toe click, hit toes together twice.
- ✿ When doing a finger snap, snap 2 times.

DOUBLE CROSSOVER
[6 sounds] [&8&123]

Traceable to clog dancing, A recognized combination of shuffle hop step and ball change. The shuffle hop step is usually done by placing the working foot ahead (e.g., R frt L) feet remaining in this pos. (R frt L) while the ball change is executed (L-R).

DOUBLE EARL
[16 sounds] [&a1 &2 &a3 &4 &5 &6&7 hold 8]

> **TO EXECUTE:**
> Shuffle step R ball change (L bk R) [&a1&2], shuffle step L ball change (R bk L) [&a3&4], scuff

hop step fwd R and L [&5&6&7 hold 8]

DOUBLE DRAWBACK. See DRAWBACK: Double

DOUBLE ESSENCE. See ESSENCE: Double

DOUBLE FLAP (Ram a Flap, Ramming a Flap, Double Slap)
[4 sounds] [e&a1]

The old term double slap is no longer used, as slap has now been defined as a step that carries no weight. To perform this step, one must lift in the air, and on landing accomplish 2 flaps, clearly and quickly, to fit them into 1 count. They were used extensively in World War I military routines.

DOUBLE GRABOFF. See PICKUP: Double

DOUBLE HEEL CLICK
[4 sounds] [1 2 &3]

Any step in which the heels are clicked together two times in succession.

> **TO EXECUTE:**
> Jump feet to 2nd position plié [1], spring into air, clicking heels tog. 2 Xs [2&], land in 2nd position plié [3]

DOUBLE HEEL STAND. See HEEL STAND: Double

DOUBLE HEELS (Double Heel Drops, Heel Beats, Heel Cramps)
[2 sounds] [&1] [a1]

Literally means the dropping of two heels by:

- ✿ Dropping first the R, then the L heel, or
- ✿ Dropping the same heel two times, or
- ✿ Dropping both heels ast.

DOUBLE HIP WING. See WING: Double

DOUBLE IRISH
[8 sounds] [&8&1&2&3] or [a8a1a2a3]

Traceable to clog dancing. See also IRISH

> **TO EXECUTE:**
> Sh hop St R, Sh bc L. Do ip, traveling or in any direction.

DOUBLE JUMP

Very old term meaning shuffle R, leap R, for in the beginning a shuffle was called a two and leap and jump were synonymous terms. Today the term would mean jump twice on both feet at the same time.

DOUBLE KNEE SPIN. See KNEE SPIN: Single, Double, Triple

DOUBLE ONE-STEP RHYTHM. See ONE STEP RHYTHM

DOUBLE PICKUP. See PICKUP: Double

DOUBLE RIFF. See RIFF: Double

DOUBLE SCUFF
[2 sounds] [a 1]

Depending upon the execution, the double scuff might be considered a nerve scuff. See HEEL SHUFFLE

> TO EXECUTE:
> Swing R foot fwd hitting the back edge of the heel [a] before it completes the lift, hit the back edge of the same heel again [1]

DOUBLE SHUFFLE. See SHUFFLE: Double

DOUBLE SLAP. See DOUBLE FLAP

DOUBLE TIME. See RHYTHM: Musical; DYNAMICS: Rhythm, Double Time

DOUBLE TIME STEP. See TIME STEP: General, 5(B)

DOUBLE TOE
[2 sounds] [1a&2]

While standing on the left foot, spring into the air and tap the toe of the right foot 2 times before landing on the left on the 2 count.

DOUBLE TOE STAND. See TOE STAND: Double

DOUBLE TOE TAP
[2 sounds] [a&] or [e&]

Strike the top of the same toe 2 times in rapid succession.

DOUBLE TRAVEL. See PARALLEL TRAVEL: 1

DOUBLE TRIPLE TIME STEP. See TIME STEP: Double Triple

DOUBLE VIRGINIA ESSENCE. See ESSENCE: Virginia: Double

DOUBLE WALTZ CLOG. See WALTZ CLOG (STEP): Double

DOUBLE WING. See WING: Double

DOWN BALL CHANGE

Old descriptive name for step ball change

DOWN HOP

Old descriptive name for step hop.

DOWN SYNCOPATED STEP
[19 sounds] [&a1&2&a3&4&a5&6&7&8]

(From *The Tap Dance Dictionary* by Mark Knowles)

> TO EXECUTE:
> Shuffle step R, ball change (L to R) [&a1&2], shuffle step L, ball change (R to L) [&a3&4], shuffle step L, chug R bk, step L [&a5&6], step R, chug bk R, ball change (L to R) [&7&8]

DOWNBEAT

Refers to the first beat in a measure or the downstroke of the conductor's hand when beating time. The ct. of 1.

DOWNSTAGE. See REFERENCE MANUAL: Performing, The Stage Area

DOUBLE TIME. See DYNAMICS: Rhythm, Double Time

DOWNWARD RHYTHMIC PROGRESSION. See RHYTHMIC PROGRESSION: Downward Progression

DRAG. See DRAW

DRAG TRAVEL

While moving (traveling) on one foot, the other foot (in this case the L is pulled or dragged along in a posé position).

TO EXECUTE:

Lunge on R to R, plié R and L extended straight and to L while holding the lunge position on R, drop toes of R foot to R, then heel of R foot to R, continue to travel to R

DRAW (Drag, Toe Draw, Toe Drag) [w/wo sound]

Standing on one foot and pulling the free foot toward the body, into any position or direction, without it leaving the floor. The ball, side, toe, tip, or whole foot may be used.

DRAWBACK [3,4 or 5 sounds] [&a1] or [a&a1] or [&1&a2]

General: Part of the genre of close to the floor work. Although the step was recognized for some years, it was Jack Stanly, a well-known New York teacher, who gave it its name. The basic or single drawback is a rather simple step, but, as its tempo increases, the sound becomes more difficult to execute quickly, at this point, the movement must be initiated by the ankle rather than stem from the knee. Using the ankle, eventually, transforms the first movement, spank, into a nerve tap. Drawbacks are a backward moving step. Listed below are some of the more recognized ones.

Drawbacks: There is much dispute about the actual existence of the double and triple drawback as such. There is no dispute about of the single drawback.

TO EXECUTE:

Begin with feet close together and parallel: spank bk R, drop L heel, step bk R [&a1] reverse

TO EXECUTE:

Spank R bk, drop L heel, flap R [a&a1] reverse

TO EXECUTE:

Spank bk R, drop L heel, Sh St bk R [&1&a2] reverse

NOTE:
In this form the triple drawback and the Cincinnati (single) are identical steps. See CINCINNATI

Straight:

✪ the direction, e.g. bkwd, diag.

✪ that the feet remain parallel and side by side—not crossing.

One-Sided (Crossed): R or L
Execute by continuously crossing one foot over the other. If the R foot leads str. bkwd on the 1st drawback and the L foot then crosses it on the 2nd drawback—the step is classified as being R sided, and vice versa for the L. These may be done par or tno.

Alternating
First one foot crosses in frt, then the other.

TO EXECUTE:

2 str. drawbacks R and L, drawback crossing R frt L, 2 str. drawbacks L and R, drawback crossing L frt R. [&a1&a2 &a3&a4&a5&a6].

The feet are usually held par on the straight drawbacks and to on the ones which cross.

NOTE:
In 4/4 time, only the cts. 1-6 are used, thus leaving cts. 7 and 8 unused. When beginning the next series of alternating drawbacks on the cts &a7, &a8, a rhythmic progression has been begun (see RHYTHMIC PROGRESSION). However in 3/4 or 6/8-time, a rhythm pattern has been created, but not a rhythmic progression, since the step in itself is in patterns of 6.

Turning

Stationary: Drawbacks can be used as a stationary turn, but may be difficult to keep in place and require rapid turning to be effective with the number of sounds being heard.

Traveling: Drawbacks may be done as inside or outside traveling turns. See TURNS: Traveling.

Drawbacks in Place: These must be executed as nerve taps, in order to remain ip. They are more comfortably done as straight drawbacks w/ the feet remaining in a closed par pos.

Twisting Drawbacks: Keeping the feet and legs close together and parallel and switching the heels and/or lower body, from side to side, such as to the R then the L.

DROP [w/wo sound] [1]

General: Means to lower a raised extremity, part of the foot, or whole body etc. to the floor; may be done w/o sound or force. For example:

Toe Drop: Starting with feet in par pos., flex toes of one foot (e.g., R), using the heel in contact with the floor as a pivot pt. Wt. is basically on the supporting leg. With a firm action, lower the R toe; weight is usually transferred [1 sound] [1 count].

DROP (continued)

Heel Drop: Starting with feet in par pos., lift the heel of one foot (e.g., R), using the ball of the foot in contact with the floor, firmly lower the R heel; weight is usually transferred **[1 sound] [1 count]**.

Backdrop, Scenic: A large piece of canvas, usually hung in the upstage area during a performance that realistically, abstractly, atmospherically, etc., helps set the mood or carries forth the idea of what is being presented on the stage.

Back drop, Dance: A movement developed in modern dance, now used in jazz and occasionally in tap. See BACKDROP

DROP CRAMPROLL. See CRAMPROLL: Drop

DRUM PICKUP. See PICKUP: Drum

DRUM PULLBACK. See PICKUP: Drum

DRUMROLL. See CRAMPROLL

DRUM SLAP (Military Flap)
[2 sounds] [a1]

Traceable to vaudeville. It was especially favored in the military dances of the day and referred to the fast flap that followed the hop.

The favorite combination was **Sh R, hop L, flap R (drum slap R) [&8 &a1] or**

Sh R, hop L, flap R, L, R [&8 &a1 a2 a3].

NOTE:
In today's terms slap does not carry weight and flap does carry weight, so, the term drum slap is literally an incorrect term, but out of respect, the term has been left in its original form.

DRUM WING. See WING: Drum

DUCK WADDLE
[w/wo sound] [a1]

Traceable to vaudeville and musical comedy. This term belongs more to the realm of eccentric and musical comedy dancing than to any other category. To be done properly, legs were kept stiff and straight and astraddle, body pitched slightly fwd, back arched, fingers flexed, arms str. The performer, retaining this pos, then proceeded to do a series of stiff heel toes, from one foot to the other, allowing the body to roll twd the performing foot, thus creating a waddling appearance. It is interesting to note that Charlie Chaplin retained this roll-like stride in his famous Charlie Chaplin walk.

DUCK WALK
[movement] [w/wo sound]

A stylized movement, with feet turned out.

TO EXECUTE:
Walk R to R, L to L etc. maintaining the turned out position, rock to the same side as the working foot. heel toe R, lean R, heel toe L, lean L while feet remain turned out.

DUET (Duo)
Two people working and/or dancing together.

DUO. See DUET

DUPLE RHYTHM
Occurs when one beat of music is divided into two equal parts. Its basis is the eighth note and it is counted as **[1&]**.

DUTCH HOP
[3 sounds] [1 2 3]
A short combination often used in a Dutch or wooden-shoe dance.

TO EXECUTE:
Step R fwd, brush or scuff L fwd, step fwd R, hop L [1 2 3]

DYNAMIC SHADING
Where tap phrases have different tonal qualities such as soft, loud, etc., thus enhancing and stressing the various rhythmic blendings; almost like creating conversations with the feet.

DYNAMICS (Tap Sounds)
Dynamics add life, form, quality, and energy to the work being performed. The principles listed below have to do with the dynamics of sound, but they could easily apply to style or presentation.

Rhythm: Rhythm is like the ticking of a clock. It is the regular occurrence of a beat and the framework upon which all accents and syncopation are placed:

On Beat: Falling exactly on the primary or major beats of the music. e.g., 1 2 3 4.

Off Beat: Falling in between the major beats (e.g., using the counts i, e, a & etc.).

Duple Rhythm: Occurs when 1 beat of music is divided into two equal parts; it is based on the eighth note and counted as [1&].

Triplet Rhythm: Occurs when 1 beat of music is divided into three equal parts; it is based on the eighth note and is counted as [1&a].

Quadruplet Rhythm: Occurs when 1 beat of music is divided into four equal parts; it is based on the sixteenth note and is counted as [1e&a].

Double Time: In dance, it expects that whatever step or sound is being executed in 4 cts, such as toe heel R and L [1234], would now be executed in 2 cts. [&1&2].

Syncopation: The displacement of the pulse or the normal accent, usually on the weak beat of the music, like on & or a etc.

Accent: To place the emphasis on a particular step or part of a step that will make it more prominent in sound than that which surrounds it. Remember, all accents are not loud, some are medium and some soft and the choice of the accent is dependent on the total phrase being executed.

Clustering: The idea of clustering is perhaps best expressed through an analogy to writing. As letters, when placed together, form words, words, together form sentences and sentences form paragraphs. Finally paragraphs express the ideas of the text. Thus tap sounds should be grouped together and through the use of accent or shading, form short or long rhythmic passages that contribute to the concept of the routine. Beale Fletcher, a fine teacher and author, proposed the idea of clustering many years ago in his book *How To Improve Your Tap Dancing.*

Shading: Shading concerns controlling sounds such as flap heels, heel drops, or shuffle step from soft to loud (crescendo) and from loud to soft (decrescendo). Practicing this control of sounds allows the performer more options and can only add to the quality of the performance.

Contrast: Learn to contrast one rhythmic pattern against another, see that the port de bras has fluidity as well as percussiveness, that the levels are not always the same. Contrast sparks interest and keeps the performance alive and vital.

Quality: This helps distinguish one dancer from another: quality of sound, presentation, concept, technique, performance.

EAGLE ROCK
[4 movements] [1234]

A social dance in which the dancer(s) held their hands out and rocked from side to side as though flying. It was named after a Baptist church in Kansas City, and soon was in dance halls all over the country. An era step derived from the sailor's hornpipe and much later used in a social fad dance called ballin' the Jack.

> TO EXECUTE:
> Interlock fingers, press palms down. Step L frt R, snap kick R to R, step R frt L, ast, leaving feet crossed and on the ground, rock ankles L, then to R [1234].

EARL
[8 sounds] [&a1 &2 & hold 3 & 4]

Origin unknown. Works well as an ending for a dance and follows the rhythmic line of "A Shave and a Haircut—Two Bits."

> TO EXECUTE:
> Shuffle step R, ball change [&a1 &2], scuff L fwd. pause [& hold 3] hop R, step L [&4]

ECCENTRIC

A dance often associated with comedy and musical comedy, it contains exaggerated gestures and movements and often portrays a character. Ray Bolger is well–known for his performances in this style.

ECHO TAP

A type of dancing in which the 2nd beat and the 4th beat of the measure are accented.

ECHO WINGS. See WING: Scatter Wings

ÉCHAPPÉ

Literally, "escaped." ballet terminology, meaning to escape from a closed position to an open one. Used in toe stands, wings, and pickups.

EDDIE
[8 sounds] [&a1 &2 &3 & hold 4]

(From *The Tap Dance Dictionary* by Mark Knowles)

> TO EXECUTE:
> Shuffle step R, ball change (L-R) [&a1 &2], spank bk L, heel drop R [&3], brush L fwd and bent-(thigh par to floor) [& hold4]

EDDIE LEONARD SOFT SHOE
[18 sounds] [&1&2&3&4&5&6&a7&8]

> TO EXECUTE:
> (A) ball change R bk L, shuffle ball change R bk L, scuff R, hop L, step R [&1&2&3&4], reverse (A) [&5&6&a7&8]

EIGHTH-NOTE RHYTHM. See DUPLE RHYTHM

ELEANOR POWELL (TURN). See TURN: Stationary, Outside

ELEVATION

- ✪ To the dancer it is ballon, or the ability to spring from the floor, the illusion of stopping at the height of the spring and then descending into the floor, ending in plié.
- ✪ May also refer to a platform or another level on the stage, such as a building or a hill, etc.

EN CROIX

Literally, "in the form of a cross." Most thought of in relation to the ballet barre where exercises are performed 4th en avant, à la seconde, 4th derrière and à la seconde, thus creating half a cross. When the other side of the barre has been completed, the full cross has been formed.

EN DEDANS

Literally, "inward." This indicates that the leg moves inward or toward the body, in a counterclockwise direction (i.e., from the back to the front). It may be executed on the floor (à terre) or in the air (en l'air). In the case of turns, the direction would be, determined by the supporting leg. In a circle of turns, the direction would be clockwise.

EN DEHORS

Literally, "outward." This indicates that the movement of the leg is outward or away from the body, as in rond de jambe en dehors. Regarding turning, an en dehors turn would take place on the supporting leg, in the direction of the working leg. In a circle of turns, the line of direction would be clockwise.

EN L'AIR

Literally, "in the air." When a part of the body or the body itself is in the air, as opposed to à terre or on the ground.

ENTR'ACTE

A short entertainment or divertissement performed between the acts.

ENTRANCE

Stage: The sides or back of a proscenium-type stage, where a performer may enter onto the stage proper.

Dance: A dance step or run–on that transports the dancer onto the stage proper.

ESSENCE
[any number of sounds] [4] [1&a2]

Both a dance and a step. It stems from an older dance called the essence of Old Virginny (Virginia), a favorite dance of black minstrelsy. The present essence, which we call the soft shoe, was conceived from the more graceful sections of this older routine. It was, at first, performed in soft shoes with no taps and frequently as a sand dance. The step, the essence, is incorrectly known as a time step, probably because of its long usage and because of its capability of being singled, doubled, and tripled. The basic step of the essence (dance) is the essence step, which is given below.

Front Essence

> TO EXECUTE:
> Single R frt essence: St R to R, Br St L frt R, St R ip-reverse for L   [&1&2]
> double R frt essence: Fl R to R, Br St L frt R, St R ip-reverse for L   [&1&a2]
> triple R frt essence: Sh St R to R, Br St L frt R, St R ip-reverse for L [&1e&a2]

Back Essence

TO EXECUTE:

Single R bk essence: Sp
St R bk L, St L to L, St R
ip-reverse for L [&1&2]
double R bk essence: Sp St
R bk L, Fl L to L, St R ip-
reverse for L [&1&a2]
triple R bk essence: Sp St R
bk L, Sh St L to L, St R ip-
reverse for L [&1e&a2]

Listed below is another popular
execution of the Back Essence.

TO EXECUTE:

Single R bk essence: Step R
bk L, brush bc L end in 2nd.
reverse [1&a2]
double R bk essence: Sp St
R bk L, brush bc L end in
2nd. reverse [&1&a2]
triple R bk essence: Sh St R
bk L, brush bc L end in 2nd.
reverse [&a1&a2]

Short Essence

TO EXECUTE:

Literally, a step followed by
a brush ball change crossing
either in frt or in back of the
supporting leg.
Step R to R, brush L frt R,
ball change L frt R [1&a2]
or
Step R to R, brush L bk R,
ball change L bk R [1&a2]

Long Essence

TO EXECUTE:

Step R to R, brush bc L frt
R. brush bc L to L, brush bc
L frt R [1&a2&a3&a4]
reverse for L.

NOTE:

✿ The long essence is usually done as a frt essence,
   not as a bk essence.
✿ To make it double replace the step R to R with
   flap R [a1&a2&a3&a4].
✿ To make it triple replace the step R to R with Sh
   St R [&a1&a2&a3&a4].

Virginia Essence

The Virginia essence involves changing every ball change
to a heel change.

TO EXECUTE:

Single: Step R to R, brush L
frt R, heel change L frt R,
Sp L to 2nd, heel change L
to 2nd, brush L frt R, heel
change L frt R
[1&a2&a3&a4]

NOTE:

To make it a double, replace the step R to R with
flap R to R [&1&a2&a3&a4]

To make it a triple, replace the step R to R with
shuffle step R [&a1&a2&a3&a4]

Riff Essence

To execute a riff essence, substitute a fwd 2 ct. riff for
each brush in any of the essences.

Single frt riff essence

TO EXECUTE:

Step R to R, two ct. fwd riff
L frt R, bc L frt R [1a&a2]

Double Riff Essence:

TO EXECUTE:

Flap R to R, two ct. fwd riff
L frt R, bc L frt R [a1e&a2]

Triple Riff Essence:

TO EXECUTE:

Sh St R to R, two ct. fwd
riff L frt R, bc L frt R
[&a1e&a2]

Essence: Turning

The basis for an essence turning is a paddle step step R to
R bc bc bc L bk R. [1&2&3&4]

TO EXECUTE:

inside R turn:Step R to R,
brush bc L fwd R 3 times.
Turn on R to R. Execute
one or more turns
[1&a2&a3&a4]
outside R turn: Step R to R,
spank bc 3 times. Turn bk to L.
Execute one or more turns
[1&a2&a3&a4]

EVEN RHYTHM

A rhythmic phrase in which all of the beats are of the same value (**e.g., waltz is 1,2,3, 1,2,3**).

EXTENSION

This is the ability of the dancer to hold an extended leg in the air at a prescribed height and in any position—front, back, side, crossed, etc.—for a designated length of time.

EXIT

Stage: The sides or back openings of a proscenium-type stage where a performer may leave the stage proper.

Dance: In dance, the performer leaving the stage proper, either with a step or a runoff.

FAKE

Literally, a false or counterfeit copy of the original step, position, etc. There is something about it that does not fulfill the total requirements (e.g., performing a double pickup, but there are no emanating sounds, only the jumping aspect).

FAKE CRAMPROLL. See CRAMPROLL: Fake

FAKE SPLIT. See SPLIT: Fake

FAKE WINGS. See WINGS: Fake

FALL

To drop purposely and with regard to technical principles from a higher to a lower level.

FALL OFF (Stumble)
[6 sounds] [1 2 3&4]

Used often as an exit and executed as if falling and having to catch one's balance.

> TO EXECUTE:
> Leap L to L (like falling), step R bk L [1 2], step L to L, shuffle step R [3 &a4], repeat until off stage

FALL OVER STEP
[10 sounds] [8 &a1 2 3 4 5 6 7]

Resembles the falling off a log step used for vaudeville exits, but begins differently and is longer in content.

> TO EXECUTE:
> Hop R, shuffle step L bk R, lift R up in frt [8 &a1], spring R to R, spring L frt R [2-3], spring R to R, spring L bk R [4-5], spring R to L, spring L frt R [6-7], reverse while step-2 M

FALLING DOWN STAIRS
[2 movements] [12]

Similar to falling off a log. Old vaudeville step in which the illusion was that the dancer was about ready to fall. Used in eccentric routines.

> TO EXECUTE:
> Begin SR and face frt, lean to L; leap R ast cut L frt R, with L leg str. (body leans to L), step L to L (body leans to L) [12], continue across stage; repetition creates the falling illusion.

FALLING OFF THE LOG
[4 or 6 sounds or movements] [1234] or [&a1234]

A very early jazz step found in the old dances of the United States, which many times described the work, play, and culture of the people. This particular step is characteristic of a logger, riding and rolling a floating log down the river. His actions describing the turning of the log or his plunge into the water. The step was originally done on one spot, cutting the feet high and sharply into the air, the body changing pos. from side to side as fully as possible. Later it was used for exits and entrances onto or off the stage.

> TO EXECUTE:
> Leap R or shuffle leap R Xd bk L, ast cut L in low battement frt R (body faces slightly to R, lean L), leap L to L, R to 2nd, leap R frt L ast cut L Xd bk R (face L frt corner), leap L to L, face frt [1234] or [&a1234]

FALLING SPLIT. See SPLIT: Falling

FALLOUT (Burpee)

Beg. feet tog. in squat position, place hands on floor, close to and dir. frt of feet. With a springing action and, keeping feet and legs tog., shoot feet bkwd until legs are stretched bk and body is in a push up, wt. balanced on hands and balls of feet. Bend knees and return to squat position.

FAN KICK (Circular Kick, Round Kick)

Traceable to the era of lines and production numbers. A fan kick is a high circular kick directed from one side to the other and passing in frt of the body, thus forming a high arc or half circle. There are three types of fan kicks, based on the dir. of the kick.

Inside

TO EXECUTE:

Stand L Xd frt R, tendu bk R or croisé bk R inside fan. Brush R thru 2nd, lift higher while creating a large arc or half circle as it passes from R to the L and crosses in frt of the body. The fan may end with a point R frt L, step R frt L, etc. The fan should reach its highest point when it is frt and in its crossing of the body.

Outside

TO EXECUTE:

Stand on L, tendu R to R or croisé bk R, brush R in tendu from R to L, crossing the body. At the conclusion of the tendu, lift R from croisé to battement, carrying it in a large outside arc from L to R. Fan may conclude with step R to R, tendu R etc. Highest point of the fan should be when the leg is in a fwd pos., passing the face.

NOTE:

Both of the above kicks may be preceded by a jump on both feet or a hop on one; this is most effective when done by a line of dancers. The prep. jump increases the excitement and, for some, helps to increase the height of the kick. These kicks may also be done w/ a heel drop during execution.

Turning

TO EXECUTE:

R Inside:
step R frt L; battement L to 2nd en l'air and perform an inside turn while executing an inside fan L (may add hop R if desired). During turn, step L frt R, leaving feet on floor, turn. Feet will end crossed with R frt L.
Outside:
step R brush L frt R and execute an outside fan kick with L (may hop if desired). Step L crossed bk R and leaving feet on the floor in crossed position, turn bk to L. End with L frt R.

Literally, the basis of a renversé turn. See RENVERSÉ TURN

FANCY BUCK
[7 sounds] [8& 1 & 2 & 3]

TO EXECUTE:

Shuffle step R, toe tap L, step L, heel dig R, step R [8& 1 & 2 & 3]

FINGER DANCING

Invented by Johnny Boyle Jr. It consists of putting thimbles on the fingers and emulating the steps of a tap dance using the proper tap technique.

FIVE
[5 sounds] [1&2&3]

An old term for a waltz clog, based on the idea that it contains 5 sounds.

FIVE COUNT. See RIFF: Conventional and Traditional

FIVE-POINT CRAMPROLL. See CRAMPROLL: Brush, Spank.

FIVE-SOUNDED (count) WING. See WING: Other Types

FLAM (FLIM FLAM)
[2 or 3 sounds] [a1] or [&a1]

There is not perfect agreement as to the execution of the flam; below are three definitions.

To execute:

- Brush R fwd and lower it with a heel toe R [&a1]—changes wt.

  or

- Brush R fwd and lower it with a slam [a1]—doesn't change wt.

or

- A touch of the inside or outside of the shoe and a rim shot, all done as one action.

FLAP (Brush Step Forward, Tap Spring, Front Straight, Slap)
[2 sounds] [a1] or [&1]

Flap is a very early step in tap. It originated when the sole of the tap shoe was purposely sewed only partly around, thus allowing it to slap the ground and create a sound. The terms slap and flap were interchangeable. Today the term slap is a flap w/o wt., while flap is w/ wt. The terms tap spring and front straight are no longer in existence.

To execute:

Raise R foot in a bkwd position; swing R foot in a fwd and downward direction making a brush sound, then step fwd R, usually on the ball of the foot.

This step may be done traveling in any dir., turning or ip. As the tempo increases and the flap becomes quite rapid, the brush changes to a nerve tap. Flaps alternate from foot to foot. Knees are relaxed and bent, according to need.

There are several types of flaps:

Walking: Flaps performed in a walking fashion, usually at a slow or moderate tempo.

Running: Flaps done in a running fashion, usually at a quick tempo and springing from foot to foot.

Flaps in Place: Executed by substituting the brush mov. for a nerve tap.

Double Flaps: 2 flaps done in rapid succession and in groupings of 2: spring in the air and execute flap R and flap L, in rapid succession to the rhythm of [a&a1] , [a&a2], etc.

NOTE:
Flap, like shuffle and ball change, is one of those basic steps that combine easily with many steps to produce a new steps, such as flap ball change, flap heel drop, etc.

FLAP BALANCÉ

Execute a balancé and substitute flaps and/or brush steps for all the steps [&1&2&3].

FLAP BALL CHANGE (Double Change, Brush Step Ball Change)
[4 sounds] [a1a2] or [&1&2]

A well-known and used step in tap; derived from step ball change.

To execute:

Flap to R to R or fwd and bc L bk R. Reverse

May be executed ip, forward, moving bkwd, or sdwd.

FLAP BRUSH BALL CHANGE (Double Essence)
[5 sounds] [a1&a2] or [&1&a2]

To execute:

Flap R to R, brush bc L frt or bk of R

Feet may vary in pos. as desired. For example, feet may remain par and movement may be from side to side or it may be done ip, traveling fwd, or turning [a1&a2] or [&1&a2]. Flap brush bc is seldom called an essence unless it crosses in frt or in bk.

FLAP CHUG
[3 sounds] [&a1]

This is really not a legitimate tap step, but an often used tap combination of two tap steps.

To execute:

Flap R, immediately chug fwd R [&a1]

FLAP CLOSE
[3 sounds] [a1 2]

A very common combination for beginners because of its simplicity and very helpful to tie steps together, for example, flap close R, shuffle hop step L frt R, and to teach beginners a change of weight.

TO EXECUTE:
Flap R to R [a1], close L to R [2], repeat [a 3 4]

FLAP CRAMPROLL. See CRAMPROLL: Brush, Flap

FLAP DOUBLE HEELS. See FLAP HEEL HEEL

FLAP HEEL (Brush Toe Heel, Brush Step Heel, Brush Ball Heel)
[3 sounds] [a1 2] or [&1 2] or [&a1]
This is an important step in fast tap work or close to the floor routines. The heel usually receives the accent.

TO EXECUTE:
Flap R high on ball of foot and forcibly lower the heel. Reverse

It may be executed in any dir. and performed to many rhythms. Can also be done turning. See TURNS: Traveling

FLAP HEEL BALANCÉ
Execute a balancé and substitute flap heels or brush toe heels for all of the steps. **[&a1&a2&a3]**

FLAP HEEL HEEL (Flap Double Heels, Brush Step Heel Heel, Brush Step Heel Heel, Brush Ball Heel Heel, Brush Toe Heel Heel)
[4 sounds] [a1a2] or [&1&2]

TO EXECUTE:
Flap R, heel drop L and R. reverse.

Note that the bk heel is dropped first to allow wt. to remain on the frt foot. This is the normal manner of execution. However, to remain on the same foot, Flap R and heel drop R and L. Repeat. Weight is left on the L foot **[a1a2]** or **[&1&2]**. May be executed in any dir., ip, or turning.

NOTE:
The term slap heel heel is no longer used. See TURNS: Traveling

FLAP HEEL HEEL TURNING. See TURN: Traveling, Flap Heel

FLAP HEEL TRAVELING TIME STEP
[15 sounds] [8 &1 &2 & 3 &4 &5 &6 &7]
A time step frequently used by teacher Al Gilbert because it is simple to understand. It's a good, smarter time step to learn.

TO EXECUTE:
(A) Shuffle step R to R, shuffle L, ball change, 2 Xs w/L, move R
(B) flap heel L and R [8 &1 &2 & 3 &4 &5 &6 &7] reverse (A) and (B)-2 M

FLAP HEEL TURNING. See TURN, Traveling, Flap Heel

FLAP STEP
[3 sounds] [a 1 2]
A well-known flap combination and used often as a predecessor to flap ball change, shuffle hop step and others. Often called flap close.

TO EXECUTE:
Flap R to R, step L to R [a 1 2]

FLAPPERS
The stylish, high–spirited women of the roaring twenties era. They wore tight or split skirts, cut rather high, so at certain times when they walked or sat, their skirts would flap open or around them.

FLASH ACT
A dance act that uses spectacular tricks.

FLASH ENDING. See BIG FINISH

FLASH FINISH. See BIG FINISH

FLASH RATTLE
[4 sounds] [e&a1]
An old flash step.

TO EXECUTE:
Stand L frt R with ball crossed bk L. Wt. is on the L. Slight spring and execute a toe stand on the L, ast scrape wing R, descend from L toe stand with a heel drop L, toe tap R bk L. Wt. on L foot to repeat [e&a1].

The toe stand may also be faked. The attention should be on the raising of the arms and on the action of the R foot.

FLASH STEP (Trick Step)

Used in routines to add a moment of excitement or brilliancy to a certain part of the music, such as the ending or loud passages that occurred in the center sections. They were strictly for applause. Most were very acrobatic and had few, if any, tap sounds. They embraced a whole realm of movement, from splits jumping off pedestals and stairways to around the world, trenches, over the tops, toe stands, and wings and their main theme was repetition—that is, until the audience applauded. Today flash steps have been replaced with turns, switch splits, and close to the floor footwork, but the reason is still the same—to get audible approval in the way of applause.

FLAT (Flat Brush, Flat Tap)
[1 movement] [1]

Stand on L, R in raised pos. bk swing R fwd striking whole of foot on floor. Foot ends raised in front. Some consider a slam as being a form of flat. See SLAM

FLAT BRUSH. See FLAT

FLAT CRAMPROLL. See CRAMPROLL: Drop

FLAT FOOT FIVE
[5 sounds] [&1 &a2]

Also a form of a round down.

> TO EXECUTE:
> Shuffle R, stamp R L R
> [&1 &a2]

FLATFOOT(ED):

Dancing on the whole or flat of the foot as opposed to performing on the balls of the feet. This a preference and a style among the traditional dancers of our country. Its past exponents were performers such as King Rastus Brown and the Nicholas Brothers. Today, Gregory Hines and Savion Glover are carrying on the tradition.

FLATFOOTED SHUFFLE. See SCUFFLE

FLAT STEP
[w/wo sound] [1] or [12]

Step on a flat foot. Carries wt. w/wo sound, or execute a flat followed by a step on the same foot.

FLAT TAP. See FLAT

FLAT TOE FLAT
[3 sounds] [1 &2]

Not a legitimate step, but a recognized form of a step ball change.

> TO EXECUTE:
> Stamp R, ball L, stamp R
> [1 &2]

FLAT TOE TURN. See TURN: Traveling, Stamp Toe

FLEA HOP
[w/wo sound]

This step is a form of a Slide, where the working leg is bent and held high to the side of the body.

> TO EXECUTE:
> Inside:
> Standing on the R, in plié, slide on the R to the L. Lift L knee higher on the slide itself and straighten R knee. Arms might swing to the L to help motivate the movement. Sliding foot remains in contact with the floor.

> TO EXECUTE:
> Outside:
> Standing on R, in plié, slide on R to R. Lift L knee higher on the slide itself and straighten R knee. Arms might swing to the R to help motivate the movement. Sliding foot remains in contact with the floor.

FLEX

A bent or contracted muscle or part of the body, such as the foot or hand.

FLEX KICK. See JAZZ KICK

FLEXED

Bent at a wrist or ankle joint. A flexed hand is bent at the wrist at a right angle to the arm, whereas a flexed foot is bent at the ankle at a right angle to the leg.

FLEXED FOOT

A term borrowed from jazz dance. The whole foot is flexed (turned upward from the ankle) forming a right angle with the leg.

FLICK
[2 sounds] [a 1]

A forward brush R, followed by a heel dig R. Almost a riff-like step, but it does not lift off the floor.

FLICK KICK. See JAZZ KICK

FLIM FLAM. See FLAM

FLIP KICK. See JAZZ KICK

FLOP

There are two source references for flop:

- An old term for slam, which implies that the working leg is straight and then lowered to the floor.

- Raise R foot with R knee bent. Strike floor with a flat foot ast straighten leg, so that it appears that the floor forced the leg to straighten.

In either context, it was used in eccentric work as an exaggerated step, walk, or movement.

FLOOR LUNGE. See LUNGE: Floor

FLOOR ROCK. See ROCK: Floor

FLOOR SPIN

A classification. A spin or turn executed on the floor, such as seat spin, knee spin, etc. See SEAT SPIN; KNEE SPIN

FLOOR WORK

Encompasses a dance mov. that is done, dropped to, or raised from the floor area, such as fake splits, knee spins, suspensions, coffee grinds. See SPLIT: Fake; KNEE SPIN; SUSPENSION; COFFEE GRIND

FLUTTER RIFF. See RIFF: Flutter.

FOCUS

Focus has to do with concentrating on the work at hand, whether it is alignment, the combination, one's performance, etc. It is one of the primary concerns of teaching that a student is well focused and remains that way throughout his training and professional life.

FOLLOW UP. See CONTAGIOUS

FOOT JUMP. See JUMP

FOOT LEAP

Old term meaning leap. See LEAP

FOOT POSITIONS

The positions assumed by the feet in dance are another means to performing well or poorly. Whether the feet and legs are turned out, remain on an oblique angle, or are parallel, certain rules still prevail.

- The weight should be evenly distributed on each foot individually and both feet collectively.

- The toes of each foot should lie flat within the shoes.

- No rolling should take place on either the inside or outside of the foot.

- The turnout of the dancer should never exceed his/her ability to turnout from the hip socket, in other words, the turnout should never be forced.

Tap requires, also, that the feet work inside the shoes, that the foot reshape itself constantly in anticipation of the sound(s) to be made. It, like most dance, must be aware of all the various positions and principles that govern them.

Turned out

The five ballet positions, 1st, 2nd, 3rd, 4th, and 5th, should be adhered to and determined by the sequence of tap steps being performed. It is not usually advisable to remain fully turned out for too long a time when tapping.

The five basic positions of the feet were established in ballet. From these, all movement would stem. The five turned-out positions are listed below:

1st Both heels touch, both legs are turned out from the hip socket, and together the feet form a straight line.

2nd Both heels are still in a straight line, with a distance of one's own foot between the heels.

3rd One foot is in front of the other, the heel of that foot touching the middle of the other foot, both are turned out.

4th Feet are parallel to each other and one step apart. One foot is parallel and ahead of the other.

5th Both feet touch so that the toe of one foot touches the heel of the other foot in a completely turned-out position.

NOTE:
The text on the five turned-out positions of the feet is from Agrippina Vaganova, *Basic Principles of Classical Ballet (Russian Ballet Technique).*

FOOT POSITIONS (continued)

Tap recognizes these turned positions as well as the feet being used with a slight turnout, parallel, or for some executions like tanglefoot even being turned in.

Parallel: All of the above five positions can be accomplished in the parallel position as well as tno. Dancing with the feet parallel is comfortable and practical for tap, especially if it is the close to the floor variety. However, female dancers wearing heels and doing a great deal of ballet stylization might want to use the feet and legs in a different manner.

Oblique: Oblique positions are described as somewhat less than turned out, but more than parallel. They are useful in tap, especially when the feet and legs have to be crossed.

Inverted: Inverted or turned-in feet are also called pigeon-toed. Although not often used in tap, they are an absolute essential when doing side travels, traveling cramprolls, tanglefoots, etc. so don't discount their potential!

NOTE:

Don't forget that in tap, many times the ankle must allow the foot to bevel and sometimes even to sickle to hit certain tap sounds, and flexed feet happen all the time with heel toes, toe drops, and back brushes, along with feet that must be arched for toe stands as well as normal technique.

FOOT SLAP

To hit the boot with the hand. Derived from folk dancing, it began as part of the male's vocabulary in Slavic and character dances of Europe.

FOOT SLIDE

Old term for slide. See SLIDE

FOOT TAP

Old term for tap. See TAP

FOOTLATURE

A tap and clog notation system developed by Ruth Pershing that charts the steps and counts on a grid.

FORMATION

The deliberate positioning of three or more dancers to form patterns such as lines, circles, squares, triangles, crosses, v's, etc. Formations may be solid and filled in or form the literal outline. They may be linear or flowing and of different levels and shapes. Putting a dance in formation makes the routine more interesting because of changing patterns, as opposed to the longtime practice of keeping dancers in a line or lines from the beginning to the end of the routine. Formations may be used to enhance or compensate for the anatomical differences in the dancers. The number of dancers a choreographer is to work with is a determining factor for the type and kind of

formations to be used. Other factors to be considered are the relative height of each dancer, the type of routine to be presented, the costume color, and the mood and design of the routine.

FORWARD BRUSH

Old term for brush to designate its direction. See BRUSH

FORWARD PICKUP. See PICKUP: Forward

FORWARD PULLBACK. See PICKUP: Forward

FORWARD RIFF

A Riff executed in a forward direction. see RIFF

FORWARD TAP

Old term meaning to tap the foot in a forward position.

FOUETTÉ ⚲ (Fouetté Rond de Jambe en Tournant) [w/wo sound]

Literally, "whipped." A whipped circle of the leg while turning. It is a popular turn whereby the circling leg and the relevé/plié are the main impetus of the series of turns. They may be executed both outside and inside, with the former being the more popular of the two.

> **TO EXECUTE:**
> Outside R: Turn maybe prefaced with R outside pirouette, upon facing frt, plié L, extend R 4th frt en l'air, relevé on L, sweep R to 2nd en l'air, turn bk R, R foot to frt of L knee, end facing frt.
> Inside R: Execute as above, but turn on R to R using an inside rond de jambe with L.

NOTE:

Upon reaching frt, the working leg can open to 4th or to 2nd. It should be kept at hip level with the foot closing to the knee of the supporting leg on each pirouette. The turn may be done w/wo a beat and w/wo sound; traveling or ip.

With a beat: On Outside, as leg passes through passé, beat R bk-frt around L leg before extending it to 4th or 2nd. On inside, as leg passes through passé, beat R foot frt-bk of L leg before it is extended.

With Sound: One might add heel drops, pickups, or wings to the supporting leg on the extension or a 3-count riff might be executed by the working leg upon completion of the turn. Be aware that to execute the riff sounds, one must distort the extension by lowering the foot to the floor.

Traveling or On the Spot: All the fouettés previously described have been on-the-spot turns. To travel fwd, sdwd, or bkwd, one must execute a chug and ast plié.

Variation: On each turn, a double inside or outside turn may be performed previous to extending the leg. The fouetté turn is often used in tap, but with the addition of sounds, usually in the form of heel drops.

FOUR (4)

An old term for a shuffle ball change, based upon the fact that the step contained four sounds.

FOUR COUNT (TAP) RIFF. See RIFF

Conventional, Traditional, 4-count

FOX TROT:

A form of ballroom dancing based on 4/4 time.

FRED ASTAIRE DRAG
[5 sounds] [12&34]

> TO EXECUTE:
> Step R to R (left in lunge position) [1], drag or draw L to R [2], ball change L to R to 2nd position [&3], step L frt R [4]

FREE FOOT

The foot that is not being used in the execution of a step.

FREEZE CHORUS

Usually occurs on the 2nd chorus of a routine. The first chorus is danced out fully; on the second chorus, the dancer freezes for all or part of the break.

FRENCH TWIST (Cigarette Twist)
[2 movements] [w/wo sound]

Traceable to early character and eccentric dance

> TO EXECUTE:
> Leap on R, face sr, ast plié R, L leg bent and raised in bk, knee inverted to floor

and L heel high. Subscribe an inside circle with the lower half of the L leg. Body faces the frt and L goes to 2nd. Continue to pivot and end facing L. Repeat. Change to L foot and raise R ready to reverse the step. A hop can be added as the leg completes the rond de jambe and extends to 2nd.

FRIGGLE. See CRUMP

FRONT-BACK

Old term for shuffle describing the action of the foot and leg, fwd than bkwd. Today, there is a step known as frt & bk shuffles. See SHUFFLE: Front Back

FRONT-BACK SHUFFLE. See SHUFFLE: Front-Back

FRONT AND BACK SPLIT. See SPLIT

FRONT ESSENCE. See ESSENCE: Front

FRONT HITCH KICK. See HITCH KICK: Front

FRONT IRISH. See IRISH Front

FRONT RIFF. See RIFF

FRONT RIFFLE. See RIFFLE

FRONT SHUFFLE. See SHUFFLE: Front

FRONT STRAIGHT

Old term for Flap. See FLAP

FULL BREAK. See BREAK: Full

FULL CRAMPROLL. See CRAMPROLL: Regular

FULL PIVOT. See PIVOT: Full

GALLOP

A very fast 2/4 tempo.

GEORGE MURPHY STEP
[&1&a2 &3 &4 &5&6 &7 &8]

Named for a dancer/actor in motion pictures for many years.

TO EXECUTE:

(A) Flap L, double shuffle R [&1&a2], ball change R bk L, flap R to R [&3 &4], repeat (A) 2 more times [2 M], shuffle heel, step L X bk R [&5 &6], flap fwd R and L [&7 &8]

GEORGIA GRIND. See BALLIN' THE JACK

GLIDE

With feet close to floor, moving or flowing along smoothly and without effort.

GOING NO PLACE. See BOX STEP

GRABOFF. See PICKUP

GRAB ROLL

TO EXECUTE:

Shuffle R to R, alternating pickup L to R, step L bk R [&1&a2]

GRACE TAP

An uncountable beat or tap that falls in between sixteenth notes (i.e. thirth-second notes).

GRAND BATTEMENT. See BATTEMENT

GRAND JETÉ

Grand jeté is used frequently in ballet and classical tap. It should adhere as accurately as possible to the ballet technique from which it stems. However, when sounds such as brush, scuff, or riff are to be used in the initial entrance into the jeté or when the landing uses footwork such as toe heel or flap heel, the dancer must be prepared to make adjustments to the line of the feet.

GRAND JETÉ TURN. See TURNS: Grand Jeté

GRAND PLIÉ

May be executed in all turned-out, parallel, and oblique positions, but should follow the technical rules of plié as stringently as possible: the passing through demi-plié, the placement and alignment of the body, etc.

GRAND(E) TOUR

Refers to a turn of the body, such as a pirouette, a turn in the air, and others. See TURN: Stationary

GRAPEVINE (Serpentine)
[w/ sound] [&1&2&3&4] or [a1a2a3a4]

The pattern woven by the feet while executing the step. The movement is in a sideward direction.

TO EXECUTE:

St R to R, St L bk R, St R to R, St L frt R [&1&2]

The body usually remains facing the frt. If a bouncing effect is desired, then each step may be substituted with a leap, much like a series of ball changes [a1a2a3a4]. It may also be executed as a series of toe heels, [a1a2 etc.], flap heels [&a1&a2 etc.]

GRAPEVINE SCHOTTISCHE
[4 movements] [1 2 3 4]

So called because of the combining of a partial grapevine with a hop.

TO EXECUTE:

Step L to L, R frt L, L to L, hop L [1 2 3 4]

GRIND

✪ A circling of the hips.

✪ A grinding of the heel into the floor, such as a heel grind. See HEEL GRIND

(THE) GUN
Jackson Gun [48 sounds]
[1&a2 &a3 &a4 &a5 &a6 &a7 &a8 &a1 &a2 &a3 &a4 &a5 &a6 &a7 &a8 &a]

This combination created by dancer Eugene Jackson relies basically on rolling shuffles and hops which are done on the ball or the flat of the feet, thus creating a louder sound. The accents are on the counts 1, 5, 1, 3, 6, and 7

TO EXECUTE:

Leap onto flat foot L, shuffle R, hop L [1&a2], shuffle R, hop L,

shuffle R, hop [&a3 &a4],
shuffle R, hop L onto flat foot
[&a5], shuffle R, hop L, shuffle
R, hop [&a6 &a7], shuffle R,
hop L, shuffle R, hop L onto
flat foot [&a8 &a1], shuffle R,
hop L, shuffle R, hop L onto
flat foot [&a2 &a3], shuffle R,
hop L, shuffle R, hop L, [&a4
&a5], shuffle R, hop L on whole
foot, shuffle R, hop L on whole
foot [&a6 &a7], shuffle R, hop
L, shuffle R [&a8 &a]

HALF BEND. See DEMI-PLIÉ

HALF BREAK. See BREAK: Half

❂ The 4th step of the shim sham shimmy.

HALF PENDULUM RIFF. See RIFF:
Pendulum

HALF PIVOT. See PIVOT: Regular

HALF PLIÈ See DEMI-PLIÉ

HALF ROUND BREAK. See BREAK: Half

HALF SPLIT. See SPLIT: Jazz Split

HALF TIME

Dancing half as fast as the beat of the music and/or
taking twice as long to do the actions. For example,
flap ball change is usually executed as **[a1 a2]**. In half
time, the count would be **[&1 2 3 hold 4]**.

HAM BONING

Creating sounds by slapping various parts of the body
with the hands.

HAMP
[1 or 2 sounds] [1] or [&1]

> TO EXECUTE:
> (1) Hop on a flat foot [1]
> or
> (2) Hop L and stamp or
>   stomp R [&1]

HANG(ING) 4 OR 8

An expression that arose from traditional tap and in
relationship to challenges, in which each dancer
performs and/or improvises his best 4 or 8 measures
of music.

HEAD POSITIONS

The positioning of the head in dancing is as basic and
as essential as the position of the feet, arms, and body.
The posture of the head is a contributing factor to
proper placement, alignment, and presentation. There
are six basic head positions, which can be combined
to create subtle variations.

Straight Forward: The neck is reached out of the
shoulder line, with the face directly fwd and with the
chin par to the floor. The bk of the head is in line
with the spinal column.

Straight Backward: The neck is lifted out of the
shoulder line and stretched backward as far as
possible.

Raised: The face, while in a fwd position, is lifted
and stretched upward and slightly bkwd with the eyes
focused diagonally on the ceiling or walls ahead.

Lowered: The head is stretched out of the shoulder
line and inclined twd the floor either on a diag. line
or with the chin pressed twd the chest.

Inclined (Tilted): W/ the face str. frt, the head is
stretched out of the shoulder line and tilted to the R
or L.

Profile (Turned): W/ the face str. fwd and pulled
out of the shoulder line, turn the head directly to the
R or L with the chin parallel to the shoulder and to
the floor.

HEEL (Heel Tap, Heel Touch) [1 sound]
[1] or [&]

A placing of the bk edge of the heel on the floor in
any dir. w/wo wt. The toes of the working foot are
flexed the working leg can be bent or str. Heel is
readily combined w/other basic steps to form
amalgamated steps, such as heel toe or heel step.

HEEL BALL.
Old term for Heel Dig. see HEEL DIG

HEEL BALL CHANGE
[3 sounds] [1&2]

Place R heel fwd, move R foot to bk and execute,
bc R–L. Can be done moving fwd, ip, bkwd, frt; par
or tno heel ball change is a well-known combination,
as opposed to a major term.

HEEL BEAT. See HEEL DROP

HEEL BEAT SWIVEL (Rocking Heels, Heel Rocks)
[1, 2 sounds] or [&]

To rock one or two heels from side to side with feet in parallel position.

HEEL BRUSH. See SCUFF

HEEL CHANGE (Heel Rock)
[2 sounds] [1 2] or [&1]

Comparable to ball change except that the heel is used instead of the ball.

> TO EXECUTE:
> Place R heel fwd, with wt. (R ft. flexed), step L back, either on half or flat foot. Can be done traveling in any dir., turning, or ip.

HEEL CLICK (Click Heels) [1 sounds] [1] or [&]

Traceable to character dancing. A heel click consists of the striking together of both heels simultaneously, while wt. is on balls of feet or while both feet are in the air.

> TO EXECUTE:
> Stand in relevé with feet several inches apart, knees are usually straight, but for character dance, may be bent. Forcibly turn heels inward, striking them together. Toes will end turning out.
>
> or
>
> Plié, spring into the air hitting both heels together simultaneously. Legs may be straight or bent. This execution may be classified as a form of Bell.
>
> or
>
> Stand on L, with R foot, Click R heel against L heel, or vice versa.

HEEL CLICK CRAMPROLL
[5 sounds] [1e&a2]

Spring into the air and click both heels together, landing in a type of a cramproll.

HEEL CLICK WALK
[3 sounds] [&a1]

> TO EXECUTE:
> While walking fwd with the R, click R heel to L heel in passing, heel drop L [&a], step fwd R, [1], and continue using the L foot [&a2]

NOTE:
Properly, the term should say heel clip walk. See CLIP

HEEL CLIP

The heel making a sound when passing by the other heel or toe. See CLIP

HEEL CRAMP. See HEEL DROP

HEEL CRAMPROLL. See CRAMPROLL:
Variations, Heel Cramproll

HEEL DIG (Heel Ball)
[1 sound] or [&]

Stand L, raise R foot. Strike floor bk edge of R heel on floor with accent. Usually done close to standing foot. Dig implies leaving the foot on the floor with no wt. See DIG

HEEL DRAG (Heel Draw)

Execute as a drag but perform with the edge of the heel rather than with the ball of the foot. Stand on L with R heel edge on floor and away from the body. Pull the heel twd the body, leaving it in contact with floor.

HEEL DRAW. See HEEL DRAG

HEEL DROP (Cramp Heel, Heel Beat, Heel Cramp)
[1 sound] [1] or [&]

Begin w/ feet flat in a close par pos., bend knees slightly and raise heel of one foot from floor. Drop heel, leaving ball of the foot on floor. There may or may not be a wt. transfer. The popular connotation of heel drop is that it carries wt. Historically, it was recognized as a heel beat, with no wt. transfer, while heel cramp implied a wt. transfer. See BEAT; CRAMP

HEEL DROP TIME STEP

Any time step in which a heel drop is substituted for the original hop.

HEEL FLAM
[1 sound]

A heel dig immediately followed by the toe drop. Old term for heel toe.

HEEL FLAP
[2 sounds] [a1]

Scuff R, heel dig R. Old term and description of the action, but incorrect technically because dig has no wt., and flap carries the wt.

HEEL GRIND (Heel Twist)
[w/wo sound]

With R heel on floor and R foot flexed, move R toes from an inward to an outward direction, using the heel as a pivot point. Can be done w/wo sound.

HEEL GRIND TIME STEP. See TIME STEP: Heel Grind

HEEL JAB (Heel Dig)
[1 sound] [1]

Dig R bk edge of R heel on floor, usually close to the supporting leg. Jab implies picking foot up after execution. Carries no wt. See DIG

HEEL JUMP
[1 sound] [1]

From a standing position, spring into air from both feet and land on one or both heels, simultaneously, toes flexed.

HEEL KICK

Old term for scuff.

HEEL LEAP
[1 sound] [1] or [&]

Traceable to character dancing. Stand on R, raise L leg bent, spring into the air, ending on the on the L heel, toes flexed.

HEEL PATTER

Series of small quick steps but executed while being suspended on the back edge of both heels, toes lifted. May be done in straight lines, circles, etc.

HEEL PAS DE BOURRÉE
[6 sounds] [a1 a2 a3]

See PAS DE BOURRÉE.

TO EXECUTE:

Heel drop L, step R bk L, heel drop R, [a1 a2], step L to L, heel drop L, step R frt [a3]

NOTE:
A Hop may be used instead of a heel drop.

HEEL PUSH
[1 sound] [&] or [1]

Place ball of R foot on floor, drop R heel and push dropped heel slightly fwd while it is in contact with the floor.

HEEL RATTLE

Old term for SCUFFLE.

HEEL ROCK. See HEEL CHANGE

HEEL ROCKS. See HEEL BEAT SWIVEL

HEEL ROLL (Alternating: Heel Beats, Cramps, Drops)
[any number of sounds] [&1] or [a1]

A series of alternating heel drops, cramps, or beats done rapidly with an even spacing of rhythm, w/wo accent. Also may involve shading, soft to loud, loud to soft, etc. Old term for cramproll.

HEEL SCUFF. See SCUFF

HEEL SHUFFLE (Double Scuff) [& 1]

TO EXECUTE:
Scuff R fwd [&], brush R bwd by hitting the back edge of the R heel in passing. [1]

HEEL SKID. See HEEL SLIDE; SKID

HEEL SLIDE (Heel Skid)
[1] or [&]

Stand w/ wt. on R heel, R toes flexed, and L foot off the floor. Execute a sliding motion on the bk edge of the R heel in any direction. Wt. remains on supporting leg. A heel slide can also be performed on both heels ast.

HEEL STAND
[1 or 2 sounds]

Standing and balancing one's weight on the back edge of the heels, with the toe(s) lifted from the floor.

NOTE:

✪ There are no sounds while in the heel stand, unless one walks, etc.

✪ A sound could be made when one steps onto the heel stand.

Single Heel Stand: To stand on one heel only with the free leg held off the floor and the toe lifted off the working foot.

Double Heel Stand: To stand on both the back edges of the heels ast, with toes lifted in the air.

HEEL STAND TIME STEP. See TIME STEP: Heel Stand

HEEL STEP
[2 sounds] [1 2]

1 Standing on L, place full wt. on bk edge of R heel with toes flexed; lift L foot, then step down L in any direction.

2 Standing on L, place bk edge of R heel on floor with toes flexed no wt. Step R usually ip.

HEEL TAP
[1 sound] [1] or [&]

Strike bk edge of heel on floor with toes flexed. May be done in any dir. or pos.

HEEL THUMP

Old term for chug. See CHUG

HEEL TOE (Heel Toe Beat, Heel Toe Cramp, Heel Toe Drop)
[2 sounds] [1 2] or [&1]

TO EXECUTE:

1 Stand L, place R foot fwd, bk edge of R heel on floor, toes flexed. Drop R toes, keeping R heel on floor. May be done w/wo wt.

2 Stand L, place bk edge of R heel on floor, frt or side, with no wt., lift R heel and toe tap R bk L.

HEEL-TOE BEAT. See HEEL TOE

HEEL-TOE CATCH. See CLIP

HEEL-TOE CLICK
[1 sound] [1]

✪ The heel of one foot and the toe of the other foot strike each other simultaneously, with equal force.

✪ The heel of the working foot strikes the uplifted toe of the L foot.

HEEL-TOE CRAMP

Old term for Heel Toe See to HEEL TOE

HEEL-TOE DROP

Old term for Heel Toe. See HEEL TOE

HEEL TOUCH

Touch the bk edge of the heel to the floor in any pos. or dir.

HEEL TWIST. See HEEL GRIND

HESITATION TIME STEP. See TIME STEPS: Hesitation

HIGH BARREL ROLL. See BARREL ROLL: Upright

HIGH HEEL BEAT. See HIGH HEEL DROP

HIGH HEEL CRAMP. See HIGH HEEL DROP

HIGH HEEL DROP (High Heel Beat, High Heel Cramp) [1 sound] [1]

A heel drop executed from a 3/4 foot.

There are two kinds of high heel drops:

High Heel Beat: A heel drop from 3/4 foot. May be left on floor or raised. Carries no wt.

High Heel Cramp: A heel drop from 3/4 foot that changes wt.

HIGHLAND FLING

A Scottish folk dance of the highlands. See STEPS AND STYLES OF TAP DANCE: Styles and Dances.

HIGH RATTLE

Old English term for hop L, shuffle R **[1&a].**

HIGH TOE BEAT

Old term for a toe drop that does not carry wt. See HIGH TOE DROP

HIGH TOE CRAMP

Old term for a toe drop that does carry wt. See HIGH TOE DROP

HIGH TOE DROP (High Toe Beat, High Toe Cramp) [1 sound] [1]

An older term for a toe drop. Beat referred to not bearing wt. Cramp to executing with a wt. transfer.

HINGE. See BACK DROP: Dance

HIP WING. See WING: Hip

HIT
[w/wo sound]

- ✪ Executed by hitting parts of the body tog.; by hitting prop w/ hand or by hitting prop to floor, the body or other object.

- ✪ Hitting one part of the foot against another part of the foot or striking two parts together.

- ✪ A star, a well-recognized and appreciated person or show.

HITCH (Catch)
[w/wo sound]

A form of a slide that moves bkwd on one foot. Stand in demi-plié on one foot, pull bkwd, making a scraping sound or w/o sound. End with supporting leg str. and on ball of foot. The free foot is placed in a definite pos. (e.g., coupé, arabesque, etc.). Free leg can be held tno, usually w/ knee bent, par to frt, or in an extended pos. such as Arabesque. Hitch is the opposite of chug. Can be done in any direction.

HITCH KICK

Traceable to acrobatics and musical comedy. A set of two kicks, the last one receiving the emphasis and being higher than the first one. There are two kinds of hitch kicks:

Front
[w/wo sound] [4 if w/ sound] [1 2 3 4]

This is the most frequently used hitch kick combination.

TO EXECUTE:

Stand L, reaching R either frt or back (on or off floor). Leap onto R extending L bk off floor (1). Leap onto L, extending R bk off floor (2). Leap onto R, raise L fwd below waist level (3). Leap onto L raising R frt, usually to a high level (4). The hitch takes place on ct. 3. The hitch kick on ct. 4.

NOTE:
Legs are raised str., tno, or par. The last kick is the one raised the highest and w/emphasis.

Back

TO EXECUTE:

Execute as a front hitch kick, but cts. 1 and 2 are done raising legs in frt. On cts. 3 and 4, raise legs in back, w/ct. 4 being the highest bk kick.

HITCH STEP. See CATCH STEP

HOOFER

An old term from the 1920s and 1930s that stems from the flatfooted style of tap, which had its beginnings in buck dancing.

HOOFING

An old term meaning several things:

- ✪ Dancing that has not been influenced by ballet, modern, ballroom, etc.

- ✪ A heavy, into the floor type of tap.

- ✪ Used to be typed as laying down iron.

HOP
[1 sound] [1] or [&]

A movement executed by standing in plié on one foot, springing into air, and landing on the same foot. The landing can be on the ball or flat of the foot. The body should not be distorted in any way or show strain from either the prep., execution, or landing. The free leg should be controlled. Landing is usually in plié but may be on str. leg.

HOP CLOG
[5 sounds] [1e&a2] or [1&2&3]

Old term for hop shuffle ball change.

HOP CRAMP
[1 or more sounds]

This term has two meanings:

- ✪ Hop L and landing ball L, heel drop L [&1] or [a1].

- ✪ Very old term for hop followed by a cramproll.

93

HOP CRAMPROLL. See CRAMPROLL: Hop

HOP DOUBLE LEAP

Old term for hop shuffle (called a double because it had 2 sounds). Not really a step, but a combination.

HOP ROLL
[3 sounds] [1&a]

> TO EXECUTE:
> Hop L, shuffle R [1&a]
> repeat continuously until a
> rolling sound is created

HOP SCUFFLE STEP
[4 sounds] [1&a2]

> TO EXECUTE:
> Hop L, scuffle R (scuff R,
> brush bk R), step R [1&a2]

HOP SHUFFLE STEP (Snap Roll, Triples)
[4 sounds] [1&a2]

> TO EXECUTE:
> Hop L, Sh St R or vice versa

HOP STEP
[1 2] or [&1]

Beginning on both feet or while standing on one foot, the other being held in the air, spring into the air, land on the same foot. Step with free foot. Used in a different context and executed in a faster form, hop step is a skipping movement.

HORNPIPE

Known in the sixteenth century, it was popular with sailors, who used wood or percussion instruments as accompaniment. It was not only recreational, but also a competitive dance and often depicted the rolling sea and chores while on ship board.

HOUSE LEFT AND RIGHT

House is to that part of the auditorium where the audience is seated. For the technicians and staff who also work there, the stage, directions are given from their position while facing the stage, house left being to their L hand (stage R to the performer) and house right to their R hand (stage L to the performer).

IMPROVISATION (Ad-lib)

To sing, dance, act, choreograph, or perform without a set plan in mind. To work from inspiration and impulse rather than from a previously thought-out plan.

IMPULSE

Traceable to modern and jazz dance. A wavelike movement involving the entire body. Many executions are possible, for example, standing with feet in 2nd, usually parallel, body erect, hands at sides, plié, knees in line with toes; thrust pelvis fwd plié, ast lift heels, project knees farther fwd, contract and as impulse is carried higher into upper body and as lower part of body is pressing fwd, upper half begins to arch bk piece by piece, ast legs beg. to str. into relevé. Body ends arched bkwd. Straighten body when in full relevé, then lower heels.

INCLINED

A body line that is not perpendicular but leaned in a direction, such as frt, bk, sdwd.

INCLINED BARREL ROLL. See BARREL ROLL: Inclined

INSIDE. See EN DEDANS

INSIDE BARREL ROLL. See BARREL ROLL: Inside

INSIDE CIRCLE. See TURN: Traveling, Turns in circles and patterns

INSIDE FAN KICK. See FAN KICK: Inside

INSIDE FLEA HOP. See FLEA HOP: Inside

INSIDE FOUETTÉ. See FOUETTÉ: Inside

INSIDE KNEE SPIN. See KNEE SPIN: Inward Knee Spin

INSIDE/OUTSIDE TURN. See TURN: Other Traveling Turns, Inside/Outside

INSIDE PADDLE TURN. See PADDLE TURN: Inside

INSIDE PIROUETTE. See PIROUETTE; TURN: Stationary Spot

INSIDE PIVOT. See PIVOT: Inside

INSIDE ROND DE JAMBE. See ROND DE JAMBE: Inside

INSIDE SLIDE. See SLIDE: Inside

INSIDE SPOT TURN. See TURN: Stationary (Spot)

INSIDE TURN. See TURN: Inside, En Dedans

INTERLUDE

- ✪ A strong or long musical strain that is used between the melody and the strong sections of a song.
- ✪ The music played between the acts of an opera, a play, or a musical.
- ✪ A short play inserted into an entertainment.

INTERVAL

The duration of time between two sounds, or distance between two notes.

INTRODUCTION (Intro)

- ✪ A chord, a note, or a measure or two of the music played before the performer enters, which acts as a cue for that entrance.
- ✪ In music, a preparatory section leading to the main part of the composition.

INVERTED (Turned In, Pigeon-Toed)

Literally, "turned inside-out." In dance, a pos. of the leg in which the whole leg is turned inwd (For inverted foot, See PIGEON-TOED).

INVERTED TOE TAP
[1 sound] [any count]

Invert the working foot inward and strike the top of the working foot on the top of the toe, heel of the working foot faces outward.

IRISH (Shuffle Hop Step, Carryover, Carryover Irish, Carryback)
[4 sounds] [&1&2]

Traceable to Irish step dancing jigs, and reels.

Single:
TO EXECUTE:

Shuffle hop step R or L
[&1&2]

Double:
TO EXECUTE:

Sh hop, St R, Sh bc L
[&1&2&3&4]

Front: (Also called a carryover, carryover Irish, shuffle hop step fwd). On the step, one foot is placed in frt of the other, the movement is normally fwd but may stay ip. A frt shuffle may be used. Feet are usually tno, but may also be par or obl.

Back: (Also called a carryback, carryback Irish, shuffle hop step back). On the step, one foot is placed behind the other, the movement is normally bkwd but may stay ip. A bk shuffle may be used. The feet are usually tno, but may also be par or obl.

(THE) IRISH BREAK
[19 sounds] [1 &a2 &a3 &4 &a 5 &6 &7 &a 8]
(From *The Tap Dance Dictionary* by Mark Knowles)

TO EXECUTE:

Step R, shuffle step L and R [1 &a2 &a3], shuffle R, hop L, heel drop L [&4 &a], step R bk L, brush L, step L [5 &6], shuffle R, hop L, heel drop L [&7 &a], toe jab R Xd bk L [8]

(THE) IRISH DOWN STEP
[48 sounds] [&a1 &a2 &a3 &a4 &a5 &a6 &a7 &a8 & repeat]

TO EXECUTE:

(A) Shuffle step R, L, R, step L R, L [&a1 &a2 &a3 &a4] reverse (A) [&a5 &a6 &a7 &a8] repeat (A) [&a1 &a2 &a3 &a4]

(B) Shuffle step R and L, shuffle R, hop L, stamp R [&a&]

IRISH JIG

A folk dance of Ireland and one of the heavy contributors to the development of tap dancing. See STEPS AND STYLES OF TAP DANCE: Styles and Dances

ISOLATION

The moving of a certain part(s) of the body alone, in unison, or in opposition to the rest of the body. Isolation exercises build technical proficiency and allow for more choreographic license. Common isolation movements are of the head, neck, shoulders, rib cage, pelvis, and hips. Arm isolations are also a valid contributor to the style and continuity of the performance. Isolation exercises in tap are beneficial in increasing the control and flexibility of the feet and ankles.

(THE) ITCH

A 1920s eccentric social dance in which dancers scratched and wiggled as though they had been bitten by fleas. Eventually, this movement became incorporated into the breakaway of the Lindy.

JAB

To retract or pick up the foot after execution of a step such as dig; more important, whether the foot is left on the floor or raised, it carries no wt.

JAZZ DANCE

A separate dance form with its own techniques, structures, and philosophies. Tap often uses its movements, steps, and styles as well as its music and principles.

JAZZ KICK (Flex Kick, Flip Kick, Snap Kick, Flick Kick)

Traceable to jazz. A jazz kick is a frequently used movement in tap as well as jazz. To execute, feet can be par, obl, tni, tno. Feet may begin in a closed or open position. When executing a true jazz kick, there are four sections to be considered:

1   The working leg is bent w/ knee raised and the lower part of the leg, retracted slightly bkwd.

2   The working leg straightens w/ a sharp, accented motion. Leg is held straight.

3   The working leg is again retracted to the position in (2).

4   The foot lowers to starting position. The supporting leg can be str., in plié, or r/p.

It can beg. in plié, rise to relevé on (2) and (3), and return to plié on (4).

JAZZ SPLIT. See SPLIT: Jazz

JAZZ STEPS

Steps found in dances such as the shimmy and the Charleston. Some were natural movements that had become highly stylized and moved onto the stages of the country, such as falling down stairs and time steps. Others became flash steps, such as bells and over the tops. Today, the term has a different connotation, meaning that we have directly borrowed steps, movements, and concepts from jazz dance, and adapted them to fit the vocabulary of tap.

JAZZ TAP

A style of tap dancing that borrows movements from jazz dance, or tap that uses jazz music for its accompaniment.

JETÉ
[w/wo sound]

Derived from the ballet jeté, meaning "thrown." Tap usually begins the initial movement by brushing the lead foot off the floor thus, adding sound: spring into air, with both legs str. and execute a petit or grand split. Land in plié on the lead foot. See GRAND JETÉ

JIG

A dance of Ireland that led to tap dancing. See AN HISTORICAL LOOK AT TAP

JIG STEP
[22 sounds] [1&a2&a3&a4&a5&a6&a7&a8]

TO EXECUTE:
Leap on R, do 6 running shuffles L, R, L, R, L, R and stamp L, R, L

JIG WALK
[3 sounds] [&a1]

TO EXECUTE:
Brush hop step fwd R, L alternately, arms str. to sides, palms flexed and fingers outwd, lean fwd, turn legs slightly outward on each brush hop step

JINGLE TAP

A metal disc or plate inserted into the toe and/or heel plate that distorts and adds to the original sounds of the taps. Unaccepted by performers, as tap demands clear and positive sounds.

JITTERBUG

A type of social dance that began in the 1930s and led to the Swing era.

JIVE

Swing music or music played in a swing style.

JOIN

Close together, as in step side close.

JUBA

Real name William Henry Lane, a.k.a. Juba. The most influential single performer of nineteenth-century American dance. His dancing blended the British system with the rhythms and syncopations of African dance. Juba is also the name of a well-known African-based circle dance.

JUMP (Foot Jump, Plain Jump)
[w/wo sound]

Usually beg. on two feet, spring into air and land on both feet simultaneously. However, it may also be considered as a spring, from one foot but must land on both. Feet may be in any pos. or dir. previous to jumping (tni, tno, par). While in air, feet may be held tog. or posed apart, Xd, open, etc. Landing should be made in plié, in any dir. or pos. Jumps may be large, allowing time for the legs to be posed while in the air, or small and purposeful as in a prep. for another movement They may land silently or with sound(s), such as toe heels, cramprolls, etc.

JUMP KICK

A jump on two feet followed by a type of kick in any direction.

JUMP(ING) RIFF

A jump followed by any kind of riff.

JUMP(ING) SPLIT
[2 sounds] [&1] or [1 2]

Traceable to acrobatic and character dancing. A split done in the air or on the floor but preceded by a jump as a prep., for example, jump on both feet (usually in a closed pos.), plié, spring into air and execute a full or fake split. Land either on feet or on floor.

JUMP OVER THE FOOT
[w/wo sound]

To execute:
Step fwd R to #1, step fwd L to outside edge of L foot Xd frt R, leap R up and over L (place no wt. on the edge of L foot) but lift wt. in air to give the effect of jumping up and over.

This is considered a trick or flash step.

NOTE:
The working leg and foot may also be circled under the supporting leg; the supporting leg responds by jumping over it at the appropriate time.

JUMP OVER THE LEG
[w/wo sound]

To execute:
Step fwd R to #1, Xd frt, bk, or side to R, plié, battement frt L (tno or par) letting battement lift the body into the air, holding L leg str. and as par to the floor as possible, lift R leg, bending it in the air and leap R over the extended L leg, landing on R in plié.

This is considered a trick or Flash step. Often it is performed by men because of its virile nature and because of the strength and elevation required.

JUMP TEMPO

A fast 4/4 tempo exceeding that of a bounce or bright tempo.

JUNE TAYLOR DANCERS

A group of dancers who appeared weekly on the Jackie Gleason television show (1970s), and whose director, June Taylor, experimented with camera angles much like Busby Berkeley did with the motion picture camera.

KAHNOTATION

A system of tap notation developed by Stanley Kahn, using "K" symbols to represent specific steps.

KAZATSKY

A Russian folk dance staple. Basically, squat in par 1st position; from this position, kick first one foot fwd, then the other. May be performed w/wo support from the hands.

KICK
[w/wo sound]

General

Prevalent in every form of dance, a natural movement occurring in the play of children, later an integral part of folk dancing (especially in the Slavic countries) and later still a technical exercise and step executed in a prescribed and precise manner, such as a chorus kick, jazz kick, etc.

Battement Kick. See BATTEMENT

Brush Battement Kick

Execute as a battement, but brush the foot off the floor. If sound is employed, a nerve tap is used.

Chorus Kick

A very general term, embracing a kick done by a chorus line. Usually preceded by a jump or a spring from both feet. The term included battements, knee kicks, fan kicks, etc., which were an applause-seeking device. However, in character dancing, they were often performed by males and executed with great force and speed.

KIMBO (Akimbo)
[w/wo sound]

A step used extensively in "era" jazz work. Execute by stepping bk on R (turn R knee out and end in R plié), L leg remains str., leave L heel on floor flex L foot body twists to L (in line with L foot). Lean slightly fwd in a flat-back pos. A clap or snap may be added after the kimbo.

KNEE BEND

Old term for:

❂ Back drop. In the early 1920s, it literally meant "to bend the knees."

❂ A bending of both or one knee in any position or direction.

KNEE BOUNCES

Starting in plié continuously straighten and bend the legs, which has bouncing effect.

KNEE CRAWL. See KNEE WALK

KNEE DROP
[w/wo sound]

Dropping on one or both knees. Included in the area of flash or trick steps. Must be controlled through the thighs and supported to the floor; therefore, the term "drop" is very misleading. If finishing on both knees, stand in wide 2nd, par, obl or tno, bend both knees

ast keeping body on inclined plane twd the bk. Continue to bend the knees and lower the body to the floor.

NOTE:
The only portion of the knee that touches the floor is the very lowest part of the knee bone; at no time is the full body wt placed on the knee caps. The back line is absolutely str. no arch or break at the waist. There is a straight, inclined line existing from the head through the knees. Hands may be used or not as desired. Knee pads are often used as a further protection. This step, as most areas of knee/floor work, is considered more desirable for males than for females, although it is used by both.

KNEE FALL
[w/wo sound]

A flash step that begins in a turned-out 2nd position. Starting as a knee hinge, midway down the knees turn inward to face each other and continue until they are on the floor in an inverted position. There is no wt. exerted on the knees, but as in the knee drop, the lowering to the floor is controlled through the thighs. Once the floor position is reached, and again using the thigh muscles, return to a standing position by reversing the knees to turned out.

KNEE HINGE (Knee bend)
[w/wo sound]

A bending of the knees and an inclining back of the body, where the body remains in one straight line from the knees to the top of the head. It may continue to the floor or be suspended in the air at a given point. See KNEE BEND

KNEE KICK

A kick that stems from the knee, rather than from the whole leg. See JAZZ KICK

KNEE KNOCKS

With feet par, slightly apart, and in the plié position, close and open knees so that they gently knock together. A Charleston movement.

KNEE LUNGE. See LUNGE: Knee

KNEE ROCK. See ROCK: Knee

KNEE SLIDE
[w/wo sound]

Traceable to jazz. Execute a knee drop and instead of stopping abruptly, continue to slide in the dir. of the drop. Momentum for the slide may be gained by preceding it with a run, both arms str. and bk of body, as slide is done, arms are shot fwd, adding a fwd thrust to the step. The final push fwd comes from the balls of the feet; as the knees are lowered to the floor, both feet push fwd ending on both knees. The body wt. is supported by the thighs. Knee pads might well be worn until the movement is perfected. See KNEE DROP; KNEE HINGE

KNEE SPIN (Knee Turn)
[w/wo sound]

Traceable to jazz and character dancing. Primarily, knee spins, falls, and other floor work are considered flash or trick steps. They are used extensively by males because of the required strength. Knee pads for protection are advisable.

Inside Knee Spin

TO EXECUTE:

Prepare by kneeling on R knee, L foot flat and to L frt corner (A2), arms to L, spot to R or fwd as desired, using the R knee cap as a pivot pt. (hold R foot slightly off floor), arms to 2nd, turn to R; arms at 1/2 way pt. (when facing bk) place L knee (L foot off floor) close to R. now transfer wt. to L knee cap and using it as a pivot pt., continue to turn to R. End facing A1, on L knee, R foot flat and to R, arms to R. Acts as a three-step turn. Step may now be reversed to L; however, if a continuous series of turns is to be executed, See Turns: chaîné, and execute as described but on knees rather than feet. Knee spins may be done as pirouettes and as singles, doubles, etc. with the working leg in a posé position such as attitude, arabesque, etc.

Outside Knee Spin

Not as commonly used as inside knee spins, for the execution is far more difficult.

TO EXECUTE:

kneel on R knee, L foot flat, fwd and slightly to L, body frt, arms to R. Using R knee cap as a pivot pt. beg. to turn bk on R to L. The R foot must be slightly off the floor or it will prevent the turn from occurring. The L leg is raised from floor and may be placed in attitude, arabesque, etc. Spot frt or to L.

A number of alternatives are possible at this pt.:

- ✿ The turn may be completed, all of it being done on the R knee cap, L foot is returned to starting pos.

- ✿ When the body is at mid-pt. (i.e., facing bk) the L knee cap may be placed closely beside the R, thus transferring the wt. and knees. The turn is completed w/ wt. on the L knee, the R foot to the R and on the floor and facing frt. To execute again it is necessary to reverse.

- ✿ May be done as a str. line of outwd chaîné turns. Execute as described but on the knees rather than the feet. See TURNS: Chaîné

Single, Double, Triple, etc.: The number of turns executed on one knee at one time without interruption. See SPOTTING

KNEE SPLIT. See SPLIT: Knee

KNEE TURN. See KNEE SPIN

KNEE WALK (Knee Crawl)
[w/wo sound]

Traceable to jazz and character dancing. While in kneeling pos. on one knee for example, the L knee, R knee bent; R foot fwd push wt. fwd, lower R knee to floor and step through and fwd L to L knee, thus ending in original starting pos. May also be executed by beginning from both knees and "walking" or "crawling" from one knee to the other.

LAMP (Shot Beat)
[w/wo sound]

Leap to a flat foot. Some sources claim that lamp is a combination of leap, stamp, or leap and lunge.

LANCASHIRE

A wooden clog dance and shoe used in the manufacturing county of Lancashire, England. See AN HISTORICAL LOOK AT TAP.

LATIN WALK. See CUBAN WALK

LAYOUT

A movement and posé position from modern dance. The body is parallel to the floor and forms a theoretical straight line. The layout may be fwd, bkwd, or sdwd.

LEANED BARREL ROLL. See BARREL ROLL: Leaned or Inclined.

LEAP (Foot Leap)
[w/wo sound]

Present in every form of dancing. Beginning on one foot, spring into air and land on other foot. Involves a change of feet and wt. Landing may be accomplished on ball or flat of foot, w/wo sound, in plié or on a str. leg. Leap may cover distance or remain on the spot; it may be the major step in a sequence or part of a step. In most springing or leaping steps, the balls of the feet and finally the tips of the toes are the last to leave the floor and the first to return. Foot leap is an old term meaning "to leap."

LEAP CRAMP
[2 or more sounds]

- ❂ Leap from one foot to the other and execute a heel drop on the landing foot **[&1]**.
- ❂ A leap ending in any kind of a cramproll.

LEAP DOUBLE HOP

A very old term for leap L, shuffle R, hop L, as shuffle has 2 sounds and was called a double.

LEAP TOE
[2 sounds] [&1 or a1]

A common combination where one leaps from one foot to the other and adds a toe tap bk with the free foot, for example leap R, toe tap L **[&1] or [a1].**

LEAP TOE TURN. See TURN: Traveling, Leap Toe.

LEAP TURN

A turn in which a leap appears in any part of the turn—at the beginning, in the middle, or at the end.

LEAPING CRAMPROLL. See CRAMPROLL: Leaping

LEAP(ING) RIFF. See RIFF: Leaping

LEFT (HANDED) TURNS. See TURN: General

LEFT PIVOT. See PIVOT

LEFT SIDED DRAWBACK. See DRAWBACK: Left-Sided

LEFT STAGE. See STAGE DIRECTIONS

LEGOMANIA

A loose-jointed movement or routine employing high kicks, rubber legs, and other eccentric leg movements.

LEVEL

To dancers it could pertain to their technical level and knowledge or their ability to change level during a routine (i.e., to change height and physical appearance, by leaning fwd, bkwd, or sideward, as well as by the use of relevé and/or plié).

The level of a performance: its consistency, calibre, and professionalism.

Level is also concerned with the quality of the sound of the taps—loud or soft—and their ability to produce rhythmic and melodic passages.

LIMBO
[w/wo sound]

Traceable to jazz and Afro-Cuban. Its basis is in tribal dances of Africa, where as part of a tribal ritual performers executed a deep knee hinge with the body inclined bkwd, feet spread and tno, the goal being to chug fwd under a low-suspended pole, the pole being lowered w/ each successful movement; today, heel drops or chugs may be used as sounds. See KNEE HINGE

LIMP TIME STEP. See TIME STEP: Traveling

(THE) LINDY
[4-5 sounds] [1 &2 3 4]

Step (flap) R to R, ball
change (L to R) [1 &2 3 4]
step bk L, step R fwd.

Named after Lindbergh's solo flight across the
Atlantic Ocean. Began as a ballroom craze and found
its way into tap and jazz as well.

LINDY HOP

A social dance of the Swing era, performed in black
ballrooms long before Lindbergh's solo flight across
the Atlantic, after which this dance was supposedly
named. Its popularity and uniqueness is credited to
George "Shorty" Snowden. See AN HISTORICAL
LOOK AT TAP. The Lindy Hop is often used in jazz
and in "era" tap numbers.

TO EXEXUTE:

Wo sound:
Step ball change R to R [1&2]
ball change L bk R [3 4]

W sound:
flap ball change R to R [&1&2]
ball change L bk R [3 4]

LINE OF DIRECTION (L.O.D.)

The line of direction is the line of travel in which the
dancer or dancers are moving, for example, from
stage right to stage left, in a right inside circle, etc. It
does not necessarily connote the direction in which
the dancer or dancers are facing.

LINE OF TRAVEL. See LINE OF DIRECTION

LONG BRUSH. See BRUSH: Long

LONG ESSENCE. See ESSENCE: Long

LONG RIFF

Straightening the working leg out after a forward riff
to its longest length, thus ending with a straight leg.

LOOKOUT

Not a step but a body position, in which you shade
your eyes while you look in a direction as though
you were searching for someone or something.

LOW HEEL BEAT

Old term for Heel Drop that carries no wt.

LOW HEEL CRAMP

Old term for heel drop that carries wt.

LOW HEEL DROP (Low Heel Beat or Cramp)

Old term for heel drop. Beat carries no wt.; cramp
carries wt.

LOW TOE BEAT

Old term for toe drop that carries no wt.

LOW TOE CRAMP

Old term for toe drop that carries wt.

LOW TOE DROP (Low Toe Beat, Low Toe Cramp)

Old term for toe drop. May be executed w/ wt.
(cramp) or wo wt. (beat).

LUNGE
[w/wo sound] [1 sound] [1]

A pose or pos.; may be done forward, sideward,
backward or in croîsse position. Supporting leg is in
plié and the extended leg is straight and usually
placed on the inside edge of the foot, in a turned-out
pos. Listed below are several types of lunges:

Side Lunge: Body faces frt, step R to R, plié R, L str. and
to the L side.

Back Lunge: Face frt, if executing R bk lunge, step bkwd
R and plié in tno position. Leave L leg fwd, straight and
tno, wt. on R; body faces frt.

Forward Lunge: Face frt, if R lunge is to be performed,
reach R foot frt and end standing on R in plié, while L
remains straight and in bk. Both legs are tno.

Standing Lunge: Any lunge that ends on the feet.

Floor Lunge: Any lunge that ends on the floor or assumes
a lunge position on the floor.

Knee Lunge: Any lunge in which the dancer is kneeling
on one knee, while the other leg is straight and extended
forward, backward, sideward, or crossed of the kneeling
leg.

LUNGE TRAVEL

Lunge travel to the right: stand in plié on R, with L
extended in lunge position, face frt, while holding
lunge position. Execute toedrop R to R then heel drop
R to R, while twisting on ball of R foot, drop R heel
to R. (Weight is always over working, or supporting,
foot).

LYRICAL

A dramatic style of dance incorporating ballet, jazz,
or modern dance that is deeply attached to the
content, structure, mood, words, and meaning of the
music. It may or may not tell a story.

MACHINE GUN

This is not a step but a sound or taps that sound like a machine gun, for example, a series of flap heels or flap heel heels done in fast succession.

MAMBO

A form of Latin music and dancing that was introduced into America in the 1940s and became very important to ballroom dancing.

MARCH

A high lifting of the knees on each step, executed in a military manner.

MAXIE FORD
[5 to 14 sounds] [1&2&3] or [1&2&a34&5e&a67]

Regular Maxie Ford

Max Ford was a fine buck and wing dancer in vaudeville and these steps are credited to him.

> TO EXECUTE:
> Leap R to R , shuffle L to L, leap onto L, tap R Xd bk L [1&2&3]

Maxie Ford Break

> TO EXECUTE:
> Leap R to R, Sh leap L, R toe bk L leap R to R, Sh leap L, R toe bk L leap R to R [1&2&3 4&5&6 7]

Maxie Ford w/ Graboff

> TO EXECUTE:
> Leap R to R, Sh alt. pickup to L, tap R bk L [1&2&a3] leap R to R, Sh alt. pickup to L, tap R bk L [4&5&a6] leap R to R [7]

Advanced Maxie Ford

> TO EXECUTE:
> Leap R to R, Sh alt. pickup to L, tap R bk L [1&2&a3]

leap R to R, Sh alt. pickup to L, heeldrop R [4&5e&a] tap R bk L, leap R to R [6 7]

MEASURE (Bar)

The interval on a musical staff between the two vertical bars. In 4/4 time there are four beats to every one measure. In 3/4 time there are three beats per measure. In dancing, owing to the inconvenience of counting each measure separately, dancers usually count by two-measure phrases: in 4/4 time, cts. 1–8, in ³/₄ time cts. 1–6.

MEDIUM BOUNCE

A medium 4/4 tempo with heavy accents on the second and fourth beats.

MEDLEY

Usually applies to music but can also apply to dance. Generally, it is a grouping of songs placed together for a specific purpose.

MESS AROUND
[any number of movements] [w/wo sound]

A typical Bill Robinson step.

> TO EXECUTE:
> Place fists on hips, remain in plié on the balls of the feet, keeping feet close together; execute tiny steps ip, while circling the hips slowly from frt to R, to bk to L

METER

The regular grouping of beats into measures. There are two types of simple meter: duple meter, groupings or multiples of 2, such as 2/2, 2/4, 2/8, etc., triple meter, groupings or multiples of 3, such as 3/2, 3/4, 3/8.

MILITARY FLAP. See DRUM SLAP

MILITARY ROLL. See CRAMPROLL

MILITARY STEP
[9 sounds] [a8 &a1 a2 a3]

Traceable to vaudeville:

> **TO EXECUTE:**
> Stand on L, sh R, hop L,
> flap R, L, R [a8&a1a2a3]

Travel in any dir. in place, turn, etc. Used extensively in military routines.

MILITARY TAP

An extremely popular style and type of tap dance that began in vaudeville and found its real popularity during World War I. See STEPS AND STYLES OF TAP DANCE

MILITARY TIME STEP. See TIME STEP: Military

MINSTRELSY

The minstrels were the most popular entertainment form of the 1860s with both black and white minstrelsy existing side by side. See AN HISTORICAL LOOK AT TAP.

MODERATE

Musically, a medium tempo, one that is neither slow nor fast.

MODULATION

In music, a process of changing from one key to another, without a break in the melody or the chords.

MUSICAL BREAK. See BREAK: Musical

MUSICAL COMEDY

A type of production that contains a plot, singing, acting, and dancing. It may be serious and realistic or light and carefree.

MUSICAL PICKUP

A few notes or measures of music played as a brief introduction, so that all dancers and musicians can begin together and at the same time.

NEGRO TIME STEP

Old term for the buck time step.

NERVE BRUSH
[1 sound] [1]

See also NERVE TAP; BRUSH

> **TO EXECUTE:**
> Working from the ankle
> only, tip R fwd, as in brush,
> striking ball of foot and
> creating one sound

The forward movement of brush may not necessarily occur—only the tap sound.

NERVE FLAP
[2 sounds] [&1] or [a1]

See also NERVE TAP

> **TO EXECUTE:**
> Nerve brush R, step ball R
> fwd rev.

Only the ankle is used in the execution, with wt.

NERVE HEEL
[1 sound] [1]

See also NERVE TAP

> **TO EXECUTE:**
> Using only the ankle and
> leaving the ball of the foot
> on the floor, raise the heel
> and lower sharply

NOTE:
Nerve heels are difficult to detect from regular heels as their normal execution is basically the same as their nerve execution.

NERVE ROLL
[any number of sounds]

See also NERVE TAP; ROLL. A continuous, rapid group of rhythmic sounds made by the toe, the heel, or alt. the two; all the sounds must stem from the ankle.

NERVE SHUFFLE
[2 sounds] [&1] or [a1]

See also NERVE TAP; SHUFFLE

> **TO EXECUTE:**
> Using the ankle only, tap the
> ball of the foot slightly fwd
> as in brush and slightly bkwd
> as in spank

A grouping of two nerve taps may be substituted for shuffle **[&1] or [a1]**.

NERVE SLAP
[2 sounds] [&1] or [a1]

See also NERVE TAP

> TO EXECUTE:
> Using the ankle only, tap the ball of the foot fwd as in brush and step with the same foot [&1] or [a1]

NERVE SPANK
[1 sound] [1]

See also NERVE TAP; SPANK

> TO EXECUTE:
> Using the ankle only, execute a regular spank, foot ends up bk.

NERVE SPANK STEP
[2 sounds] [&1] OR [a1]

See also NERVE TAP; SPANK STEP

> TO EXECUTE:
> Using the ankle only, do a nerve tap bkwd as in spank and step. [&1] OR [a1]

NERVE TAP

- ✿ A single sound made with any portion of the foot—heel toe, ball, tip, etc.—in any dir. or pos. It is used for close to the floor work where leg movement must be restricted to a minimum, thus allowing the maximum number of tap sounds to be produced. All movement, therefore, must be constricted and stem from the ankle, that is, a tense and controlled working leg and a very relaxed ankle.

- ✿ Can be executed in 2 ways:
  a) It may follow the path of movement of the step it is emulating, for example, if a shuffle is being executed as a nerve tap, using the ankle only, tap the ball of the foot fwd as in brush and bkwd as in spank with no unnecessary movement of the leg.
  b) Execute two nerve taps, with no direction as to frt or bk, as a substitute for the shuffle.

Nerve taps began around the early 1920s when John Bubbles introduced rhythm tap and a whole new area of experimentation took place. His influence is still felt today.

NERVE TOE
[1 sound] [1] See also NERVE TAP; TOE

> TO EXECUTE:
> Execute as for a regular Toe, moving only the ankle, to create the sound [1]

(A) NINE
[9 sounds] [&a1 &a2 &a3]

> TO EXECUTE:
> Execute 3 running shuffles R, L, R

NOTATION

Notation is a system or method of recording by symbols, signs, or abbreviations, dance works in their totality, including steps, counts, style, movement, and staging.

OBLIQUE (Diagonal, 45 Angle, Turned Out)

The angle of the feet, arms, body, dir. of step, etc. If standing in 2nd pos., the feet would be pointed toward the corners, rather than str. fwd or tno. Arms raised to the obl would lie halfway between perpendicular and horizontal. Oblique may also refer to the angle of the leg, as being neither on the same plane as the floor or at R angles to it, but in between. Directionally, obl would refer to traveling on the diag., usually from cor. to cor. An obl body pos. might be inclined or leaned fwd, sdwd, or at an angle.

OFF BEAT

- ✿ A legitimate and intentional playing or dancing of a step off the direct beat of the music, in order to set up a syncopated rhythmic pattern. It often avoids the strong beats of the music and dances in-between the beat.

- ✿ Used derogatorily to identify a performer who has an inability to keep in time with the music.

OFF-BEAT BREAK. See BREAK: Other Breaks, Soft Shoe 7

OFF-BEAT TIME STEP

Old term for buck time step.

OFF STAGE

Any area that is not on the stage proper.

OFF TO BUFFALO. See BUFFALO STEP

ON BEAT

Opposite of off beat. Playing or dancing directly on the beat of the music, sometimes known as dancing on a square beat. Also means of being in time with the music.

ON THE FLOOR

There are two meanings:

✿ To physically sit or lie on the floor in order to continue class.

✿ To move to the center of the floor and wait for further instructions.

ON STAGE

Any area on the stage itself.

ONE
[1]

Old term for a step, so named because it created one sound.

ONE-MAN DANCE

A dance in which several dancers are pressed together in one line and dance in unison.

ONE-SIDED DRAWBACK. See DRAWBACK: One-sided

ONE-STEP RHYTHM
[7–9 sounds]

Traceable to vaudeville.

> TO EXECUTE:
> Sh hop St R, Sh St L. [8&12&3&] Feet may be par or tno
>
> Double One-Step Rhythm: Sh R, hop L, Fl R, Sh St L [8&1&2&3&]
>
> Triple One-Step Rhythm: Sh R, hop L, Sh St R, Sh St L [8&1&a2&3&]

OPEN THIRD
[3 sounds] [&a1] or [ea1]

> TO EXECUTE:
> Brush fwd R, bend R as though to brush R bk and execute a bkwd scuff or a tap R, then brush bk R

OPPOSITION

A natural, yet necessarily learned movement, used extensively in dancing for keeping the body centered and in balance. It involves such things as placing the L arm with the R foot, using the hips to L when upper torso is to the R, or executing plié (and lowering the body to the floor) while the torso is lifting upwd.

ORCHESTRATION

Music that has been scored, selected or arranged for an orchestra or band to play at a specific event,

OUTSIDE. See EN DEHORS

OUTSIDE BARREL ROLL. See BARREL ROLL: Outside

OUTSIDE CIRCLE. See TURN: Traveling

OUTSIDE FAN KICK. See FAN KICK: Outside

OUTSIDE FLEA HOP. See FLEA HOP: Outside

OUTSIDE FOUETTÉ. See FOUETTÉ: Outside

OUTSIDE KNEE SPIN. See KNEE SPIN: Outside

OUTSIDE PADDLE TURN. See PADDLE TURN: Outside

OUTSIDE PIROUETTE. See TURN: Stationary: Outside

OUTSIDE PIVOT. See PIVOT: Outside

OUTSIDE RENVERSÉ. See RENVERSÉ: Outside

OUTSIDE ROND DE JAMBE. See ROND DE JAMBE

OUTSIDE SLIDE

✿ A slide that moves from underneath the body line to 'out' or away from its starting point.

✿ A slide that uses the outside edge of the foot in its execution.

OUTSIDE TURN. See TURN: En Dehors; Outside

OVER THE TOPS
[2 movements] [w/wo sound]

A flash step popularized by the dancer Toots Davis during World War I. It is one foot leaping over the other foot or leg and may be done in several ways:

TO EXECUTE:

Basic over the tops

Place the L leg frt of R on outside edge, or in high battement croisé position. L is as straight as possible and horizontal to frt of body. Leap R foot over L, landing in frt of it [1 2].

Toe stand over the tops

Execute a toe stand L Xd frt R and leap R over L w/o releasing the toe stand position [1 2].

Fwd and bkwd over the tops

Stand on L frt of R, leap R foot over L, landing R frt L, then leap R bkwd on L, ending in starting position [&1&2].

Pendulum over the tops

Brush fwd R, hop L, brush R frt L, hop L, toe tap R frt L (in toe stand pos.), leap L over the R and then leap L bkwd over R [&1&a234].

A coffee grind or around the world is also considered a form of over the tops.

NOTE:

In many descriptions of over the tops the word jump was used rather than the word leap. In the past, the terms jump and leap were used interchangeably. Today, we are aware that jump entails two feet, while leap engages one foot. See COFFEE GRIND(ER).

OVERTURE

The music that is played prior to the opening curtain of a musical production, or concert. It usually contains excerpts of the melodies and strains of the music within the show.

PADDLE AND ROLL (Tommy Gun)

Known in New York City around 1937. Its original form was toe/heel taps produced by the rocking and alternating movement of one foot (the roll section), while the paddle section consisted of accents which, when interjected, varied the content of the roll section. Some claim that it was always a paradiddle, others that the name is a paddle and roll. It is a product of traditional tap. See also PARADIDDLE

PADDLE STEP (Buzz Step)
[7 or 8 sounds] [a1&2&3&4]

Traceable to soft shoe and sand dancing.

TO EXECUTE:

Step, leap or flap R to R, adding 3 bcs (L-R) [1] or [a1&2&3&4]

It may remain par beside R or Xd bk of R and is usually a step of travel; when on the R, move or turn to the R. It is also possible to alt. the pos. of the L from frt to bk to frt.

NOTE:

A double paddle step began with a flap before the 3 ball changes [a1&2&3&4].

PADDLE TURN (Buzz Turn) [7 sounds] [1&2&3&4]

Execute as paddle step See PADDLE STEP but do turning R to the R and L to the L.

R Inside

TO EXECUTE:

Step R to R, execute 3 bcs (L-R, L-R, L-R), while turning forward, on the spot, to the R [1&2&3&4]

R Outside

TO EXECUTE:

Step R to R, execute 3 bcs (L-R, L-R, L-R), while turning backward, on the spot, to the L [1&2&3&4]

NOTE:

Brushes, flap heels, etc. may be added on the R inside turn, and spanks, spank toe heels, etc. on the outside turn.

PARADIDDLE (Perrididdle, Hollywood Roll, Paddle and Roll)
[4, 8 or 12 sounds] [1e&a] or [1e&a2e&a] or [1e&a2e&a3e&a]

The basis of much of the close to the floor work. It offers many sounds to a beat and easily lends itself to syncopation. Its exponents were John Bubbles, Bunny Briggs, and Honi Coles. The single, double, and triple paradiddles are listed below:

TO EXECUTE:
Single Paradiddle
 Heel dig R, spank toe heel R [1e&a]

Double Paradiddle
 Heel dig R, Sp St R, heel drop L, heel dig R, Sp toe heel R [1e&a2e&a]

Triple Paradiddle
 Heel dig R, Sp St R, heel drop L. Repeat. Heel dig R, spank toe heel R [1e&a2e&a3e&a]

There is a second manner of execution suggested for double and triple paradiddles:
(Courtesy of Barbara Denny, Lancaster, NY)

Double Paradiddle
 Heel dig R, Sp ball R, heel drop L and R heels [1a2&a]

Triple Paradiddle
 Heel dig R, Sp ball R, heel drop R, L, R heels [1&a 2&a]

PARALLEL

A position of the arms, body, head, or feet in relationship to each other or to a surface. Literally, "side by side," "having the same course."

PARALLEL TRAVEL (Side Travel)
[2 to 4 sounds or movements] [&1] or [a1] [&1&2] or [a1a2]

Travel that takes place to the side with the feet parallel during its execution.

TO EXECUTE:
Body faces frt
(1) Drop both toes to the R ast, then both heels to the R ast [&] or [a1]
or
(2) drop R then L toe to the R, drop R, then L heel to R [&1&2] or [a1a1]

NOTE:
Also known as a (1) double travel (2) a flat or drop cramproll.

PAS DE BOURRÉE ⚲ (Ride Out)
[3 sounds] [1 &2]

Borrowed terminology from ballet, may be done with or without tap sounds.

TO EXECUTE:
Step R bk L (legs str), step L to 2nd position in relevé, step R frt L (plié), reverse.

NOTE:
Pas de bourreé may be done making a ½ turn or a full turn, inside or outside, with or without sound.

PASS CRAMPROLL. See CRAMPROLL: Alternating

PASSÉ ⚲

- A ballet position in which the working leg is bent, turned out and away from the supporting leg.
- In a jazz passé, the passé leg is bent but remains held in par position, not turned out.

PATTER (SHOE PATTER)

- A series of small steps, executed high on the balls of the feet, on the bk edge of the heel or as small heel drops resembling chugs. The steps are taken close to the floor and may go in any direction or pattern.
- In vaudeville acts, the dialogue or conversation between performers as part of their act. The idea for this exchange was born in minstrelsy.

PATTER RHYTHM

- A series of small steps, usually performed on the balls of the feet and without accents.
- Rhythmic accompaniment that merely marks the tempo and does not mimic the patter rhythm.

PEANUT BUTTER AND JELLY SANDWICH

A teaching technique that promotes quicker and more permanent learning for a child. The image created is that the stamp is a piece of bread; the shuffle ball change, the jelly; and the last stamp, the other piece of bread. (From *The Tap Dance Dictionary* by Mark Knowles)

TO EXECUTE:
Stamp L, shuffle ball change R, stamp L   [1&2&34]

PEARL ROLL

Not a step, but a 2-ct. combination that through usage became accepted as a step.

TO EXECUTE:
Single Pearl Roll
Step R, shuffle L, heel drop R [1 &a 2]

Double Pearl Roll
Flap R, shuffle L, heel drop R [a1 &a 2]

Triple Pearl Roll
Shuffle step R, shuffle L, heel drop R [&a1 &a 2]

PEDESTAL DANCING. See STEPS AND STYLES OF TAP DANCE: Styles and Dances

PEG LEG TIME STEP

Actually, this is the Ruby Keeler time step performed often by Peg Leg Bates in his act as a flash step, spectacular looking because of his peg leg. See TIME STEP: Ruby Keeler
(Courtesy of Helen Horsey, Vineland, NJ)

PENCIL TURN

A stationary turn, usually executed en dedans, but may be en dehors as well.

TO EXECUTE:
Inside R: Step R to R in plié, pull L to beside R and ast relevé. Spin on the balls of both feet, simultaneously. The supporting leg the R is carrying most of the wt. with the ball of the L grazing the floor. May be done as singles, doubles, etc.

Outside R: Step R to R in plié, pull L beside R and ast relevé. Spin with both feet on the ground, bkwd to the L. The supporting leg, the R, is carrying most of the wt. with the ball of the L grazing the floor. May be done as singles, doubles, etc.

PENDULUM OVER THE TOPS. See OVER THE TOPS: Pendulum

PHRASING

A musical composition or choreographic piece can be viewed from many positions. It may be thought of in its entirety, in sections, in bars, or note for note. Phrasing might be considered a section with an idea. These sections and/or ideas are held together by some common tie; usually a theme or a similar rhythmic pattern, etc. After the performer has learned each movement and step separately, he often thinks then of the phrases to solidify the total look and sound of the routine. The expression "his phrasing was excellent" means that the performer had a fine control and understanding of each section or idea.

PICKOVER
[2 sounds] [&1] or [a1]

A form of a forward pickup. See PICKUP: Forward Pickup

TO EXECUTE:
While standing on the R, add a brush fwd R, followed by a hop R, as you move fwd

PICKOVER CHANGE
[2 sounds] [&1] or [a1]

A form of a forward pickup. See PICKUP: Forward Pickup

TO EXECUTE:
While standing on the R, add a brush fwd R and land on the L foot

PICKUP (Pullback, Graboff, Snatch)
[2 sounds to many] [&1]

Pickup and pullback are the same term as are graboff and snatch (the latter are older terms, the former more current). Some claim that there is a slight distinction between the first two, offering the argument that even though the execution is identical a pickup does not cover space, but a pullback does. Regardless, we will consider them interchangeable, but use pickup as the major heading for this dictionary.

Descriptively, the single pickup is performed by executing a spank step on one foot, thus creating two clear sounds. Eventually, in a very advanced form, we expect these sounds to transform themselves into a nerve tap and a landing made on the ball of the supporting foot—the same two sounds, but a different execution. This new approach was demonstrated by exponents of classical tap such as Paul Draper, Danny Daniels, and Michael Dominico.

The pickup family is vast and contains many variations. Once it was discovered that the simple hop could produce two sounds with the addition of spank, the experimentation was under way. Described below are the five basic types of pickups: the single, double and échappé double, alternating, forward, and drum, which serve as the foundation for all the other pickups.

NOTE:

1 Never double bounce, (i.e., plié on the landing and plié again in preparation for the second pickup). The landing plié is also the preparation plié.

2 The basic count of a pickup is [&1]. This allows the pickup to be evenly spread in sound and not snapped. The "a" count is usually used when there are many other sounds involved and where the emphasis and attention has been placed on the rhythmic content of the step and not on the pickup alone.

3 There are many other sounds that may be added to the pickup, such as shuffle, brush, scuff, riff, etc., before they are executed and other sounds may be added during and after their execution, such as toe taps, heel drops, stamps, toe heels, etc.

4 Continuous pickups may be done in patterns such as straight lines, diagonals, circles, zigzags, etc. and may be executed moving fwd, bkwd, to the side, turning, and ip.

5 Whereas the pickup once was used only in conjunction with a tap combination, today it has turned into a flash step and appears in routines as a display of technical proficiency.

Single Pickup

TO EXECUTE:
Begin with the back to the lod. Stand in R/P on the R with the L held in par or tno passé. Spring into the air and execute a nerve tap or spank on the R and land in R/P on

the R. The movement is bkwd [&1].

Double Pickup (Delayed "4")

TO EXECUTE:
Begin with the back to the lod. Stand in R/P on both feet. Spring into the air and execute a nerve tap or spank with first the R foot and then the L. Land on the ball of the R followed by the ball of the L This is a R double pickup because the R foot leads off first and lands first. The order of the feet is very important. The movement is bkwd [e&a1].

NOTE:
Some claim that there is another execution of a double pickup, as follows:

✿ Stand on both feet in R/P, spring into the air and execute both spanks ast, landing on both feet ast [&1]. There are no written sources that confirm this is a double pickup and it does not fulfill the requisite 4 sounds being emanated. However, many teachers claim using this as a practice exercises.

✿ To alternate a double pickup, change the last landing step to dig and then begin the next pickup with the dig foot: **Double pickup R: Sp R & L, land R, dig L. Double pickup L: Sp bk L & R, land L, dig R [e&a1 e&a2].**

✿ The term "delayed 4" is traceable to Canadian terminology. It is another term for double pickup.

Échappé Double Pickup

Based upon the structure of a ballet Échappé.

TO EXECUTE:
Begin facing mirror or travel across the floor. R frt L, plié, execute a R double pickup to 2nd position [e&a1]
do a double pickup crossing the R in frt of the L in 5th position [e&a2].
do a R double pickup crossing L frt R [e&a4].

PICKUP (continued)

May be done traveling or remaining ip, turned out or parallel.

Alternating Pickup (pickup changes, changing pickups, swap pickups, changeovers, changing pullbacks, alternating pullbacks, shuffle alternating graboffs, shuffle alternating pickups, shuffle alterating pullbacks)

TO EXECUTE:

Begin with the back to the lod. Stand in R/P on the R with the L held in par or tno passé. Spring into the air and execute a nerve tap or a spank on the R and land in R/P on the L. The movement is bkwd [&1].

Forward Pickup (Forward Pullback)

TO EXECUTE:

Begin by facing the lod. Stand in R/P on the R with the L held par or tno passé. Spring into the air and execute a nerve tap or fwd brush with the R and land in R/P on the R. The movement is forward [&1].

A forward pickup is sometimes referred to as a pickover.

Drum Pickup (Drum Pullback)

Any pickup in which a heel drop(s) is added upon the landing. R drum pickup

TO EXECUTE:

nerve tap or brush on the R, land on the R in R/P and add heel drop with R [&a1]. R Double Pickup

TO EXECUTE:

nerve tap or spank R and L, land R and L and heel drop R and L. Movement may be fwd, sdwd, bkwd, or ip (all sounds done within 1 count, the last heel drop ending on the 1 count).

NOTE:

To alternate a R drum pickup, spank R & L, land R & L, drop L & R heels and renversé.

The following are some variations that may be executed within the basic pickups described above:

Variations

Single Pickup Variations

These may be done traveling bkwd or fwd. They are described as beginning on the R foot.

1	Pickup on the R, tap L bk R	[&a1]
2	Shuffle L, pickup R	[e&a1]
3	Shuffle L, pickup R, toe tap L	[ie&a1]
4	Shuffle L, pickup R, toe tap L, heel drop R (drum pickup)	[&1a&a2]
5	3-ct. riff fwd L, spank bk L, pickup R	[&a1&a2]
6	Pendulum pickup: brush L fwd with str leg, pickup R, Sp bk L (bent or str), pickup R	[&a1&a2]

The following are single pickups executed facing the lod:

1	Spank step L frt R, brush battement R to 2nd, pickup L (waltz pickup)	[&12&3]
2	Brush L fwd, pickup R, step fwd L (walking pickup)	[a&a1]
3	Shuffle L, pickup R, brush battement L to L, pickup R, step L to L (pickup time step)	[a&a1a&a2]

Double Pickup Variations

These are done with the back to the lod.

1. Feet par and side by side. Execute double pickup diag. bk R, then L (zigzag pickup) [e&a1] or [e&a2]
2. Double pickup in 2nd, double pickup; cross R frt L [e&a1, e&a2]

NOTE:

You may repeat above or on 2nd set cross L frt R.

3. Double pickup R, drop R and L heels (double drum pickup) [e&a1&2] or [iea&a1]
4. Two double pickups R, stamp R and L to 2nd (prep), do low bk aerial to R, turn on spank R and L, face lod with step R and L [e&a1 e&a2 &3 e&a4]
5. Stamp R and L in 2nd, execute a double pickup, but do not end stamp R and L. End in a double toe stand [a1e&a2]. Repeat
6. Stamp R and L to 2nd, 2 double pickups, travel bkwd, 1 double pickup, turn bk R and end facing the lod in a double toe stand [a1e &a2e &a3e &a4]

Alternating Pickup Variations (Swap Pickup, Swap Graboff, Swap Pullback)

These may be done traveling bkwd or fwd. They are described as beginning on the R foot.

1 Alternating pickup R to L, add toe tap R bk or frt of L   [&a1]

2 Alternating pickup R to L, add heel drop L (alt. drum pickup)   [&a1]

3 Shuffle L, alternating pickup R to L [1&a2]

4 Shuffle L, alternating pickup R to L, add toe tap L bk R (swap toe) [&1&a2]

5 Shuffle L, alternating pickup R to L, ball R bk, drop R, & L Heels [&1ie&a2]

6 Shuffle R, diag bk R alternating pickup L to R, step L to R (grab roll) [&1&a2]

The following are alternating pickups executed facing the lod:

1 Brush R fwd, alternating pickup L to R (running pickups) [&a1]

2 A running pickup keeping knees bent, front parallel and high in the air (treadmills) [&a1]

3 Brush R to R, alternating pickup R to R (coupé L bk R) (jeté pickup) [&a1]

4 Brush R to R, alternating pickup L to R ball L bk R, (Xd) drop L & R heels (brush cramproll pickup) [1ie&a2]

5 Brush R fwd, alternating pickup L to R, heel drop R) (running drum pickup) [e&a1]

Pickups to a Toe Stand

In executing pickups to a toe stand, it should be noted that the toe stand ending is (a) substituting for the normal landing on the ball of the foot or feet, (b) that it is a difficult technical execution, and (c) that not all tap shoes are built for toe stands.

1 A single pickup R to a toe stand R [&1] stand on R, L in held position, execute a pickup on the R, but after the 1st sound [&] do not land on the R foot, but land on the R toe tip (R toe stand) and balance, reverse for L.

2 A R double pickup to a double toe stand [e &a1] starting from a par 1st demi-plié, execute the nerve tap R, then L (if it is a R double pickup) [e&] and land on the R toe tip, then the L [a1], thus ending in a double toe stand.

3 An alternating pickup from R to L [&1] starting from a par 1st demi-plié, R, execute the nerve tap R and land on the L in a toe stand position [&a1]

NOTE:

Any pickup, frt, side, bk, double alternating, etc., can be substituted with a toe stand for the landing foot or feet. However, the difficulty lies in executing a number of pickups in succession, for you would have to take the next preparation and pickup from a toe stand position. Pickups to a toe stand could well be classified as a flash step.

Aerial Pickup

If a pickup such as a single, double, or alternating is used, the following points should be kept in mind:

1 If an aerial movement is preceded by a pickup of any kind, the elevation will be lower because of the sounds to be executed.

2 If an aerial movement ends in a pickup of any kind, the feet, at the same point, must be relaxed to execute the sounds.

NOTE:

All pickups noted here have been given in their usual form. Note that there are many more pickup combinations, but for brevity, they have not been presented here. All pickups may be executed as nerve pickups and all may be executed ip or while moving fwd, sdwd, bkwd, or turning.

Musical Pickup

A note or notes that may be played prior to the actual downbeat of a piece.

PICKUP CHANGES. See Pickup: Alternating

PICKUP HEEL. See Pickup: Drum

PICKUP RENVERSÉ. See Renversé: With Sound

PICKUP TIME STEP. See Pickup: Single, Variations

PICKUP TOE. See Pickup: Variations, Single and Alternating

PIGEON TOE TRAVEL

May be executed on one or both feet, in any rhythm, w/wo sound; the usual direction is to the side.

One Foot Side Travel

While standing on the left foot, with the R held up in any posé position, raise the L toes; using the L heel as a pivot point, drop the L toes to the R, then raise the L heel, spin on the ball of the L foot, so that the L heel faces to the R and drop the L heel to the R. Repeat until travel is accomplished to the R.

PIGEON TOE TRAVEL (continued)

Two-Foot Side Travel

a) While standing on both feet, toes in, heels out (pigeon-toed): to travel to the R, release L heel, spin on ball of L and drop L heel to R, ast, release R toes, spin on R heel and drop toes to R (heels are together in tno, 1st position twd each other in 1st position).

b) Using L toe as a pivot, pick up L heel and drop it to the R, ast using R heel as pivot point, pick up R heel and drop it inward. Feet are now in and in 1st position. Continue to repeat.

Single Pigeon-Toe Travel

To EXECUTE:

While standing on R, with the L knee bent and L foot up: using the R heel as a pivot point, pick up R toes and place them to the R, then using the R ball, as a pivot point, pick up R heel and place it to R. Continue alternating, first the R toe, drop to the R, then the R heel drop to the R. Use any rhythm [1 2 3 4 etc.]

Double Pigeon-Toe Travel

To EXECUTE:

Using both toes ast then both heels ast, begin par in 1st pos. Using both heels as pivot points, lift both toes ast and drop them to the R [1]. Then using both balls of feet as pivot points pick up both heels ast and drop them to the R [1]. Continue alternating the toes, then the heels and travel to R. Use any rhythm [1 2 3 4 etc.]

PIGEON-TOED (Turned In)

See also INVERTED The toes are turned twd each other in an inward pos. Heels face outward.

PIKE

A gymnastic movement, used many times by male dancers as a flash step within their routine.

To EXECUTE:

Feet begin tog., plié, spring into the air. Thrust both feet up and fwd, keeping legs str. Bend fwd and touch fingertips to toes, land with both feet tog in plié.

PIQUÉ

Literally, "pricked," "stung." Stepping directly onto the pointe or onto the demi-pointe of the supporting leg, with the working leg placed in any desired position or direction. May be performed while turning.

PIQUÉ TURN
[w/wo sound]

A Piqué position on the supporting leg with the working leg raised sur le cou de pied or passé. The turn may be executed inside or outside.

PIROUETTE
[w/wo sound]

From the medieval French word "pirouelle" or "pierette," literally, "pier that wheels." In dancing, it is a complete turn on one foot. It may be executed in relevé, r/p, or flatfooted. It may be performed on the R or L side, en dedans or en dehors, on center or off center. Pirouettes, as stationary turns are discussed under TURN: STATIONARY (SPOT) TURNS. See SPOTTING

PITTER PATTER. See BALL CHANGE DOUBLE

PIVOT (About Face, Pivot Turn, Push Turn)
[w/wo sound] [2] [1 2]

General: Received its popularity during World War I because of its resemblance to a right about face. Through the years, it has absorbed various styles, including the use of the sugarfoot in the swing era and the lofty relevé and plié of ballet tap. The pivot involves a ½ turn, and is classified as R or L depending on the direction in which it turns, not the first foot being used.

R Pivot: Facing frt step fwd L, using the ball of the R as pivot point, execute a ½ turn to R, ending to face the back wt. on R. May step on R when facing bk or leaving wt. R.

L Pivot: Facing frt step fwd R, using the ball of the R as pivot point, execute a ½ turn to L, ending to face the back wt. on L. May step on R when facing bk or leaving wt. R.

Regular: Either R or L pivot as described above, a ½ turn.

Full: ❂   Can be the regular R or L pivot, as described above, or

    ❂   Can expect two ½ pivots, either R or L, therefore, completing a full revolution, beginning and ending to the front.

Inside: Pivots are normally executed on the inside (i.e., in the direction of the supporting leg), which in the case of a R pivot would be the L, the beginning foot. The general movement, therefore, is fwd or twd the direction of the turn.

Outside: The outside pivot turns in a backward direction, or one that is away from the supporting leg. Thus in a R outside pivot, step bkwd on the L, execute a ½ turn bk L, step ip on R.

NOTE:
Pivots may also be executed as a ¼ or ¾ revolution. These are the unusual, not the normal.

PIVOT TURN

Another term for pivot. See PIVOT

PLACEMENT

The proper weight distribution on one or both feet in preparation for the movement or step to be executed. It is also concerned with alignment and posture. Good placement prevents injuries and allows the feet to be agile, while the body weight is easily controlled and used to the best advantage. When the proper placement is present, the style and technique of the exercise or the routine flows easily.

PLAIN JUMP. See JUMP

PLAIN THREES (3s). See SHUFFLE STEP

PLIÉ ⚲

Plié is a basic movement and present in all forms of dance. It can be as minute as a slight bending of the knees or as highly technical and placed as a ballet plié. It may be executed in any of the 5 pos. or with the feet parallel, oblique, or even turned in. During the plié, the upper torso is held erect, and as the body descends, the torso continues to stretch upwd. However, through the influence of jazz and modern, the torso may be contracted, released, inclined, etc. Pliés are normally performed with the knees in a direct line over the toes, not only for appearance, but also for proper alignment and control. In instances where the knees are not in line with the feet or where the torso is not erect, it is important to allow another part of the body to take over the function of supporting the weight. In tap, a relaxed knee is one

that is not held in a fixed plié position. Plié may be used as an exercise, to precede and finish steps of elevation and turns, for the fluidity of a step, and for a change of level. See DEMI-PLIÉ; GRANDE PLIÉ; BODY PLACEMENT; RELAXED KNEE

POINT
[w/wo sound]

Literally, to arch the foot and place the tips of the toes on the floor. May be a movement or accompanied by sound; in either instance the toes are reached and extended.

POINT STEP (Tap Step, Touch Step)
[1 2] [w/wo sound]

Standing on L, reach R foot fwd in any direction touching ball, with or without a sound. The working leg is usually str. Step R to beside L to finish.

POLKA

A Bohemian folk dance in 4/4 time that originated in the 1830s and became popular in Eastern and Central Europe. Later, it was performed as a ballroom dance.

POLYRHYTHMS

The use of two or more rhythms occurring at the same time, such as a waltz clog step being executed **[1&2&3]** to a 4/4 tempo, thus creating a polyrhythm of **[1&2&3]**, **[4&5&6]**, **[7&8&1]** etc.

PORT DE BRAS (Carriage of the Arms)

Carriage of the arms is as technically significant to the tap dancer as it is to the ballet dancer, for it gives any performance meaning, individualism, and expression.

POSITIONS OF THE FEET. See FOOT POSITIONS

POSITION OF THE HEAD. See HEAD POSITIONS

PRIMARY ACCENT

The first beat in the measure.

PRODUCTION

A complete show or an extended musical number employing a large group of singers, dancers, actors, and technicians; usually contains a plot or story line centered around a theme.

PRODUCTION NUMBER

A large number, usually based on a theme, with lavish costumes, sets, and music.

PROGRESSIVE CRAMROLL. See
CRAMPROLL: Progressive

PROPS

Theater: Usually handheld articles that are used in
the rendering of the plot. (Stairs, tables, and chairs are
considered part of the set and scenery.)

Dance: Usually a cane, stairs, maracas, scarves, hats,
etc. that are used within the number extensively.

PULL
[w/wo sound]

A one-footed slide, executed in a bkwd dir.,
supporting foot kept in contact w/floor, supporting
leg str. or in plié. May be done on ball or flat of foot.
If pull is done on both feet, it is called catch. See also
SLIDE

PULLBACK. See PICKUP

PULLBACK CHANGE. See PICKUP:
Alternating

PULLBACK HEEL. See PICKUP: Drum, Single,
Alternating, and Double

PULLBACK TIME STEP. See TIME STEP:
Pickup

PULLING THE TRENCHES. See TRENCH

PULLBACK TOE. See PICKUP: Variations,
Single and Alternating.

PULLOVER

This is an old term describing any pickups that move
forward.

PUMP BARREL ROLL. See BARREL ROLL:
Pump

PUNCH
[1 sound] [any count]

Striking the floor with the toe tip of the shoe, often
behind the standing leg. It may be executed in any
direction or position and usually assumes that the
working foot is lifted directly after the sound has
been executed.

An old term meaning a toe tap back of the
supporting foot, which is quickly lifted.

PUSH
[1 sounds] [&a1]

TO EXECUTE:
Slide fwd on the ball of the
working foot and do not
allow the heel of that foot to
strike the floor

PUSH BEAT

An accented tap executed on a count that falls in
between the beat (i.e., on the ct. of i, e and /or a).
Therefore, classifiable as an off-beat.

QUADRUPLE. See SHUFFLE TOE HEEL

QUADRUPLE RHYTHM

When one beat of music is divided into four equal
parts. It is based on the sixteenth note and is counted
1e&a.

QUARTER-NOTE RHYTHM

A tap, sound, or movement for each note in the
measure, for example, in 1 measure of 4/4 music
there are 4 quarter notes and, therefore, 4 counts. If a
tap is executed on each one of them, the count
would be 1 2 3 4.

QUARTER PIVOT. See PIVOT

QUARTER TURN

Turn only 1/4 of the way around (i.e., if facing frt
turn L to face the L wall).

QUINTET

A five-count riff is also known as a quintet.

QUINTUPLE

Old term and combination meaning and containing
5 sounds, for example, shuffle toe heel R, heel
dig L **[&1&a2]**

QUINTUPLET
[5 sounds] [1e&a2]

TO EXECUTE:
Stand on L and execute a
double shuffle with R
[1e&a], step R **[2]**

RAILROAD STEP

"Train" steps were very popular in the days of vaudeville. Anything that resembled the sound of a train was automatically named a railroad or train step. The following is one of them:

> TO EXECUTE:
> Begin at SR, face frt and travel to the L, Sh bc R bk L Sh bc, bc R bk L, Sh bc, bc R bk L [16 sounds] [&8&1&2&3&4&5&6&7]

RAGTIME

A popular musical form of the 1890s and early twentieth century. Scott Joplin was one of its most prolific and recognized composers.

RAM(MING) A FLAP

An old tap expression meaning to execute two flaps in rapid succession, as though they were one unit. **[e&a1].** Often used in the military numbers. See DOUBLE FLAP

RAP TAP

Tap work performed to rap (spoken) music. Because of its rhythmic and nonmelodic composition, this style of music is quite appropriate for tap, as it allows the tap sounds to bleed through.

RAT-A-TAT
[10 sounds] [1&a2&a3&a4]

A combination whose rhythm reminds one of a machine gun firing. (From *The Tap Dance Dictionary* by Mark Knowles)

> TO EXECUTE:
> Chug R, shuffle L, hop L shuffle L, hop L shuffle L, hop L

NOTE:
Chugs maybe substituted for all the hops.

RATTLE. See SHUFFLE

RATTLE STEP. See SHUFFLES STEP

REEFER WALK
[2 sounds] [1 2]

Plié, feet tog. and par, knees bent and slanted twd L, dig R beside L as a starting position, step on R to R diag., keeping knees together, swing knees and legs to R and end with L in dig position. Later became the jazz Shorty George. May be done on flat or balls of feet.

REGULAR CRAMPROLL. See CRAMPROLL: Regular

RELAXED KNEE

Sound as well as dance is a requisite in tap as well as in flamenco dancing. Because of this, the tap dancer will often use a relaxed knee, sometimes referred to as a natural knee. In this position, the knee is allowed to remain soft, not in a fixed plié, so that it may respond to the tap sounds to be executed. Along with this, the tap dancer must also be capable of staying within the technical confines required by other fields.

RELEASE

Music:

The release or the bridge is another name for the odd strain of music that appears in a standard chorus. In this musical form of 32 bars, 3 strains have the same melody (usually the 1st, 2nd, and 4th), while the 3rd strain of music has an entirely different melody, thus relieving the pattern.

Dance:

1   To contract means to tighten and constrict the muscles, making them shorter. When a contraction takes place in the abdominal muscles, the front of the body appears to be concave or scooped out while the spinal muscles are released and lengthened. When the contracted muscles are released, the body returns to a normal state.

2   Release means to disengage or to stretch, for example, if the back is arched, the stomach muscles are stretched or released while the vertebra muscles are constricted.

RELEVÉ (Rise)

Present in all forms of dance. It literally means to rise on the points or the balls of the feet. In ballet, it may be executed in two different manners:

1   A slow rising to the position (French school) or accomplished with a little spring onto the position.

2   Stepping directly onto the position (Italian school). The body wt. is lifted via the spine and the elongation of the muscles in the body, so that the wt. is virtually removed from the balls or points and ejected upwd. See RELEVÉ-PLIÉ

RELEVÉ–PLIÉ

Tap has borrowed the r/p position from jazz. It is executed by maintaining a high relevé with the feet, while the legs are in a plié. It is also known as ¾ foot or toe.

RENVERSÉ ⚹
[w/wo sound]

In General: Renversé turns may be done w/wo sound, arched or straight, on the spot or traveling, inside or outside, spotted straight ahead, at the other end of the room, or on the floor. They are based on the ballet renversé, but executed in a different manner. In tap, the opposite arm and foot are employed: when the R leg is executing the circular fan, the L arm is circling into third. This opposite tension helps keeps the body centered and facing the front. The placement of the feet is also a consideration because of the sounds that must be executed.

Stationary Right Renversé: Executed as an outside turn.

To execute:
Prepare by facing front and using a spot that is directly ahead and at eye level.

(1) Step R frt L to corner #2, L arm to 2nd, R to prep. pos. Body twists momentarily to #2, head remains frt, step l Xd bk of R [7 8]

NOTE:
This is a preparation and only appears at the beginning of the first turn and is not used for any successive turns.

(2) Spring up from L, ast execute an outside fan with the R and carry it to 2nd. The L arm to 3rd, R arm to 2nd, body faces frt and spot is frt [1]

(3) St R Xd bk L, body and head are frt, L arm goes to 2nd, R remains in 2nd [&]

(4) Turn bk R, leave both feet on the floor at the beg. of this turn, look over L shoulder at spot, snap head and as body faces #2, Step L bk R, arms remains in 2nd (head is frt) [2]

NOTE:
This crossing of the feet is the preparation for the next turn. See SPOTTING and TURNS: Stationary, Traveling

Right Traveling Renversé: Executed as a R outside turn beginning sr and traveling in a straight line sdwd until sl is reached. The spot is frt and a traveling spot is used (i.e., using an imaginary str. line, eye level and str. ahead, move the spot on each turn to another spot slightly to the L of the one before).

To execute:
Follow the same general directions given for the stationary right renversé but movement to the L may be gained by:
• Moving the hop to the L on each successive turn.
• By over stepping with the R a little on each turn.

NOTE:
Be sure the body remains erect, as the tendency will be to lean to the left.

Right Renversés in a Circle: All renversés may be executed in a circle. The following directions are given for the right renversé:

Inside Circle: Inside circles revolve counterclockwise. Begin dsr, face frt and following the rules for traveling renversés and a traveling spot, progress the turns across the frt to sl, face sl and progress to usl, across the bk and to usr, finishing the circle by facing sr and traveling ds to starting point. The body remains facing outward for the complete circle, while the back remains to the center.

NOTE:
In all outside circles the body faces inward and the circle is clockwise in direction.

Arched/Leaned Renversé: The following describes a right stationary outside renversé. It is executed on the spot in the following manner: Follow the same format as for a right stationary renversé, but *if an arch is desired*, do so when the R foot has stepped Xd bk of the L and the body is beginning to turn bk R, as the head is snapped, arch the body bkwd holding onto spot as if in a back bend, then straighten upon returning to the frt. *If a lean is desired,* proceed as above, but after the R has crossed bk of the L, lean to the L side, remaining there until the body can no longer hold the image, then str. in readiness for the next turn.

Renversé with Sound: The following are described as stationary right renversés with tap sounds; the same sounds may be made while traveling.

1 Make an audible sound on the hop or substitute a pickup or wing for the hop and make a sound on each step R Xd bk L and step L [1&2] or [&1&2] or [&a1&2]

2 Accent the hop, accent the step R Xd bk L, add toe heel L Xd bk R [1&a2]

3 Accent the hop and add heel drop L, step R bk L, drop R and L heels as the turn is being done. Leave the feet on the floor during the turn [1&a2] or [&1&a2]

4 Execute the hop and finish the turn with brush bc bk R [1& a2]

5 Execute the hop and finish the turn with spank toe heel R and step L [1e&a2]

6 Execute the hop but pull R foot to bk of L (sur le cou de pied), upon facing frt execute a 3-ct. riff [1&a2]

REPEAT

In dance, as in music, repeat refers to doing the same thing over exactly as it was executed the first time.

REST

A musical term meaning silence.

RETARD (Ritardando)

Musical term for a gradual slowing down of the tempo.

RETIRÉ

In retiré, the thigh is raised to 2nd position, with the toe touching and placed in front of or behind the knee.

REVERENCE

In performance, the acknowledgment of the performers to the applause. In the classroom, the ending to the class in which the students express their thanks to the teacher and the teacher to the students. It takes the form of a curtsy or bow.

REVERSE

In dance, doing a step or combination in the same order but with other foot.

RHYTHM

Music: The regular occurrence of the beat. It is the framework upon which all other principles, such as accent, syncopation, etc., are based. Rhythm is intricately tied to its time signature and is involved with tempo. It includes such things as double time, 3 against 4, etc. Briefly described below are some of these usages:

Syncopation: A type of rhythm and timing that became popular during the ragtime era, dixieland and blues; involves accenting the usually unaccented beats, that is, playing in between the beats (1/8th and 1/16th notes) and accenting the weak beat (the 2nd and 4th beats) - thus, playing off-beat, rather than on-beat.

Single Time: Acknowledging each beat as it is in accordance with the time signature.

Double Time: Playing or dancing twice as many beats within the same time framework (i.e., in one bar of 4/4 time there are 4 beats; double time would allow for 8 beats played during that interval. In dance, we would count this new beat as 1&2&3&4&).

3 Against 4: This is only one of a number of possibilities of interesting rhythmic patterns that are at the tap dancer's command. As the musical background of 4 beats per measure is being played, the performer is dancing 3 beats to that measure. Thus, the ct. 4 musically will be the dancer's next ct. of 1. This procedure creates downward Rhythmic Progression patterns and a counterpoint of overlapping taps. See RHYTHMIC PROGRESSION

Individual Rhythm: The individual's ability to feel a beat, timing, and tempo with or without the music being present. More advanced types of rhythm must be practiced, but much natural rhythm seems to be present in certain individuals either because of inherent qualities or environmental exposure.

RHYTHM BREAK. See BREAK: Buck

RHYTHM BUCK

Rhythm Buck was a modified form of buck dancing that was introduced around 1910. See STEPS AND STYLES OF TAP DANCE: STYLES AND DANCES

RHYTHM TAP

Introduced by John Bubbles in 1922, it contained very complex footwork and substituted the normal fast-moving 2/4 tempo for a much slower 4/4, thus allowing the footwork to become more complex. Today, it is associated with highly syncopated, rhythmic dancing and fast footwork, many times using improvisation.

RHYTHM TIME STEP. See TIME STEP: Buck

RHYTHMIC PROGRESSION

Downward Rhythmic Progression

Occurs when the number of cts. in a step are less than the number of beats in the measure: in 4/4 time, if a step is executed to 3 cts. rather than 4 and the step is repeated over and over, with no pause left in between, the step would end on the ct of 3 the 1st time, then ct. 2 the 2nd time, and ct. 1 the 3rd. time because the step is underphrased and the ct. upon which the step ends is on the descent.

Upward Rhythmic Progression

When the number of cts. in a step is more than the number of beats in the measure: in 4/4 time, if a step is executed to 5 cts. rather than 4 and the step is repeated over and over, with no pause left in between, the step would end on the ct. of 1 (or 5) the 1st time, then ct. 2 (or 6) the 2nd time, and ct. 3 (or 7) the 3rd time because the step is overphrased and the ct. upon which the step ends is on the ascent.

RHYTHMIC SHADING

Changing the timbre and a rhythmic pattern, sounds, and textures of a step by using off-beats, rests, syncopation, and loud and soft sounds.

RIFF
[2 or more sounds] [a1] or [&1]

A riff consists of two sounds, one rendered by the ball of the foot and the other by the heel of the same foot. However, they may be executed in the following manners: brush R, scuff R; ball R, scuff R; or nerve ball R and scuff R. All of them are acceptable but, in the advanced form, the last is the one favored.

Some students slur the riff by grounding the ball of the foot and then pushing it fwd into the scuff, whereas others hit two clean sounds by executing the first sound, then tilting the ball of the foot upward and executing the scuff. Again, both executions are acceptable, but the cleaner sounds are preferred.

Lastly, when one arrives at the 3-ct. riff, there are two totally different systems of execution: the Traditional and the conventional, the former being the original and based on flatfoot dancing and the latter found in the English and Irish systems.

The two systems are contrasted below:

Conventional

2 ct. - ball R, scuff R	[a1]
3 ct. - ball R, scuff L, HlDr L	[&a1]
4 ct. - 3 ct. R &hl dig R	[e&a1]
5 ct. - 3 ct. R & Hl toe R	[&a1&2]
6 ct. - 5 ct. R & HlDr R	[&a1&2]
7 ct. - 5 ct. & HlDr L, R	[e&a1&2]

Traditional

2 ct. - ball R, scuff R	[a1]
3 ct. - ball R, scuff R, Hl dig R	[&a1]
4 ct. - 3 ct. & toe dr R	[e&a1]
5 ct. - 4 ct. & HlDr R	[ie&a1]
6 ct. - 4 ct. & HlDr L, R	[do in 1 ct.]
7 ct. - HlDr L & 6 ct.	[do in 1 ct.]

NOTE:

1 A 5-ct. riff is also known as a quintet.

2 A 2-ct. riff and a step R **[&a1]** is known as a three tap riff walk.

3 Both count and tap refer to the number of sounds contained in the riff (i.e., a 5-ct. riff and a 5 tap riff contain 5 sounds) See RIFF

4 The traditional 4-ct. riff became a walking riff, whereas the conventional riff did not walk until its 5-ct. riff.

5 The conventional riff extended to 2 cts. on its 5-ct. riff, while the traditional riff has remained within the framework of 1 ct. for all the riffs presented here. Thus, the later riff produces more sounds per musical beat than the former one.

6 The words beat, count, point and sound are all interchangeable words.

Conventional Riffs and Related Terms

Regular Riff (Forward or Front)

Any riff in which the working leg begins in a backward position and then swings forward to execute the riff, like the basic 3-ct. riff.

Back Riff (Backward)

Place R fwd and in the air, swing R bk, ast strike the bk edge of the R heel, then spank R bkwd **[&a] or [1&]**.

Walking Riffs

Any riff that is capable of being executed on one foot and then the other in an alternating fashion, for example 4-ct. traditional or 5-ct. conventional riff.

NOTE:
Any walking riff may turn into a running riff.

Leaping Riffs

Any riff preceded or ended by a leap, for example, leap R, 3-ct. riff L [1&a2] or 2-ct. riff fwd Sp leap R frt L [e&a1]

Flat Riff

Any traditional riff.

Straight Riffs

- ✪ Any riff that is executed in a straight line.
- ✪ Any riff that is executed in its original basic form and not in combination with any other riffs, like a 6-ct. riff.

Alternating (Changing) Riffs

Any riff, walking or leaping, that changes from one foot to the other, for example, leap R, 3-ct. riff L.

Crossover Riff

A riff in which the working leg crosses over the supporting leg. See PENDULUM RIFF

Double Riff

There are two versions:

TO EXECUTE:

- Dig toe R, dig heel R, dig toe R, scuff fwd R [4 sounds] [e&a1].
- Dig toe R, dig hl R, br fwd R, drop hl L [4 sounds] [e&a1].

Fwd/Bkwd Riff

TO EXECUTE:

2-ct. riff fwd followed by a 2-ct. riff bkwd [e&a1]. Executed rapidly it becomes a rolling riff.

Scissors Riff

TO EXECUTE:

2-ct. riff R, alt. pickup from L, ending in heel stand R, tap L toe bk end w/ wt on L toe & R heel stand

(Courtesy of Barbara Denny, Lancaster, NY)

Rolling Riff

TO EXECUTE:

- Repeat rapidly a 2-ct. riff R, Sp R bk but invert R foot inward [&a1]
- Fwd/bkwd riffs executed rapidly

Pendulum Riffs

Pendulum riffs are so called because the working leg swings fwd then bkwd during its execution. They may be executed in a parallel or turned-out position.

Parallel Pendulum

TO EXECUTE:

3-ct. riff fwd, followed by a 3-ct. back riff. Working leg remains parallel [&a1&a2]

1/2 Turned out Pendulum

TO EXECUTE:

3-ct. riff fwd R with the working leg remaining in a parallel position, followed by a 3-ct. back riff R frt L, with the working leg turned out [&a1&a2]

Full Turned Out Pendulum

TO EXECUTE:

3-ct. par riff fwd R, a 3-ct. tno bk riff R frt L, a 3-ct. tno riff to DSR corner and a 3-ct. par bk riff R [&a1&a2&a3&a4]

Walking Pendulum Riff Combinations

Using the 6-ct. conventional riffs

Parallel Pendulum Walking Riff

TO EXECUTE:

parallel pendulum riff , followed by a 6-ct. riff [&a1&a2&a3&a4]

Double Parallel Pendulum Walking Riff

TO EXECUTE:

Sh R, heel drop L, followed by a par pendulum riff walk [&a1&a2&a3&a4&a5]

Triple Parallel Pendulum Walking Riff

TO EXECUTE:

Sh R, heel drop L, followed by a parallel pendulum riff, Sh R, heel drop L, followed by a 6-ct. riff R fwd [&a1&a2&a3&a4&a5&a6]

RIFF (continued)

Turned-Out Pendulum Walking Riff

TO EXECUTE:

3-ct. riff fwd R, with working leg remaining in a parallel position, a 3-ct. back riff R frt L (tno), a 3-ct. fwd riff R to DSR corner (tno) and a 3-ct. par bkwd riff R, followed by a 6-ct. riff [&a1&a2&a3&a4&a5&a6]

Double Turned-Out Pendulum Walking Riff

TO EXECUTE:

Sh R, heel drop L, a full tno pendulum riff followed by a 6-ct. riff [&a1&a2&a3&a4&a5&a6&a7]

Triple Turned-Out Walking Pendulum Riff

TO EXECUTE:

Sh R, heel drop L, a full pendulum riff, Sh R, heel drop L and a 6-ct. riff [&a1&a2&a3&a4&a5&a6&a7&a8]

Hollywood Walking Riff

3-ct. riff R, step R [&a1 2]

Other Steps Containing Riffs
Riff Essence

Using the essence step as a basis (step R to R, Br bc L frt R), change every brush to a 2-ct. riff [1e&a2]. This use of the riff is possible in all the essence steps: the single, double, and triple forms well as in the short, long, and Virginia essence. See ESSENCE

Flutter Riff

Actually a fake riff. Using only the ankle and keeping the foot close to the floor, execute a toe drop R with no wt. then a heel drop R with no wt. Continue to do at a rapid speed.

Syncopated Riff Step

TO EXECUTE:

heel drop L, a 3-ct. riff R, step fwd on ball R, step L beside R, step R fwd, brush L fwd [1&a2&3&4]. Reverse

Riff Turns: Stationary

(All begin facing the frt.)

TO EXECUTE:

- 3-ct. riff R to A1, Sp St R Xd frt L. Leave feet on floor and Xd while turning to L, drop R and L heels on turn, bc R-L on facing frt [&a1&2&3&4]
- Sp R bk, drop L heel, turn bk R placing R frt L sur le cou de pied, face frt and execute 3-ct. riff R [&1&a2]
- R renversé ending in a 3-ct. riff R [1&a2]
- pump barrel roll ending in a 3-ct. riff [1&a2]

Riff Turns: Traveling

The following turns are all based on the execution of R chaîné turns.

TO EXECUTE:

- Step R to R, 3 ct. riff L, begin to turn R, turn ending in leap L, tap R bk L [ea1&2]
- Step R to R, scuff L, begin to turn R, leap L turning to R, 3 ct. riff R to finish turn [&1e&a2]
- 4-ct. flat riff R, face frt, 4-ct. flat riff L, face bk, turn and repeat [ea&a1ea&a2]

RIFF BARREL ROLLS. See BARREL ROLL: Riff

RIFF ESSENCE

Substitute a 2-ct. frt riff for every brush or a 2-ct. bk riff for every spank. See ESSENCE

RIFF FOUETTÉ. See FOUETTÉ: Riff

RIFF HOP STEP
[5 sounds] [e&a12]

TO EXECUTE:

Riffle R, hop L, step R

RIFF SHUFFLE. See Riffle

RIFF SHUFFLE HOP STEP. See Riffle Hop Step

RIFF RENVERSÉ. See Renversé; Riff: Turns

RIFF SHUFFLE. See Riffle

RIFF SHUFFLE STEP. See Riffle Step

RIFF TURN. See Riff: Turns

RIFF WALK. See Riff: Walking

RIFFLE (Riff Shuffle)
[3 sounds] [&a1] or [a&1]

Riffle is a combination of a 2-count riff fwd and a spank R (the last sound of shuffle). May be done in any position or direction.

RIFFLE HOP STEP
[5 sounds] [&a1 & 2]

> To execute:
> Riffle R (1-ct. riff fwd,
> spank bk R)   [&a1]
> hop L   [&]
> step R   [2]
> reverse

RIFFLE STEP (Riff Shuffle Step)
[4 sounds] [&a1 2] or [e&a1]

Execute a riffle R, step R. May be done in any position or direction. See RIFFLE

RIGHT (HANDED) TURN. See Turn: General

RIGHT PIVOT. See Pivot

RIGHT-SIDED DRAWBACK. See Drawback: One-Sided, Right

RIGHT TURN. See Turn: Right

RIM SHOT
[1 sound]

> To execute:
> Strike the floor using the inside or outside of the heel.

Usually the foot is crossed over or under the supporting leg.

RING SHOUT (The Shout)

An old American group dance that arose from the African circle dance. It used vocalization, clapping, flatfooted shuffles, and stamping. The early Baptist Church prohibited drumming and dancing. African–Americans substituted clapping and stamping, as dancing was described by Baptists as a crossing of the legs. The ring shout did not cross them. A form of this dance, the walk around, became an integral part of minstrel shows and influenced the cakewalk and the Big Apple.

RING THE TAPS

Not often used today, it means trying to create various tones and pitches with taps. Often taps are tightened or loosened to create tonality, or a small metal plate or circle is or occasionally a small fiber plate is added for musical pitch.

RIP

An old English name for some forms of pickups.

> To execute:
> 3 tap fwd rip (brush R, alt. pickup L to R) [&a1]
> 4 tap fwd rip (brush R, alt. pickup L to R, heel drop R) [a&a1]
> back rip (brush bk R, brush bk L, step R) [&a1]

RIPPLE

✪ A continuous, wavelike movement of the body beginning and ending where desired. It may be executed by the arm or hand, or by the entire body. It is different from a pulse, which is an isolated throbbing or systematic beat. An impulse may involve the total body, beg. at the feet and ending w/ the head. The ripple relies on dividing the part(s) of the body to be used and contracting and releasing them in rhythmic succession: contract the pelvis, and as the pelvis pushes fully under, the upper torso contracts, finally the chest and shoulders; then the shoulders release, next the upper torso and finally the pelvis. A ripple may be begun by one part of the body and transferred to another: after the shoulders are contracted, the arms contract, bend and come close to the shoulders, later to be pushed out or released.

RIPPLE (continued)

✿ A very loose, floppy movement done with a very relaxed foot and lower leg, as in a shuffle step ripple, the outside edge of ball of the foot would create a brush sound by scraping away from the body, the inward scrape would come toward the body on the inside of the tap scraping and the step would end by stepping on the ball of the same foot.

RITARDANDO. See Retard

RIVER BOAT SHUFFLES
[10 sounds] [&a1 &2 &a3 &4]

No origin for the name found.

> To execute:
> (A) Shuffle R X frt L [&a1]
> heel drop L, toe heel R
> to R [&2]
> Reverse (A) [&a3 &4]

ROCK
[w/wo sound]

Music: A type of music; short for rock `n' roll. Also a type of dancing that accompanies this form of music.

Dance: Generally, a rock is a movement in which both knees are bent, held tog. or slightly separated, and slanted to the R or L. Borrowed from jazz, it may be done moving from side to side, remain ip, or travel fwd or bkwd. Rocks may be accompanied w/ snaps and claps and moved about by the use of chugs or small steps on the ball or flat of the foot. It can be motivated by or involved in the movement of the hips, or the body may remain in one piece. Generally, a rock is a pose, and as such comes to a momentary stop.

Knee Rock: A rock done while kneeling on one knee, or a movement involving only the knees.

Floor Rock: A rock position that is near or on the floor or drops to the floor.

ROCK DROP
[4 sounds] [e&a1]

Traceable to vaudeville. Drop R and L toes to R, drop R and L heels to R., creating 4 sounds. Can be done maintaining one level, legs can be str. and/or bent, body can rock fwd and bkwd, toes may invert inward, then heels inward like the Charleston, etc. Same as parallel travel. See Alternating Toe-Heel Drops

ROCK DROP SIDE TRAVEL
[4 or more] [&1&2&3&4 etc.]

See Rock Drop; Parallel Travel

ROCKETTES

A famous company of dancers noted for their high kicks and precision dancing, which performs at Radio City Music Hall in New York City.

ROCKING HEELS. See Heel Beat Swivel

ROLL

A continuous repeating of a constant rhythm, beat, etc. that produces an uninterrupted, even series of sounds, like the rolling of a drum. In tap, this may be done with toe or heel drops or heel chugs. Often associated with cramprolls, paradiddles, and close to the floor work.

ROLL SHUFFLE
[18 sounds] [&1 &2 &3 &4 &5 &a6 &a7 &8]

A short 2 M combination that has a rolling look and feel to it.

> To execute:
> Stand on R with L foot fwd.
> spank L bk, leap L, brush R
> fwd, hop L [&1 &2], spank
> R bk, leap R, brush L fwd,
> hop R [&3 &4], spank L bk,
> leap L, shuffle R fwd, hop L
> [&5 &6], shuffle R, hop L,
> brush R fwd, hop L [&a7
> &8]

ROLLING
[4 sounds] [1 & 2&]

Probably named for its rolling rhythm. Possibly imitative of the sound of a train.

> To execute:
> (A) Step L, heel grind
> R (twist R toes in
> and out) [1&], step L,
> step L [2&]
> reverse (A) as desired

ROLLING OFF A LOG. See Falling Off the Log

ROLLING RHYTHM

Any rhythm that is continuous and has a repetitive count, such as running shuffles **[&a1&a2 etc.]**, running flap heels **[&a1 &a2 etc.]**.

ROLLING RIFF

A type of a riff. Execute 2-ct. riff R, Sp bk R, turning R inward **[&a1]**. Repeat continuously to create a rolling sound.

ROLLING SHUFFLES

Common name for hop L, shuffle R **[1&a]**. It is repeated over and over at a very fast tempo and low to the ground, creating a rolling rhythm.

ROND DE JAMBE
[w/wo sound]

A circular movement of the leg, used as a barre exercise, in the center, or in an adage. May be done demi or grand, on the floor (à terre) or in the air (en l'air), inside (en dedans) or outside (en dehors).

Inside: Working leg circles inward, twd the supporting leg (i.e., in a counterclockwise direction).

Outside: Working leg circles outward, away from the supporting leg (i.e., in a clockwise direction).

ROOM DIRECTIONS (Stage Directions)

Cecchetti Method	Vaganova Method
#1 Right downstage cor.	#1 Mirror/ Audience
#2 Left downstage cor.	#2 Right downstage cor.
#3 Left upstage cor.	#3 Right wall, right stage
#4 Right upstage cor.	#4 Right upstage cor.
#5 Mirror/ Audience	#5 Back wall
#6 Left wall, left stage	#6 Left upstage cor.
#7 Back wall	#7 Left wall, left stage
#8 Right wall or right stage	#8 Left downstage cor.

See diagram on page 175.

ROUND BREAK

An old term for a full 2 measure break. It is unclear whether this pertained to the buck, or standard break, or both.

ROUND KICK. See KICK: Fan

ROUND THE LEG

Derived from Highland dancing; literally, "to hop on one leg" (e.g., the left, while the right executes a high passé in front of the knee; on the next hop, the passé would move to the back of the working leg).

ROUND THE WORLD See OVER THE TOPS

ROUTINE

A series of steps created to a mood, feeling, rhythm, and phrasing of the music used. A standard routine, performed to standard music, is one chorus in length. It is comprised of 32 measures, with 8 measures to a step, thus four steps to the routine. Generally, two choruses of music are used—64 measures or 8 steps.

RUBBER LEGS

A form of movement, usually associated with eccentric or comedy dancing, in which the legs are loose and exaggerated, as if they are made of rubber.

RUBY KEELER TIME STEP. See TIME STEP: Ruby Keeler

RUMBA

A Cuban dance of African origin.

RUN-ALONG TIME STEP. See TIME STEP: Traveling

RUNDOWN
[4-5 sounds] [1&a2] [a1&a2]

Traceable to vaudeville. Flap fwd, stamp L, R, L, usually fwd **[a1&a2]** or stamp R, L, R, L, only 4 sounds **[1&a2]**.

RUNNING FLAPS. See FLAPS: Running

RUNNING IN PLACE

Any step or short combination that allows the dancer to remain in one spot during its execution and has the appearance of running or leaping (as in running flaps, running shuffles, etc.).

RUNNING PICKUPS. See PICKUPS: Running

RUNNING PULLBACKS. See PICKUPS: Running

RUNNING SHUFFLES. See SHUFFLES: Running; ALTERNATING SHUFFLES

RUNNING SLAPS

Old term for running flaps. See FLAPS: Running

RUNNING WALTZ CLOG. See WALTZ CLOG STEP: Running

RUNOFF

Literally, exiting by running off the stage.

SABOT

(Pronounced sah-BO.) The original wooden clog shoe made from one solid piece of wood, used for work and recreation as well. It became the dancers' clog shoe.

SAMBA

A Brazilian dance, executed in polyrhythms over 2/4 or 4/4 time. The name was derived from a dance performed by African slaves. It was introduced in a modified ballroom form at the New York World's Fair in 1939.

SAMMY DAVIS

[16 sounds] [a8a1 a2a 3a4 a5 a6 a7]

A short, into the floor, 2 M combination that works as a step to be repeated or as a break, used by Sammy Davis.

> To execute:
> Step R, step L, stamp R, stamp L [a8a1], spank R, stamp R, stomp L [a2a], spank L, stamp L, stomp R [3a4], spank R, heel drop L, flap R to RL [a5 a6], flap L to R [a7]

(From *The Tap Dance Dictionary* by Mark Knowles)

SAND DANCE

A popular dance in vaudeville and the predecessor to the soft shoe. The dancer executed slides and glides in the sand, in soft shoes with no tap sounds. See STEPS AND STYLES OF TAP DANCE: Styles and Dances.

SASHAY. See CHASSÉ

SAUTÉ

Literally, to spring or jump. When springing into the air, the last area of the foot to leave the floor is the tips of the toes and on the descent, they are the first to return.

SAW WING. See WING: OTHER TYPES, Saw Wing

SCATTER WINGS. See WINGS: Scatter

SCHERRER SPINNER

[16 sounds] [1e &a 2&3 &4 &hold 5 &6 a7 &8]

Created by Bob Scherrer.

> To execute:
> Hop L, shuffle R, drop L heel [1e&a], toe tap R bk L, snap fingers 2 times [2 &3], clap, snap fingers 1 time [&4], stomp R, stamp R, step bk [& hold 5 &6], flap R, step L, tap R [a 7&8]

SCHOTTISCHE

A German round dance using Polka music. It includes waltzlike turns and many hopping and gliding movements. It was extremely popular in the United States in the mid–1800s.

SCIFFLE

[3 sounds] [&a1]

No written sources found, but some dancers claim that it is a scuff, followed by a back riff on the same foot.

SCIFFLE HOP STEP

[5 sounds] [&a1&2]

> To execute:
> Scuff fwd R, 2 ct. bk riff R, hop L, St R [&a1&2]

SCIFFLE STEP

[4 sounds] [e&a1]

> To execute:
> Scuff fwd R, 2-ct. bk riff R, St R [e&a1]

See SCIFFLE

SCISSORS (Abe Kabbible)

[4 sounds] [&1&2] or [a1a2]

Traceable to vaudeville. Used in eccentric, musical comedy, jazz, and tap. (Already noted as a secondary term.)

> To execute:
> Leap R to R. leap L Xd frt R, leap R to R, extend to L, L leg str., bk edge of L heel on floor, R in plié rev

SCISSORS RIFF. See RIFF: Scissors

SCISSORS SPLIT. See SPLIT: Straddle

SCOOT
[1 sound] [1]

A form of slide. Stand on L, slide a short distance in any dir. Scoot implies a quick, contracted movement, whereas slide is longer and smoother. See SLIDE

SCOOT BACKS

Distribute weight evenly on both feet, knees bent, jump bkwd, quickly straighten legs, bend slightly fwd then land on both feet ast in plié, bk straight.

SCRAPE

See WING: Scrape Shuffle; SCRAPE KICK A sound produced by dragging any edge of the foot along the floor, usually just the outside or inside edge of the great toe w/ heel raised. In executing wings, it is the outside edge of the sole that is scraped. May be done in any dir. by dragging free foot, or by standing on foot to be scraped. At end of a scrape, foot may be left on floor or lifted in air.

SCRAPE KICK
[1 sound] [1]

While executing a kick, scrape the foot being kicked. Sound may be short or prolonged.

SCRAPE SHUFFLE See WING: Scrape Shuffle

SCUFF (Heel Brush, Heel Scuff, Heel Kick, Back Heel Brush) [1 sound] [1]

Regular: Working leg in bk pos., swing leg fwd, striking bk edge of heel in passing. Foot ends in raised pos. May be done in any dir.

Back Scuff (Backward, Reverse): The opp. of regular scuff. With working leg raised in fwd pos. swing leg bkwd, striking bk edge of heel on floor in passing. Foot ends raised off floor in bkwd pos. May be done in any dir.

SCUFF CRAMPROLL. See CRAMPROLL

SCUFFLE (Heel Rattle, Flatfooted Shuffle) [2 sounds] [a1] or [&1]

Scuffle is a contraction of scuff and the spank sound of the shuffle. Stand on L, R raised in bk pos., swing R fwd ast scuff R, swing R bkwd, execute spank R. R ends in raised pos. See SCUFF; SHUFFLE

✿ Some consider heel dig R, spank bk R the same as scuffle grounded. However, when executing a fast, close to the floor scuffle, one must resort to seel dig and not scuff. Incidently, there is no name for the heel dig, spank sequence.

SCUFFLE HOP STEP
[4 sounds] [&1&2] [1&a2]

Stand on L, R in bkwd, pos, swing R fwd, execute scuff, swing R bk, execute spank, hop L, step R. Rev. May be done in any dir. or pos. See SCUFFLE

SCUFFLE STEP
[3 sounds] [1&2] or [&a1]

Stand on L, R in bkwd pos, swing R fwd, execute scuff, swing R bk, execute spank, step R beside L. Rev. See SCUFFLE

SEAT SPIN

Traceable to jazz. A turn or spin executed on the derrière, usually done in a jackknife or contracted pos for balance and control. May be begun from any starting pos., for example, 4th on floor (L frt R), push w/ hands or by twisting to R as spin is begun, take feet off floor and hold in any pos. desired (e.g., arms clasped around knees, legs in side split pos., frt v, etc.

SEGUE

A smooth musical connection between musical numbers or passages without any hesitation or loss of beats, even though the tempos and styles of music may vary greatly.

SERPENTINE. See GRAPEVINE

SET DE FLO. See SET THE FLOOR

SET THE FLOOR (Set de Flo)

A very old practice in which a circle would be drawn or inscribed on a dance floor so that the dancers would remain within. Usually, this was done for competition purposes.

SEVEN
[7 sounds] [1&a2&a3] or [1&2&3&4] or [&a1&2&3]

Traceable to clog dancing. Stand L, step R, shuffle step L and R or Sh St R, Sh bc L (triple waltz clog). Unfortunately, there are no other written verifications.

SEVEN COUNT TAP RIFF. See RIFF: Seven Count Riff

SHADING

Best described in connection with art. If one were to do a pencil drawing, using the pencil lightly in some areas, heavier in others, and extremely dark in others,

SHADING (continued)

tones or different levels of darkness and lightness would be obvious. Toning is also possible with the sound of taps. Some sounds are light yet clear, others of medium intensity, still others extremely loud. The loudness of taps alone in a grouping is known as accent, the gradual approach to loudness and the decrease of this loudness to softness is shading. In accenting or shading, various parts of the foot may be used: the ball, tip, edge, flat, etc. See DYNAMICS: Shading

SHAG

A ballroom dance, built around the shag step, that was comprised of hopping movements that rhythmically changed from foot to foot.

SHAKE

To shimmy or shake a certain part of the body such as the shoulders, hips, foot, etc. See SHIMMY

SHANNON
[21 sounds] [&a1 &a2 & 3 &a 4 &5 &a 6 &a 7 8]

An Irish combination.

> TO EXECUTE:
> Shuffle step L, shuffle step R frt L [&a1 &a2], chug bk R, step L, shuffle step R while, [& 3 &a], kicking L out to L, step L, shuffle step R [4 & 5&a], chug R (ast lift L knee), shuffle L [6 &a], drop both heels to the R, then to the L [7], drop L heel ast lifting R knee [8]

SHAVE AND HAIRCUT
[9 sounds] [12&a34 567]

Traceable to vaudeville. Used as a finish or break. There are 2 popular executions:

> TO EXECUTE:
> Stomp R fwd, double pickup bk R, step fwd R, Br L fwd, hop R, slam L fwd.

> TO EXECUTE:
> Stomp R, shuffle ball change L, step L, step R, leap L, slam R fwd.

SHIFT(S)

A change of weight to another foot or a change of direction. A step or a ball change would shift the weight and/or direction. See BALL CHANGE

SHIM SHAM
[12 sounds] [8&12&34&56&7]

Original

> TO EXECUTE:
> Stomp R, spank step R bk
> Rev. [8&12&3]
> stomp R, Br bc R, stomp Sp
> St R [4&5&6&7]

Variations

> TO EXECUTE:
> Sh St R and L, Sh bc R, Sh St R, reverse [8&12&34&5&67]

> TO EXECUTE:
> Heel dig R Sp St R. rev. L, heel dig R, Br bc R, heel dig R, Sp St R [8&12&34&5&67]

> TO EXECUTE:
> Scuffle St R and L, scuffle bc R, scuffle St R [8&12&34&5&67]

NOTE:
For first step of the shim sham shimmy, execute the original 3 times, but on third time, substitute spank dig step R for spank step R, ending on ct. 8 (6M) and add the shim sham break See SHIM SHAM BREAK

SHIM SHAM BREAK

> TO EXECUTE:
> Dig L to R, St L [1 2], drop R heel, St bk R [3& hold 4], drop R heel, St bk L [&5], step R and L ip [6 7]

SHIM SHAM SHIMMY

In the 1920s, Leonard Reed and his partner, Willie Bryant, were searching for a routine as a finale for their act, one in which the whole cast and the audience could participate. Drawing on an old eccentric dance of theirs called goofus, they created the shim sham. It consisted of four 8-measure steps: 1, the shim sham; 2, the crossover; 3, the tack Annie; and 4, the half break. The routine was held together by a break known as the shim sham break. It was an instant success. The name shim sham came about later when they performed in a club of that name, and the word shimmy was added to the beginning when a chorus girl exited one night, shaking her shoulders. Reed, age 85 at the time of this writing, added two more choruses to the original, which are available on video See Bibliography: Video

STEP I (SHIM SHAM)		
8	(A)	Stomp R fwd
& 1		Spank step R bkwd
2 & 3		Reverse (A)
4	(B)	Stomp R fwd
& 5 &		Brush ball change R bkwd
6		Stomp R fwd
& 7		Brush step R bkwd
8 - 7		Reverse all of the above
8 & 1		Repeat (A)
2 & 3		Reverse (A)
4 - 6		Repeat (B) cts. 4 - 6
& 7	(C)	Spank dig R to L
8		Stamp R to R
Break		
1		Dig L to R
2		Step L to L
3		Heel drop L
& (4)		Step RXBL
&		Heel drop R
5		Step LXBR
6 7		Step R, L (2nd)
8		Clap

STEP II (CROSSOVER)		
1	(A)	Ball R to R
2		Step L IP
3 4		Repeat (A)
5	(B)	Step R to R
& (6)		Scuff LXFR
&		Heel drop R
7		Step LXFR

8		Step R to R
1M		Reverse (A) 2 times
1M		Reverse (B)
2M		Repeat (A) 2 times, Repeat (B) 1- time
Break		
1	(*)	Step L to L
& (2)		Scuff RXFL
&		Heel drop L
3		Step RXFL (*)
4		Step L to L
5 & (6) & 7		Reverse (*) to (*)
& 8		Stamp R & L (2nd)

STEP III (TACK ANNIE)		
a 1	(A)	Brush dig R to L
2		Step R to R
a 3 4		Reverse (A)
a 5 6		Repeat (A)
a7 a 8	(B)	Spank step ball change L (2nd)
2 M		Repeat all of the above
1 - 6		Repeat all thru ct. 6
a 7	(C)	Spank step L to R
8		Step R to R
1 - 5		Repeat Break from Step I, thru ct. 5 only.
6 7	(D)	Stamp R & L (2nd)

STEP IV (HALF BREAK)		
8	(A)	Leap R fwd R
1		Step L bkwd L
a2 a 3		Shuffle ball change R bkwd L
4 5 a 6 a7		Repeat (A)
8	(B)	Step R fwd R
1 - 7	(C)	Repeat Break from Step I thru ct. 7
4M		Repeat all of Step IV

NOTE:

- ✿ This chorus plus the two new choruses may be found on the video *Leonard Reed's Shim Sham Shimmy*.
- ✿ The whole routine is repeated but there is a freeze chorus in which part of the step is left out and the dancers assume a still pose.

SHIMMY

A type of dance from the 1920s in which the body shakes.

SHINGLES

Planks of wood used to build the platform for dance competitions or demonstrations. The finished area was five to six square feet and created a portable stage. Many times, spectators held these planks together.

(THE) SHIRLEY TEMPLE
[14 sounds] [&12&34&5&6&7&8]

This step is actually a short combination, repeated in so many Shirley Temple movies that it became known as The Shirley Temple.

> **TO EXECUTE:**
> Face SR: flap heel R & L to SR, flap heel R (face frt), heel dig L, Sp L, drop R heel, tap L bk R, drop R heel

SHOE MUSIC

The name comes from the Irish step dancers and the wonderful sounds they produce during their routines. As they were considered musicians and dancers, the term shoe music was a normal consequence.

SHOE PATTER. See PATTER

SHOE RIFF
[2 sounds] [&1]

Sounds of a riff are made on the shoe, rather then the floor.

> **TO EXECUTE:**
> Stand on L, as R foot brushes by L shoe, strike the inside of the R ball on L side of L shoe, then strike the inside of the R heel on L side of L shoe.

SHOES (TAPS)

Tap shoes began as clog shoes. Later, they progressed to a split clog shoe, in which the sole was split into three sections with hollow heels of honeycomb wood. By the 1800s, leather was available and with the popularity of sand dancing and the essence, it became the shoe of choice. Its name, the soft shoe, and the dance became synonymous. Most clog dancers, however, continued to wear wooden shoes for performing. By 1915, metal taps had been placed on the toes and heels, and the tap shoe as we know it was born. See SABOT

SHOO SHOO (Shoe Patter)

Used in soft shoe routines in early vaudeville. See PATTER

SHOOT. See CHUG

SHOOTING THE PISTOL. See SHUFFLE SIDE TRAVEL

SHORT BRUSH. See BRUSH: Short

SHORT RIFF

Usually performed in a par position and to the front.

> **TO EXECUTE:**
> Do a 2-ct. riff on the R, to the frt, with the R leg par (ball R, scuff R fwd) [&1]. At the end of the riff, bend and lift the leg to a parallel passé position

SHORTY GEORGE

Named after George "Shorty" Snowden, a self-taught dancer who steadily performed at the Savoy ballroom in Harlem, and who is credited with doing the Lindy years before it became popular.

> **TO EXECUTE:**
> Press the knees together, r/p, and with each small step R and L shift the knees R and L

Such variations as walking down stairs, where with each step the body got lower to the floor, and walking up stairs, where the body grew taller, quickly followed.

SHOT BEAT. See LAMP

(THE) SHOUT. See RING SHOUT

SHOVELING COAL
[7 sounds] [&a1e &a2]

TO EXECUTE:
Stand on L: chug L fwd to
2nd position, toe tap R bk L
[&a], step R bk L, heel toe L
to 2nd pos. [1e&], tap R bk
L, chug L to 2nd pos. [a2]

SHOW TAP

A wide variety of styles and periods of tap dancing,
but basically the tap performed in motion pictures
and on the stage.

SHOW TIME. See CURTAIN TIME

SIDE SPLIT. See SPLIT: Straddle

SIDE TRAVEL

An old term. Any step that uses toe and heel drops to
travel sideward. See PARALLEL TRAVEL

SHUFFLE (Rattle, Two, (2), Double, Front-Back)
[&1] or [a l]

Traceable to clog dancing. With R foot in a bkwd
position, brush the foot fwd striking the ball of the
foot on the floor, then spank R bkwd. shuffle, and its
amalgamates, is one of the most fundamental and
most frequently used steps in tap.

Single Shuffle

TO EXECUTE:
Stand L, R bent and bk,
execute brush fwd and spank
bkwd. Can be done in any
pos or dir., using whole leg,
lower leg, or ankle only.
Supporting leg can be str. or
bent, feet can be obl, par,
tno, etc.

Nerve Shuffle: Shuffle executed by using the ankle
only. See NERVE TAP

Double Shuffle

TO EXECUTE:
Stand on L, using the inside
edge of the tap, execute 2
single shuffles w/ R in rapid

succession. The shuffle foot
is kept close to the floor and
is not raised until the 2nd
shuffle is completed. The
supporting leg may aid the
shuffle by remaining in plié
until the last sound of the
2nd shuffle is being
executed, at which time it
partially or fully straightens.
When shuffles are done
singly, the accent is usually
on the 2nd sound, but in
double shuffles, the accent is
on the 4th sound. May be
done in any pos. or dir. [4
sounds] [e&a1].

Triple Shuffle: Six even sounds created by executing 3
single shuffles in rapid succession; accent on last sound
[1ie&a2].

Front Shuffle

TO EXECUTE:
[2 sounds] [&1] or [a1].
Stand L, R bk L, R leg tno,
R knee bent, brush R to R
(str. R leg), spank R frt L,
R remains tno, knee bent.
Lower part of leg works in
isolation, R knee remaining
to R [&1&2] or [a1a2].

Back Shuffle

TO EXECUTE:
[2 sounds] [&1] or [a1].
Stand L, R knee bent and
tno, R Xd frt L, brush R to
R (leg str.), spank R bk L.
Keep R tno. Lower part of
leg works in isolation.

Side Shuffle: Refers to a shuffle(s) that are done to the side
of the body [&1&2] or [a1a2].

Front-Back Shuffles: [4 sounds] [&1&2] or [a1a2].
Combine frt shuffle w/ bk shuffle. Working leg is tno;
movement comes from lower part of leg. As movement
becomes faster, working leg stays closer to supporting leg
and around supporting ankle. Frt-bk. shuffles resemble petit
battement.

SHUFFLE (continued)

Alternating Shuffles: [6 or more sounds] [&a1&a2]. Executing a shuffle step on one foot and then the other. May be done while walking or running.

Rolling Shuffle: A popular combination belonging to the roll family. Hop L, shuffle R [1&a] and repeat over and over, creating a continuous and rolling rhythm [1&a].

Running Shuffles: (Alt Shuffles, Shuffle Steps, Triples, Threes (3)) [6 sounds] [&a1&a2]. Stand L, shuffle R, leap R, shuffle L, leap L, etc. Should be done w/ springing motion. Shuffles should be executed away from supporting leg, so step can be made directly under body, to prevent feet from being too far apart. May be done in any dir. or pos. A rolling rhythm is produced.

Snapped Shuffles: Exactly as the name implies, each shuffle is snapped, using the "a" count.

Square and Round Shuffles: Old term for the positioning of the leg.

Square Shuffles: Place R frt L, brush R straight out and spank R directly bk. Execute with staccato movement.

Round Shuffle: Execute the same as for square shuffle, but let the movement flow.

Walking Shuffles: [6 sounds] [&a1&a2]. See ALTERNATING SHUFFLES

Running Shuffles: [6 sounds] [&a1&a2]. See ALTERNATING SHUFFLES

SHUFFLE ALTERNATING CRAMPROLL. See CRAMPROLL: Alternating

SHUFFLE ALTERNATING GRABOFF.
See PICKUP: Alternating

SHUFFLE ALTERNATING PICKUP. See PICKUP: Alternating

SHUFFLE ALTERNATING PULLBACK.
See PICKUP: Alternating

SHUFFLE BALL CHANGE (Four (4)) [4 sounds] [&1&2] or [a1a2]

While standing on the L, execute a shuffle R, then ball change R bk L. The shuffle and the ball change may be done in any pos. or dir.

SHUFFLE BALL HEEL. See SHUFFLE TOE HEEL

SHUFFLE CHUG [3 sounds] [&a1]

> TO EXECUTE:
> Stand on L: shuffle R, chug L [&a1]

SHUFFLE CRAMPROLL. See CRAMPROLL: Shuffle

SHUFFLE EN CROIX

A barre exercise in which one does a shuffle or shuffles to 4th frt, to 2nd, to 4th rear, and to 2nd.

SHUFFLE GRABOFF

Old term for shuffle pickup. See PICKUP

SHUFFLE HOP STEP (Irish, Carryover (if frt); Carryback (if back)) [4 sounds] [&1&2] or [a1a2]

Shuffle R, hop L, step R. done in any position or direction. See IRISH

SHUFFLE OFF TO BUFFALO. See BUFFALO STEP

SHUFFLE PICKUP. See PICKUP

NOTE (3); PICKUP Variations.

SHUFFLE PULLBACK. See PICKUP

NOTE (3); PICKUP Variations.

SHUFFLE SIDE TRAVEL (Shooting the Pistol) [6 sounds] [&a1 &a2]

> TO EXECUTE:
> Parallel travel w/ L foot, moving to R, stand on L foot, shuffle R, heel drop L twd R [&a1], Shuffle R, toe drop L twd R [&a2], Repeat as in a parallel side travel to R

SHUFFLE STEP (Triple, Three, (3), Rattle Step, Plain Threes (3s)) [3 sounds] [&12] or [a12]

Stand on L, shuffle R, step R, rev. May be done in any pos. or dir .

SHUFFLE STEP HEEL. See SHUFLE TOE HEEL

SHUFFLE STEP TURN

Execute shuffle steps R and L, using as a basis a chaîné turn.

SHUFFLE TAP HEEL

No longer a valid term, as tap does not carry wt. See SHUFFLE TOE HEEL

SHUFFLE TOE HEEL (Quadruple, Shuffle Ball Heel, Shuffle Step Heel, Shuffle Tap Heel)
[4 sounds] [&1&2] or [a1a2]

Stand on L, shuffle R, toe heel R, rev. May be done in any position or direction. Feet may remain side by side or crossed.

SHUFFLE WING. See WING: Shuffle

SIDE CLOSE (Side Together, Step Join)
[2 sounds] [1 2]

Step R to R, Close L to R.

SIDE DIG

To dig one foot beside the other. See DIG

SIDE JOIN. See SIDE CLOSE

SIDE SLAP

A slap executed to the side of the standing foot. See SLAP

SIDE TOGETHER. See SIDE CLOSE

SIDE TRAVEL. See TRAVEL; PARALLEL TRAVEL

SIMPLE DRAWBACK. See DRAWBACK

SIMPLE TIME STEP. See TIME STEP: Standard (Basic)

SINGLE ESSENCE. See ESSENCE: Single

SINGLE HEEL STAND. See HEEL STAND: Single

SINGLE IRISH. See IRISH: Single

SINGLE ONE STEP RHYTHM. See ONE STEP RHYTHM: Single

SINGLE SHUFFLE. See SHUFFLE: Single

SINGLE TIME. See RHYTHM: Single Time

SINGLE TIME STEP. See TIME STEP: Single

SINGLE TOE STAND. See TOE STAND: Single

SINGLE TRAVEL. See TRAVEL: Single

SISSONNE
[w/w sound]

Named after the man who originated it. It may be done from both feet to one foot—ouverte—or from both feet to both feet—fermé. It may be executed in a fwd, bkwd, or sdwd direction in either 4th or 2nd position. In tap, the preparation and/or the landing may be made with sounds, such as progressive cramprolls or heel drops.

SISSONNE FERMÉ. See SISSONNE

SISSONNE OUVERTE. See SISSONNE

SIX (6, Walking Shuffle)
[6 sounds] [123456] or [&a1&a2]

See SHUFFLE Walking, Stand on L, shuffle step R and L; usually done w/ feet par or tno, crossing or straight.

SIX COUNT (TAP) RIFF. See RIFF: Six Count (Tap)

SIX POINT CRAMPROLL

A 6-ct. cramproll, which is a shuffle followed by any kind of 4-ct. cramproll.

SIX-SOUND PADDLE
[6 sounds] [&1&2&a3]

Part of the paddle and roll family. However, it only partly meets the criteria of a steady and continuous count: **1a&a, 2a&a, etc.** See PADDLE AND ROLL

> **TO EXECUTE:**
> Scuffle R, heel drop L [1&2], flap heel R [&a3]

SIXTEENTH-NOTE RHYTHM

One count of music divided into 4 equal parts, or sixteenth notes, with the count being **1e&a**.

SKID
[1 sound] [1]

- ✿ A slide on one or both heels in any dir. or pos.
- ✿ A slide on the ball(s) of one or both feet, ending in a heel drop(s).

SKIFFLE

[3 sounds] [&a1]

A combination of a fwd brush and a bk 2-ct. riff.

SKIFFLE STEP

[4 sounds] [&a1 2]

> TO EXECUTE:
> Stand on L, brush R fwd, bk 2-ct. riff R,
> step R

SKIFFLE HOP STEP

[5 sounds] [&a1&2]

> Stand on L, brush R fwd, bk 2-ct. riff R, hop L, step R

SKIP STEP (Hop Step)

[2 sounds] [&1] or [a1]

Traceable to character and folk dancing. Stand L, hop L, step R (usually fwd). Reverse.

SKUTCH

[16 sounds] [1&a2 &3&4 5&a6 &7&8]

> TO EXECUTE:
> Step L, shuffle step R [1&a2], shuffle ball change L [&3&4], hop shuffle step R [5&a6], shuffle ball change R [&7&8]

SLAM

[w/wo sound] [1]

An accented movement used frequently in country and eccentric dancing. Stand on L, keeping R str. and stiff, raise R off floor and forcibly lower w/ accent created on flat foot. No wt.

SLAP

[2 sounds] [& 1] or [a1]

At one time flap and slap were synonymous. Today, it is recognized that flap carries weight and slap does not.

> TO EXECUTE:
> Stand on L, R bent and held in bk, brush fwd R striking floor, place foot fwd, no wt.

SLAP BALL CHANGE

Old term for flap ball change.

SLAP DOUBLE HEELS

[&1&2] [a1&2]

> TO EXECUTE:
> Slap R in any direction, drop R & L heels (or L and R heels).

SLAP HEEL

Executed the same way as a flap heel, but carries no wt.

> TO EXECUTE:
> Stand L, raise R in bk pos, swing R fwd executing a brush fwd R, place ball R on floor and drop R heel (or L heel).

Slap Heel Bk.:

> TO EXECUTE:
> To move bkwd, raise R fwd, spank R bkwd, place ball of R on floor and drop R heel with no wt. [&1 2] [&a1].

Slap Heel Heel:

> TO EXECUTE:
> Slap R in any direction, drop R and L (or L and R Heels). Because slap does not carry wt., the wt. will remain on the supporting leg no matter which foot slaps or which heel is dropped first [&1&2] [a1a2].

NOTE:

In all of the above executions, there is no weight transfer on the slap.

SLAP JACK

[w/wo sound] [1 2]

> TO EXECUTE:
> Raise knee to par passé position and slap it with one or both hands, step R

SLAP STEP (COMBINATION)
[18 sounds] [&a1&2 &a3&4 5 & 6 & 7 & 8]

(From *The Tap Dance Dictionary* by Mark Knowles)

TO EXECUTE:

Shuffle step R, ball change L [&a1&2], shuffle step L, ball change R [&a3&4], chug bk L, ast extend R leg fwd [&], chug L bk, swing R Xd frt L, slap R foot w/ R hand [5], chug L bk, uncross R leg, extend R frt [&], chug L bk, swing R to R, side bent and slap R foot w/ R hand, chug L [6], chug L bk, extend R str. bk [&], chug L bk, swing R bk bent and crossed bk L [7], chug L, swing R bent to R [&], slap foot with R hand [8]

SLIDE (Foot Slide, Fleahop)
[w/wo sound]

In its broadest sense, it means to skim the floor w/ the whole or part of the foot remaining in contact with the surface throughout. Although usually executed on one foot, it may be performed on both. The normal sliding area is on the ball, but choreographically it may be done with the edges of the feet or the edge of the heel, toe, or whole foot.

The following explanation describes the Slide on the ball of the foot.

TO EXECUTE:

Stand L, raise and hold R, in any desired pos, plié L, slide on L in any dir.

The impetus for the slide may come from a number of sources:

- ✪ By beginning with the supporting leg in plié and then straightening it.
- ✪ By beginning with the working leg held close to the body, then thrusting it outward.
- ✪ By leaning away from the direction of the slide and by using the prep. pos. of the arms in the opposing direction from the slide and then switching them to the same dir. as the slide.

Listed below are some members of the slide family and their outstanding characteristics:

Fleahop: A slide on ball or flat of foot, executed from side to side and on the spot, Al Jolson style. May be done inside or outside. See FLEAHOP

Scoot: A short slide done on ball of foot. See SCOOT

Skid: A slide done on one or both feet; could end in a heel drop. See SKID

Inside Slide: Stand R, slide L.

Outside Slide: Stand R, slide R.

Hitch: A backward slide on one foot. See HITCH

Pull: A backward slide on one foot.

Catch: A backward slide on one or both feet.

SLIP STEP
[w/wo sounds] [1 2]

Used eccentrically to look like one is slipping or falling.

TO EXECUTE:

Step L to L, ast extend (or brush) R to R [1] step R to beside L [2]

SLOW DRAG

A popular couple dance in the ragtime era, in which the couples would stand close together using grinding movements with their bodies while not moving their feet.

SNAKE HIPS

A movement of the hips using the same hip lifted as foot that is disengaged from the floor, for example, while sliding the L foot to the L, raise the L hip to the L, then reverse movement. Next, step on the L and reverse all to the R.

SNAP

Finger Snap: To create a snapping sound w/ fingers while dancing. May also be used to set tempo.

Knee Snap: Beginning with the working leg bent, with care straighten the leg with energy. May be done as an isolation.

Head Snap: A quick turning or snapping of head for emphasis.

SNAP ROLL
[4 sounds] [1 &a2] [a&a1]

- ✪ Old term for hop shuffle step. See HOP SHUFFLE STEP
- ✪ When a shuffle is snapped.

SNAP KICK. See JAZZ KICK

SNATCH

Old term for pickup. See PICKUP

SOFTSHOE

A dance that was named after the soft shoes that were worn for its performance. In the beginning it was executed with no taps but with graceful slides, glides, and poses. It had its roots in sand dancing, in minstrelsy, and was the basis for the class acts. Its main step was the essence and it has, unlike other dances of its era, survived the passage of time. See AN HISTORICAL LOOK AT TAP; STEPS AND STYLES OF TAP DANCE.

SOFTSHOE BREAK. See BREAK: Soft Shoe

SOFTSHOE KICK HOPS
[4 sounds] [&1 &2]

A short movement in soft shoe; was done w/wo sound, in tap shoes or soft slippers.

> TO EXECUTE:
> Spank bk R, hop L flap fwd R [&1&2], reverse [&3 &4]

SOFTSHOE TIME STEP. See TIME STEP: Soft Shoe

SOFTSHOE WALK
[4 sounds] [&1 &2 &3 &4]

A short movement in soft shoe; was done w/wo sound, in tap shoes or soft slippers.

> (1) TO EXECUTE:
> (A) Hop L (bend R bk), brush R fwd [&1], hop R (leave R frt) step R fwd [&2], reverse (A) [&3 &4]

> (2) TO EXECUTE:
> (A) Hop L (bend R bk), toe heel fwd R [&1&], brush L straight fwd [2], reverse (A) [&3 &4]

SOLO

A dance performed by one person.

SONG AND DANCE

A popular act in vaudeville where performers sang and danced.

SOUND LEVEL. See DYNAMICS

SOUTENU ⦵

The quality of sustaining.

SOUTENU TURN. See TURN: Stationary, Soutenu

SPANISH BARREL ROLL. See BARREL ROLL: Arched; SPOTTING

SPANISH CHUG

Any continuous rhythm. Plié and with knee bent and maintaining one level, drop the heels alternately and continuously to any rhythm.

SPANK (Brush Back, Backward Tap, Backward Brush)
[1 sound] [1]

Stand L, raise R in fwd pos., swing bk striking ball of foot on floor (brush bk R), R ends bk in air. Spank is the bkwd version of brush and is classified as a movement whose normal action is twd the body, whereas brush moves away from the body.

SPANK BALL CHANGE
Brush Ball Change
[3 sounds] [&12] or [&a1]

Stand L, spank R and ball change (R-L). Working foot ends in a bkwd position or in 2nd. See ESSENCE; SPANK; BRUSH

SPANK BALL HEEL. See SPANK TOE HEEL

SPANK BALL HEEL HEEL. See SPANK STEP HEEL HEEL

SPANK CRAMPROLL. See CRAMPROLL: Brush or Spank

SPANK STEP (Back Tap Step, Back Brush Back Brush Step, Brush Step Back, Brush Back Step, Back Flap)
[2 sounds] [&1] or [a1]

Execute spank and step on ball of the same foot. It moves bkwd.

SPANK STEP BALL CHANGE (Back Essence) [4 sounds] [a1&2]

Traceable to vaudeville and sand dancing, spank step R usually ends in a bkwd position, then ball change (L-R), feet can remain in a frt-bk position, open to 2nd, etc. Some possibilities are listed below:

> TO EXECUTE:
> • Spank step R Xd bk L, ball L to L, step R, ip rev. Original bk essence. Rev. to L.

- Spank step R Xd bk L, ball change L Xd Frt. Rev.
- Spank step R bk, ball change L fwd R. Rev.

NOTE:
Brush or spank may be added before each ball change, thus spank step R, Brush (Spank) L, ball change (L-R). Successive spank step ball changes may travel bkwd, remain ip, or may be done turning.

SPANK STEP HEEL. See SPANK TOE HEEL

SPANK STEP HEEL HEEL (Back Flap Heel Heel, Spank Ball Heel Heel, Spank Toe Heel Heel)
[4 sounds] [&1&2] or [a1a2]

TO EXECUTE:
Spank step bk R, drop L & R heels, reverse.

NOTE:
If the heel drops are R then L, the step must be repeated and cannot be reversed.

SPLATTER WINGS. See WINGS: Double, Scatter

SPANK TAP HEEL. See SPANK TOE HEEL

SPANK TOE HEEL (BACK FLAP HEEL, Back Ralph, Spank Ball Heel, Spank Step Heel, Spank Tap Heel)
[3 sounds] [a12] or [&a1]

Stand L, R raised in fwd pos., spank bk R, place ball R on floor to rear, heel drop R. Rev. Spank toe heel is the bkwd version of flap heel. May be done in any pos. or dir.

SPANK TOE HEEL HEEL. See SPANK STEP HEEL HEEL

SPATTER WING. See WING: Double, Scatter

SPIN

A turn on one or both feet, inside or outside, traveling or stationary, etc. Usually a fast turn.

SPIN AROUND. See TURN: Stationary

SPIRAL
[w/wo sound]

✪ A special manner of turning that visually resembles the effect of a barber pole and therefore has a three dimensional quality. Many stationary one-footed turns can have this effect, which is gained by leaning off center and/or changing level (i.e., beg. in plié and rise to relevé, beg. relevé, lower to plié, bk to relevé, etc).

✪ A spiral may be thought of as a rounded zigzag, looped, or conical pattern or movement emanating from a fixed point.

SPLIT

The regular split comes from an acrobatic split and its technique. Splits may be executed fwd, bk, side to side, cor to cor, changing, or revolving, etc A regular split stretches the muscles of the leg, foot, and hip sockets and should be done w/ care, knowledge, and understanding. It may be performed from a standing pos., ending on the floor, or begin when the body is already on the floor, stem from another step or be a step unto itself. It is used as both an exercise and a movement.

Front and Back Splits: So called because one leg is fwd and the other is back; if R is fwd, then it is called a R front split.

TO EXECUTE:
Stand on both feet, par or tno, R ahead for R split, body erect, legs str. Slowly lower body to floor by sliding both feet ast and equally, or one foot splitting while the other remains stationary.

Straddle Split (Scissors Split, Side Split): See general information on SPLITS.

TO EXECUTE:
Face frt stand in 2nd, tno, slowly slide both legs ast to sides, keeping body centered and erect. When split has been accomplished the knees and top of legs should be facing ceiling. Straddle Splits are very difficult and should be executed with a great deal of care and knowledge.

Jazz Split (Fake Split, Half Split): Very often used in jazz-tap routines. Jazz splits are many and varied. The usual ending position is sitting with the frt leg str. and turned out, and the bk leg bent and turned out. It may start from a standing turned-out 4th pos., with the R fwd and str and the L twd the rear, slowly slide the R fwd, bend the L

SPLIT (continued)

knee, lowering the body to the floor. It is extremely important to keep the bk knee lifted. Hands may or may not be used.

Fake Splits: These splits, in some way, do not adhere to the rules of a regular split. A Jazz split is an example of a fake split.

Floor Split: A split that beg. and ends on the floor, such as:

Knee Split:

> ### To execute:
> R split, kneel on L knee, if R front split is to be done, then place R directly fwd and straight. Body remains erect throughout, hands may be used or not. Remaining on L knee, begin to slide R to split pos. At final moment, straighten L, ending in full split.

Crawling Split:

> ### To execute:
> R split as described. After completion of split, sit on R hip, bend R knee in, place wt. on R (L extended bk), pass L fwd and through to frt pos. Execute L split from knee.

Falling Split: A split that beg. from standing pos. and appears to fall into a split. May be used as an ending or flash step.

Air Split (Aerial Split): Any split that is executed in the air; may be frt, bk, straddle, switch, fake, etc. Traceable to Slavic and character dancing.

Jumping Split: Any split that is done from a prep. that involves jumping or a split that contains jumping as a part of its execution.

SPLIT SISSONNÉ

Executing a full split in air before landing a sissonne.

SPOT

One's spot on the stage or in the program, the special spotlight used to isolate a performer, or the use of a focal point when executing a turn. See SPOTTING

SPOT BARREL ROLL. See BARREL ROLL: Stationary

SPOT RENVERSÉ. See RENVERSÉ

SPOT TAP

A tap done in any place but remaining on the spot (i.e., not traveling).

SPOT TURN

A stationary turn done on the spot; not traveling, but remaining in place.

SPOTTING

Selecting a fixed point or spot when executing pirouettes or turns, thus allowing the body to rotate under the head. At a point where the head can no longer remain attentive to this spot, it snaps, rotating faster than the body and returning to the focal point sooner. Therefore, it is the last to leave and the first to return. This procedure helps in the dancer's overall balance, aids in preventing dizziness, and because of its rapid rotation gives the illusion that the face is always front

There are many factors that enter into the ability to turn properly. The following is of physiological significance to the mechanics of spotting. Within the inner ear lie 3 semicircular canals, aligned at right angles to each other and containing a viscous fluid. Reaching into this fluid are hairlike cilia that act as nerve endings and transmitters. The canals respond immediately when the head is tilted or turned. The nerve endings, upon receiving the message, transfer it to the brain through impulses, and the brain alarms the body to react. Thus, in the initial learning how to spot process, the student is inevitably dizzy. By repeated and proper repetition, the body begins to accept the new motion, the fluid and the nerve endings begin to adapt, and dizziness becomes less prevalent, until finally it disappears. However, this dizziness will recur if the speed is increased, the type of turning is changed, there is sharp change of direction, or the turns are not practiced often enough. In the more advanced student, the extent or length of the dizziness is shortlived, requiring only a change of habit rather than a new learning experience.

Spotting a Straight Line:

> ### To execute:
> R-handed chaîné turns: Beg. sl spot sr, arms 2nd. Step R to R, head over R shoulder, body faces frt, execute 1/2 turn to R, step L beside R, arms in 1st, face bk, head now over L shoulder. Snap

head to R, ast, regain focal pt., body executes 1/2 turn to R and step to R—this is the beginning of the next turn.

Spotting a Pattern: R–handed chaîné turns: all patterns may be based upon str. lines. After the pattern is decided upon, find the closest str. lined, geometric line of travel possible (i.e., if a circle is to be performed, consider it to be a square). This geometric layout will determine the number of different focal points necessary to accomplish the pattern. In this case it will be 4 that are necessary. Begin dsl with the body facing the inside of the circle. Choose a spot (point **#1**) directly in a straight line and us of the starting position. Turn as far us as desired until this spot (point **#1**) is reached. As the last turn is being completed and as the head is being snapped, relocate the eyes on a new spot (point **#2**), which lies on a direct line to usr, turn in a straight line to **#2** and upon reaching it, select a point **#3**, dsr, upon reaching this point, select point **#4** or the original starting position and complete the last line of the circle/square, which will end where the turn was begun.

Reversing Straight Line: R–handed chaîné turns: beg. sl, execute a straight line of turns across the room to sr, as head snaps on last turn, do not look to the sr spot, but instead spot sl.

NOTE:
The turn in which the spot is changed, may be ½ turn or 1½ turns. Return along str. line to starting point.

Stationary (On the Spot) Turns: Observing the rules of spotting, and with body facing directly fwd, select spot that is directly ahead of center of body, execute turn, snapping head bk to same spot each time.

Traveling Spot: Used to keep the body facing the front while it is traveling in a straight line to the side, for example, beginning on sr and ending on sl. To locate the traveling spot, visualize an imaginary horizontal straight line, located on the frt wall or in the audience, at eye level, and extending from sr to sl. We will assume an outside R barrel roll is being executed. Upon the snapping of the head on the first turn, do not return the eyes to the first spot, but choose one slightly to the left and move the feet to the L. When this turn is completed the body should end directly in frt of the new spot. Continue the turns until SL is reached.

Spotting the Floor: When executing arched or leaned turns, the Spot is directly ahead or in frt of body on floor, the focus is down, top of head to audience, as body turns, eyes remain focused on spot as head snaps, it is dropped bkwd, as in a bk bend or kept level, with eyes to ceiling, the head snaps bk to original focal pt., if turn is to be repeated. See BARREL ROLLS: Arched

SPREAD EAGLE WINGS. See WINGS: Double

SPRING ⚲

Projecting the body into air. Springs are normally preceded w/ plié with the tips of the toes the last to leave the floor; legs become str. or posed in the air. The landing reverses the process with the tips of the toes, then the ball, and finally the whole foot reaching the floor. The ending is in plié.

SPRING JOIN

Spring from one foot, landing on both feet in closed par pos. See also SPRING.

SQUARE DANCE

Four couples face each other in a square and usually a caller rhythmically calls out the steps to be executed.

SQUATTHRUST. See BURPEE

STAG LEAP
[w/wo sound]

Stand on L in plié, R bk L. Jab R knee into air (par pos.) ast raise L to an arabesque pos. in air (tno or par). This position is referred to as a stag, based on the movement of a deer or stag as it leaps over an obstacle.

STAG TURN

Following the rules for turning, and assuming that the stag turn being performed is on the R, face frt, execute stag leap R, step L beside R (½ turn, face bk) turn bk R and repeat. **[1 2]**. See SPOTTING, TURNS

STAMP
[1 sound] [1]

A forcefully executed step using the whole foot. Reverse w/ wt. May be done in any dir. or pos.

> **TO EXECUTE:**
> Raise R (R knee usually bent), lower entire R foot to floor w/ wt. Reverse.

STAMP CRAMPROLL TURN (Chaîné Cramproll)
[5 sounds] [1e&a2]

If R, stamp R, alt. cramproll R. See TURN: Traveling

STAMP SCUFF CRAMPROLL TURN
[6 sounds] [&1e&a2]

If R, stamp R, scuff L, alt. cramproll R. See TURN: Traveling

STAMP (STEP) SCUFF LEAP RIFF TURN
[6 sounds] [&1e&a2]

If R, stamp R, scuff L, leap L, 3-ct. conventional riff R. See TURN: Traveling

STAMP SCUFF (STEP SCUFF) LEAP TOE TURN
[4 sounds] [&1&2]

If R, stamp R, scuff L, leap L, tap R bk L. See TURN: Traveling

STAMP SHUFFLE STEP TURN
[4 sounds] [&1&2] or [1&a2]

If R, stamp R, shuffle step L. See TURN: Traveling

STAMP TOE TURN
[2 sounds] [12] or [1&]

If R, stamp R, ball L. See TURN: Traveling

STANDARD

An established or authorized manner by which a step, movement, etc. is recognized and/or performed. There are certain standard time steps, such as the buck and basic, that represent a model by which all the others time steps are judged. Some terms and steps have become standardized through years of usage, for example, we accept shuffle ball change as being standard, understood by everyone in the same way and manner.

STANDARD BREAK. See BREAK: TIME STEP: Standard

STANDARD CRAMP BREAK. See BREAK: Other Breaks, Louie DaPron

STANDARD MUSIC

A music form that was popular in the 1920s and 1930s. It consists of a 32-measure chorus, with 4 equal phrases of 8 measures each. The first, second, and fourth strains were the same melody, with the third strain (the bridge or the release) a completely different melody.

STANDARD TIME STEP. Also known as basic and simple time step. Originally, it had the name rhythm time step as well. This has now been designated a buck time step. See TIME STEP Standard, history (1)

STANDING CRAMPROLL

A cramproll executed in one spot.

STANDING LUNGE. See LUNGE: Standing

STATIONARY (On the Spot)

A step, turn, combination, etc. that does not travel, but remains on the spot or the same place.

STATIONARY TURNS. See TURNS: Stationary

STEP (One, (1)) [1 sound] [1]

Dance: A step of a routine, which in standard music is equal to 8 measures. This, however, is only a framework, as the music of today is not necessarily confined to this pattern.

Movement: To place a raised foot on the floor, usually on the ball, w/ wt., w/wo sound.

Types of Dance: Such as Irish step dancing.

Prop Type of Dance: A dance performed on a pair or flight of stairs; popular during the early stages of vaudeville.

STEP BALL CHANGE (Down Ball Change)
[3 sounds] [1&2]

Simple form of essence or flap ball change. Step R to R, ball change (L-R). Rev. May be done in any dir or pos.

STEP BALL CHANGE TURN
[6 sounds] [1&2&3&4]

> TO EXECUTE:
> If R, step bc R (face frt), step bc L, execute 1/2 turn R to face bk turn bk R. Repeat.

STEP DANCING

A type of English folk dancing that created rhythms with the feet. It is said to have been perfected in Ireland and was a competitive dance for many years in both countries.

STEP DRAW
[a movement] [wo sound]

> TO EXECUTE:
> Face frt: step to R, plié, draw R foot to R foot, remain in plié R, may hold this lunge position or draw L to beside R.

STEP HEEL. See Toe Heel

STEP HEEL HEEL. See Toe Heel Heel

STEP JOIN. See Side Close

STOMP
[1 sound] [1]

A stamp carrying no wt. Also a type of dance, the stomp.

STOMP BREAK. See Break: Buck Time Step

STOMP ROLL
[1 to many sounds]

> To execute:
> Stomp R (or L) and continuously drop heels, alternatively for a designated period of time or number of counts

STOMP TIME STEP. See Time Step: History (1); Buck

STOMPLE
[2 sounds] [&1] or [&a]

> To execute:
> Stomp R, spank bk L [&1]

STOP TIME

A melody, broken by silence, to allow the taps to bleed through, often described as a chord on the 1st beat of the measure only. In 4/4 time, the chord would fall on 1 and the beats 2, 3, and 4 would remain silent.

STOPPING THE TRAFFIC
[8 sounds] [&1 &2 &3 &4]

A short combination.
(From *The Tap Dance Dictionary* by Mark Knowles)

> To execute:
> Brush R fwd, heel dig R, toe drop L and R [&1 &2] brush L fwd, heel dig L, toe drop R and L [&3 &4]

STRADDLE SPLIT. See Split: Straddle

STRAIGHT KICK

A kick executed with a straight leg and directly forward.

STRAIGHT TAP

Any tap done with a straight leg and straight forward.

STRATHSPEY

A Scottish dance known for its smooth, elegant movements.

STRIKE

Dance: See Click

Stage: To strike the set: to take it down or disassemble it.

STRUT

A style of dance that is proud, lifted, and pranced. The cakewalk was a fine example of strutting.

STRUT STEP
[2 or 3 sounds] [1 2] or [&1]

Traceable to vaudeville. A series of toe heels or flap heels in any dir. with the body very erect and lifted.

STUB. See Clip

STUB TOE WALK
[6 sounds] [&1&2&3]

This step originated with the lancashire clog.

> To execute:
> Drop L heel, hit R heel against L toe which is flexed and raised, drop L toe, Step R frt L, catch and hit L toe against R heel, step L to L

STUD
[1 sound] [1]

Strike floor with the ball of the foot, with accent and no wt., release immediately.

STUMBLE. See Fall Off

STYLE

A manner of presentation and performance individualizing expression and execution. Having a recognized style, such as Bob Fosse's.

SUGARFOOT (Sugars, Ball-Of-Foot Strut)
[1 sound] [1]

Traceable to jazz. A twisting movement executed on the balls of the feet, turning the heels from an inward to an outward position. Step fwd ball R, R heel turned in, twist R heel outward as step on ball L with L heel inward, feet apart, remain in plié.

SUGARS. See SUGARFOOT

SUPPORTING LEG

The leg upon which the weight is placed.

SUR LE COU DE PIED ("On the Neck of the Ankle")

Literally, a placement of the foot in which one foot is placed above the ankle bone of the supporting leg. The working knee is bent and tno. In devant, the working foot is in frt; in derrière, it is in bk.

SUSPENSION

Traceable to jazz. The act of raising the body fully or to a halfway position from the floor with the use of one or both hands.

SUZIE-Q
[2 sounds] [12] or [&1]

Traceable to early jazz. Stand on L with R heel on floor to the R, toes of R flexed and turned out.

> **TO EXECUTE:**
> Step R frt L with R turned in, heel grind on R as L steps to L, toes of R now tno, to R

Hands may be clasped or arms may swing from side to side. Original basis for the bombershay (bumbishay). Also a dance craze of 1939.

SWABBING THE DECK
[5 sounds] [&1&a2]

Used in shipboard dances, pretending to swab the decks. Often used for an exit.

(THE) SWANNEE
[39 sounds] [1&a2&a3&4 5&a6&a7 a8 1 &a2 &a3 &4 &a5 &a6 &a7a8]

> **TO EXECUTE:**
> (A) Step R to R, frt and bk shuffle L, ball change L bk R,

flap L to L [1&a2&a3&4] repeat (A) [1 M], (B) step R, (C) L frt and bk shuffle L, ball change L bk R [1&a2&a3], repeat (C) 2 times [&a4&a5] [&a6&a7], flap L [a8]

SWANNEE BREAK. See BREAK: Other Breaks, Soft Shoe#5

SWAP GRABOFF. See PICKUP: Alternating

SWAP PICKUP. See PICKUP: Alternating

SWAP PULLBACK. See PICKUP: Alternating

SWAP WING. See WING: Other Types

SWAY

To shift the wt. of the body from side to side.

SWING

Jazz music in which the musician often improvises rather than playing the music exactly as written.

SWING AND SWAY

A later name for Tack Annie, the third step of the Shim Sham Shimmy. See SHIM SHAM SHIMMY

> **TO EXECUTE:**
> Using the tip of the R toe, create outward or inward circular patterns resembling a ballet rond de jambe. Also refers to swirling a full skirt.

SWIVEL

Half or quarter turns executed on ball of one or both feet. Turn foot or feet inward, then outward.

SYNCOPATED RIFF STEP. See RIFF: Syncopated Riff Step

SYNCOPATED SWANNEE BREAK. See BREAK: Other Breaks, Soft Shoe #6

SYNCOPATED SHUFFLE BALL CHANGE
[16 sounds] [a8 a1 a2 a3 a4 a5 a6 a7]

Literally not a step, but an often used short shuffle ball change combination.

TO EXECUTE:

Shuffle ball change R (travel) [a8 a1], shuffle R, 2 shuffle ball change R (travel) [a2 a3 a4], shuffle R, 2 shuffle Ball change R (travel) [a5 a6 a7]

NOTE:

Because this combination is one count short of a 2-measure phrase, it will end on **7** the first time, **6** the next time, etc. Therefore, it will always sound syncopated and overlapping.

SYNCOPATION (Cross Rhythm)

A temporary displacement or shifting of the regular metrical accent to an unaccented beat, such as the beat of **2** or the **a** or **and** count.

T.O.B.A.

The Theater Owner's Booking Association, which booked African-Americans on a vaudeville circuit throughout the southern United States.

TACET (Tacit)

The part of the music that comes to a complete stop, no music existing at all. At this time the tap dancer has a chance to perform, without musical background, allowing his feet to be both melody and rhythm section. Usually the music is resumed upon cue from the performer or after a certain number of counted beats or bars have passed.

TACIT. See TACET

(THE) TACK ANNIE
[13 sounds] [&12&34&56&7&8]

The third step of the shim sham shimmy.

TO EXECUTE:

Spank dig step R to L, L to R and R to L, spank St bc L Xd bk of R and stamp R and L to end position. Repeat 2 more times, however on second repeat change last stamp R and L to stamp R. (6M) Add shim sham break

See SHIM SHAM BREAK

TAG

An added sequence of music and/or dance, usually a repeated ending, that is literally tagged onto the end or conclusion of the music. Many times such a tag is used for the effect of repetition or it is used to allow the performer an exit w/ musical accompaniment.

TAKE AWAY
[3 sounds] [&a1]

Traceable to vaudeville.

TO EXECUTE:

Stand on L, tap R toe Xd frt L, tno, plié L, hop L, spring into air ast passé R from frt to bk, step R bk L. Reverse. Usually travels bkwd

TAKE ME OUT (Take Me Out)

A cue that a dancer would give to the orchestra to end the music.

TANGLEFOOT

A descriptive term connoting that the feet twist and in some cases cross and tangle with each other. No written sources or references were found, but verbally, dancers lay claim its existence. See also CORKSCREW

Here are two quite different combinations.

TO EXECUTE:

(1) Start L and travel to R; face frt
Leap L, heel toe R to R, leap L, heel toe R to R, leap L to R, ball R (toe inward), heel drop R (R toe inverted), toe drop R to R, leap L, heel toe R to L, leap L, heel toe R to L [&1&2&3e&a4&5&6&7],
(2a)
Sp R, heel L, Sh R, St R and L (tog), toe click (tog), toe drop R and L, Sp bc R [&a1&a2&a3&a4],
(2b)
Click R toe to L heel, heel drop L, Sh heel St R frt L. Reverse [&a5&a6&a7&a8],

TANGLEFOOT (continued)

(2c)
Click R toe to L heel, heel drop L, heel dig R, Sp bc R [&a1&a2],

(2d)
Click R toe to L heel, heel drop L, St R, Sp St L, heel dig R [&a3&a4],

(2e)
Sp bc R, click R toe to L heel, heel drop L, St R, Sp St L, heel dig R, Sp bc R [&a5&a6&a7&a8]

(2a–d submitted by Ann Freeman, courtesy of Mrs. Peggy Fletcher; as taught by Beale Fletcher, beloved teacher)

TANGO

A Latin dance or music played in 4/4 time and used for character tap numbers.

TAP (Ball Tap, Touch, Toe Ball, Foot Tap)
[1 sound] [1]

A sound created by striking the tap to the floor, usually using the ball of the foot or the tip of the toe. When the term foot tap is used, the meaning could include the heel edge, heel, etc. Does not include sound made by swinging the foot, as in brush, spank, etc. Originally, tap meant that after executing the sound, the foot was lifted from the floor.

TAP DANCE CONCERTO

An actual concerto with a classical score, created, choreographed, and originally performed by Danny Daniels, with music composed by Morton Gould. This performance premiered in 1952, with the Rochester Symphony. Tap sounds were notated on the score as percussion beats. Michael Dominico from Buffalo, New York, also performed it in concert.

TAP DANCING

A form of a dance in which wooden or tap shoes are used to create rhythmic sounds and patterns by striking the tap or sole against the floor.

TAP HEEL. See TOE HEEL

TAP HEEL HEEL. See TOE HEEL HEEL

TAP LINDY
[6 sounds] [a1&2 3 4]

Based upon the Lindy step: step (flap) R to R, ball change (L to R) [1 &2 3 4]. The tap Lindy has merely added sounds to the structure.

TO EXECUTE:
Flap ball change R to R, ball change L bk R [&1&2 3 4]

TAP MAT

Wood strips backed by canvas, which may be rolled up for transporting and unrolled for the tap dancer to use as a practice mat.

TAP RIFF WALK. See RIFF: Walking

TAP SHOES. See SHOES: Taps

TAP SPRING. See FLAP

TAP STEP (Ball Step)
[2 sounds] [1 2]

Place ball of R foot on floor, in any dir., then step R.

TEMPO

The rate of speed at which the music is played.

TENDU ⅋

Literally, "extended reaching, stretched." The working leg slides from closed to open position without lifting the toe from the ground.

THE MESS AROUND. See BALLIN' THE JACK

THREE (3). See SHUFFLE STEP

THREE BALL CHANGE
[5 sounds] [&1&a2]

Literally, a shuffle step R, followed by a ball change (L bk R). This was a well-known combination with the old term three, meaning shuffle step (because it had three sounds), followed by a regular ball change.

THREE POINT CRAWL
[3 sounds] [&a1]

TO EXECUTE:
Ball R (inverted, ball faces L), heel drop R to R (toe inverted), toe drop R to R [&a1]

THREE-STEP TURN (Walking Turn) [3 sounds] [1 2 3]

Traceable to folk dancing. This turn seems to be basic and present in all forms of the dance. A complete turn is executed in three steps.

TO EXECUTE:

Step R to R, face frt, execute ½ turn to R by turning R and stepping L beside R, body is now facing the bk, execute another ½ turn by turning bk R and stepping R to R, body is now facing the frt, wt. on R

THREE-QUARTER FOOT

With all the toes of one or both feet on the floor, raise the insteps(s) as high as possible, thus creating a continuous and straight line from the leg through the foot.

THROUGH THE TRENCHES. See TRENCHES

THRUST WINGS. See WING: Thrust Wings

TILLER LINE

The Tiller line was a famous high-kick chorus line created by John Tiller, an English choreographer, who trained the dancers in England and sent them to America to perform in American shows and productions.

TIME STEP

History: The whole area of time steps is vast, redundant, and overlapping, owing to the number of sources from which they stem, the lack of written notation, the hand-me-down process with which they were learned and the great amount of experimentation that did and has taken place. During the vaudeville era, they were extremely popular and explored. With the death of vaudeville, the collapse of the movie musical, and arrival of Broadway with its new concepts and expectations in the 1940s and 1950s, the time step underwent fewer changes and finally fell into oblivion, only to be kept alive by the local dancing teacher and older dancers.

Today we are seeing a revival—time steps are being taught again, relived, and remembered. As a rhythmic composition they are basically simple, repetitive, and pleasantly syncopated—a possible reason for their great acceptance earlier. At one time, they were used by dancers in vaudeville to express to the orchestra the tempo of the act, thus the name time step.

Time steps may be short or long depending on their character, and stationary or traveling depending on their intent. The standard ones come with their own breaks (full breaks are the last 2 measures of an eight-measure phrase) and, to the traditional tap dancer (See A HISTORICAL LOOK AT TAP), the break was a time for improvisation and creativity—this was a place where he could display his skills, ingenuity, and technical virtuosity—and he took total advantage of it by ad-libbing a new and different break each time.

Time steps were well established by 1915 and grew out of buck and Irish dancing. The former was executed in a flatfooted fashion with few arm movements and limited use of the upper body. The latter was based on Irish tradition and performed high on the balls of the feet with clear, clean accented sounds. King Rastus Brown, a well-known buck dancer, was noted not only for the many time steps that he developed, but also for his prodigious execution and his unsuspected, rhythmic surprises on the 2-measure endings. Bill Robinson, on the other hand, brought the time step off the flat of the foot and onto the balls of the feet. Robinson is credited with simple yet extremely light and clear footwork and with creating whole routines comprised only of time steps.

Through the years, a standardization process has taken place and, through this, we are now aware of certain properties and facts surrounding this vast collection of steps we call time steps.

General

- There are two recognized types of time steps: the **buck (rhythm) (off-beat) (negro)** or **(stomp)** time step, and the **standard (basic)** time step, the first stemming from flatfoot buck dancing so named because dance was then very masculine, and the latter from Irish step dancing.

- These two time steps actually have the same structure and counts, but differ in their beginnings, style, and intent. A comparison, in single form, is given in the following chart.

NOTE:
An excellent reference for further study of other time steps is Diane Gudat's *The Time Step Dictionary*.

BUCK	CTS.	STANDARD
stomp R, spank R	[8&]	shuffle R
hop L	[1]	hop L
step R	[2]	step R
brush step L fwd	[&3]	brush step L fwd
step R ip	[&]	step R ip

143

TIME STEP (continued)

NOTE:

✿ The only difference in the buck and the standard time step is the very beginning, **8&**.

✿ The cts. **8&** (stomp, spank R) of the buck time step may be replaced with scuff spank, heel dig spank, stomp draw, scuffle, etc. and the hop L may be replaced with heel drop L or chug L, all of which keeps this type of execution grounded. Substitutions within the standard time step are quite possible, but are seldom used.

✿ Both of the above time steps may be done in their double form by changing the step R to flap R **[&2]** or their triple form by changing the step R to shuffle step R **[&a2]**. See **#** (5), Part (B)

   ✿ The structure for a standard(ized) time step is as follows:
   a) The first two sounds are on the lead foot. [8&]
   b) These are followed by hop. [1]
   c) Followed by hop heel drop. [2]
   d) Followed by changing feet so that the time step may be reversed. [3&]

      ✿ The two time steps listed, the buck and the standard, are the sole pattern by which all stationary, standard(ized) time steps are judged.

NOTE:

Unfortunately the name standard is very misleading for it describes the time step previously discussed, plus it is the categorical name for any time step that fits that pattern.

✿ All standard(ized) time steps must fit the following criteria:
   a) They must begin on the ct. of 8.
   b) They must be capable of being singled (s), doubled (d), or tripled (t). This is decided by the number of sounds that follow hop: if it is one sound, the hop will be followed by a step (s); if it is two sounds, the hop will be followed by a flap (d); if it is three sounds, the hop will be followed by a shuffle step (t).

NOTE:

Some believe that the time step may also be quadrupled by following the hop with a shuffle toe heel on the free foot **[4 sounds] [e&a2]**. In accordance with this theory, it must also have a break that can be singled, doubled, tripled, and/or quadrupled.

   c) It must also have a break which can be singled, doubled, or tripled. See (B)

NOTE:

A heel drop may be substituted for the hop on the 1st ct. of the time step.

Below, the full 2-measure breaks of both the buck and the standard time steps are compared in their single form. For the double, change step R to flap R; for the triple, change step R to shuffle step R.

NOTE:

The endings are the important difference between the two breaks.

BUCK BREAK (FULL)	CTS.	STANDARD BREAK (FULL)
Stomp R, Spank R	[8&]	Shuffle R
Hop L, Step R	[12]	Hop L, Step R
Sh St L, *Sh R, Hop L*	[&3&4&5]	Sh St L, *Sh St* R
Flap BC R	[&6&7]	*Sh BC L*

NOTE:

The following time steps are a mere sampling of the numerous time steps that are in existence today. Hopefully, the reader will be inspired to further investigate this vast field on his/her own.

Listed below are the stationary buck and standard time steps in their single, double, and triple forms.

Buck (Rhythm) Time Step

Single	Double	Triple
8 – Stomp R fwd	8 – Stomp R fwd	8 – Stomp R fwd
& – Spank R bk	& – Spank R bk	& – Spank R bk
1 – Hop L	1 – Hop L	1 – Hop L
2 – Step R bk	& 2 - Flap R	& a - Shuffle R
& 3 - Flap L fwd	& 3 - Flap L	2 – Step R
& – Step R ip	& – Step R ip	& 3 - Flap L fwd
		& – Step R ip

Standard (Basic) Time Step

Single	Double	Triple
8 & – Shuffle R fwd	8 & – Shuffle R	8 & – Shuffle R
1 – Hop L	1 – Hop L	1 – Hop L
2 – Step R bk	& 2 - Flap R fwd	& a - Shuffle R
& 3 –Flap L fwd	& 3 - Flap L fwd	2 – Step R
& –Step R ip	& – Step R ip	& 3 - Flap L fwd
		& – Step R ip

Double Triple Time Step

Buck	Standard
8 – Stomp R fwd	
& – Brush R bk	8 & – Shuffle R fwd
1 – Hop L	1 – Hop L
& a - Shuffle R fwd	& a - Shuffle R fwd (to R side)
2 – Step R (to L ft)	2 – Step R bk
& a - Shuffle L fwd	& a - Shuffle L fwd (to L side)
3 &- Ball Change L bk R	3 & – Ball Change L bk R

NOTE:

❍ The double triple time step is presented here in its usual form. There are many other variations possible: adding wings and/or pickups to the hop (ct. 1), heel drop(s) on the ball change, etc.

❍ Another form of double triple time step occurs when the Sh St R **[cts. &a2]** is replaced by a flap R **[cts. &2]**.

TIME STEP (continued)

Toe Tap Time Steps

Toe tap time steps appear in both the buck and standard version, but in the singular form only. However, they do have variations, which are listed below:

Buck		Standard	
8	– Stomp R fwd		
&	– Spank R bk	8 &	– Shuffle R fwd
1	– Hop L	1	– Hop L
&	– Toe tap R bk	&	– Toe tap R bk
2	– Step R bk	2	– Step R bk
&	3- Flap L fwd	& 3	– Flap L fwd
&	– Step R ip	&	– Step R ip

Variation #1

Buck		Standard	
8	– Stomp R fwd		
&	– Spank R bk	8 &	– Shuffle R fwd
1	– Hop L	1	– Hop L
&	– Toe tap R bk	&	– Toe tap R bk
a	– Hop, Heel drop or Chug L	a	– Hop, Heel drop or Chug L
2	– Step R bk	2	– Step R bk
& 3	– Flap L fwd	& 3	– Flap L fwd
&	– Step R ip	&	– Step R ip

Variation #2

Buck		Standard	
8	– Stomp R fwd		
&	– Spank R bk	8 &	– Shuffle R fwd
1	– Hop L	1	– Hop L
&	– Heel drop L	&	– Heel drop L
a	– Toe tap R bk	a	– Toe tap R bk
2	– Step R bk	2	– Step R bk
& 3	– Flap L fwd	& 3	– Flap L fwd
&	– Step R ip	&	– Step R ip

Cramproll Time Steps

Cramproll time steps are not as clearly standardized as the steps mentioned before. They may be executed in both the buck and the standard version, with the buck being preferred. They come in two variations: both heels are dropped; one heel is dropped.

NOTE:

To change any of the variations listed below to their double or triple form, change ct. 2 (step) to flap for double **[& 2]** or shuffle step for triple **[& a2]**.

Variation #1

BUCK		STANDARD	
8	- Stomp R fwd	8 &	- Shuffle R fwd
&	- Spank R bk	1 2	- Hop L, Step R
1 2	- Hop L, Step R	& 3	- Flap L fwd
& 3	- Flap L fwd	& a	- Drop L & R Heels
& a	- Drop L & R Heels		

Variation #2

BUCK		STANDARD	
8	- Stomp R fwd	8 &	- Shuffle R fwd
&	- Spank R bk	1 2	- Hop L, Step R
1 2	- Hop L, Step R	& 3	- Flap L fwd
& 3	- Flap L fwd	&(&a)	- Heel Drop R or Toe Heel R
&(&a)	- Hl Dr R OR Toe Hl R		

Pickup (Pullback) Time Step

Pickup time steps require the replacement of the hop (ct. 1) with a pickup on that same foot. In reality a time step of any kind can be converted into a pickup time step by this process. To change the single pickup time step, shown here, to its double form replace the ct. 2 (step R) with a flap R **[& 2]**, and for its triple form replace the ct. 2 (step R) with a shuffle step R **[& a2]**.

BUCK		STANDARD	
8	- Stomp R fwd	8 &	- Shuffle R
&	- Spank R bk	a 1	- Pickup on L
a 1	- Pickup on L	2	- Step R
2	- Step R	& 3	- Flap L fwd
& 3	- Flap L fwd	&	- Step R ip
&	- Step R ip		

TIME STEP (continued)

Wing Time Steps

The wing time step may be executed in several ways—as a fake wing or a real wing. The real wing does not have any known variations. There are two possible executions of the fake wing; the first variation is preferred. All of these time steps maybe doubled by changing ct. 2 (step) to flap R [& 2] or tripled by changing ct. 2 (step) to shuffle step R [& a2].

Fake Variation #1

BUCK	STANDARD
8 - Stomp R fwd	
& - Spank R bk	8 & - Shuffle R fwd
1 - Hop L	1 - Hop L
2 -Step R	2 - Step R
3&a - Flap L fwd (ast do 3-ct. wing on R overlapping the first sound of the wing w/ the landing of the flap)	3&a - Flap L fwd (ast do 3-ct. wing on R overlapping the first sound of the wing w/ the landing of the flap)

Fake Variation #2

BUCK	STANDARD
8 - Stomp R fwd	8& - Shuffle R fwd
& - Spank R bk	1 - Hop L
1 - Hop L	2 - Step R
2 - Step R	a3 - Flap L fwd (L down before wing)
a3 - Flap L fwd (L down before wing)	e&a- 3-ct. Wing R (L foot is down)
e&a - 3-ct. Wing R (L down)	

Real Wing

BUCK	STANDARD
8 - Stomp R fwd	8 - Shuffle R
& - Spank R bk	& - Hop L
1 - Hop L	1 - Step R (stand on R)
2 - Step R (stand on R)	i e& - 3 ct. Wing on R (hold L up)
i e& - 3-ct. Wing (hold L up) or R	a3 - Flap L fwd
a3& - Flap L fwd, step R ip	& - Step R ip

Traveling Time Steps

Traveling time steps are twice as long as regular stationary time steps and done in both the buck and standard versions. They may be executed as single, double, or triple in accordance with the rule for regular time steps: what follows the hop is step (single), flap (double), and shuffle step (triple). The most popular versions are the single and the triple; the double is seldom used. There is no legitimate break. However, a nonstandard break is offered after the description of the standard traveling time step. These time steps were also known as the Boston or limp time step, cubanola glide, runalong, and the bambalina, a creation of Eddie Rector.

Buck Traveling Time Step

SINGLE		DOUBLE		TRIPLE	
8	– Stomp R fwd	8	– Stomp R	8	– Stomp R
&	– Spank R bk	&	– Spank R bk	&	– Spank R bk
1	– Hop L	1	– Hop L	1	– Hop L
2	– Step R	& 2	– Flap R	&a2	– Shuffle Step R
& 3	– Flap L to L	& 3	– Flap L to L	& 3	– Flap L to L
& 4	– Shuffle R	& 4	– Shuffle R	& 4	– Shuffle R
& 5 & 6 & 7	– 3 BCs R bk L (travel to L)	& 5 & 6 & 7	– 3 BCs R bk L (travel to L)	& 5 & 6 & 7	– 3 BCs R bk L (travel to L)
&	– Step R ip	&	– Step R ip	&	– Step R ip

Standard Traveling Time Step

SINGLE		DOUBLE		TRIPLE	
8 &	– Shuffle R	8 &	– Shuffle R	8 &	– Shuffle R
1	– Step R	1	– Step R	1	– Step R
& 2	– Shuffle L	& 2	– Shuffle L	& 2	– Shuffle L
& 3	– Ball Change L-R (to R)	& 3	– Ball Change L-R (to R)	& 3	– Ball Change L-R (to R)
& 4	– Ball Change L-R (to R)	& 4	– Ball Change L-R (to R)	& 4	– Ball Change L-R (to R)
5	– Hop R	5	– Hop R	5	– Hop R
6	– Step L	& 6	– Flap L	&a6	– Shuffle Step L
& 7	– Shuffle R	& 7	– Shuffle R	& 7	– Shuffle R
&	– Step R	&	– Step R	&	– Step R

TIME STEP (continued)

Nonstandard (Illegitimate) Break

Execute standard traveling R, L, R—6 M.

BREAK
8 &   - Shuffle L
1   - Hop R
2   - Hop R
&3   - Flap L fwd
&   - Step R ip
4 &   - Shuffle L
5   - Hop R
6   - Step L
& 7 &   - Shuffle Step R

Other Time Steps

Listed below in alphabetical order are some other time steps. Most of them are nonstandard or illegitimate. All of them are old and some are quite well known.

BOJANGLES TIME STEP		BOJANGLES BREAK	
8	- Hop L	Execute the Bojangles Time Step as described 3 times - R - L - R (6M)	
& a 1 &	-Sh BC R		
2	- Stomp R fwd	**BREAK:**	
&	- Spank R	8	- Stomp L fwd
3	- Hop L	& 1	- Sp Hop Sh St bk L
		& a2	
& a 4	- Shuffle St R	& 3 &	- Sh St R & L
		4 & 5	
& 5 &	- Shuffle St L	& 6 & 7	- Sh BC R or Flap BC R
6 a 7	- Shuffle St R		

Buggy Ride Time Step

This is *not* a time step, but a wonderful older method of teaching the rhythms found in the single, double, and triple forms of the buck and the standard time steps. The words are said out loud by each student as he practices each time step.

NOTE:

The opening shuffle may be changed to stomp, spank for the buck time step on the **8&** ct. and are the last two words of the sentence.

Single

Ride and	*thanks*	*for*	*the bug*	*gy*
shuffle R	hop L	step R	flap L fwd	step
[8 &]	[1]	[2]	[& 3]	[&]

Double

Ride and	*thank*	*you for*	*the bug*	*gy*
shuffle R	hop L	flap R	flap L fwd	step R ip
[8 &]	[1]	[& 2]	[& 3]	[&]

Triple

Ride and	*when*	*will we take*	*the bug*	*gy*
shuffle R	hop L	Sh step R	flap L fwd	step R ip
[8 &]	[1]	[& a2]	[& 3]	[&]

Double Triple #1

Ride and	*thank*	*you for*	*the great bug*	*gy*
shuffle R	hop L	flap R	Sh St L	step R
[8 &]	[1]	[& 2]	[& a3]	[&]

Double Triple #2

Ride and	*thank*	*you all for*	*the great bug*	*gy*
shuffle R	hop L	Sh St R	Sh St L	step R
[8 &]	[1]	[& a2]	[& a3]	[&]

HEEL GRIND TIME STEP	
(A) 1 - Hop L	1 M Repeat (A)
& a2 - Shuffle St R	(B) & 5 Heel grind R, St L
& - L heel on floor (toe in)	& 6 Spank St R
3 - Step R (HL grind L to L)	& 7 Heel grind L, St R
& 4 - Spank St L	& 8 Spank St L
1 M Repeat (A)	

HEEL STAND TIME STEP	HESITATION TIME STEP
8 & a1 - Hop L Sh R St L	8 & - Shuffle R
2 3 - Heel stand L and R	1 - Hop L
& 4 - Step bk L & R	2 3 - Step R & L (2nd)
& 5 & 6 - Sh BC L frt R	4 & 5 - Sh Hop St R
& 7 - Step L and R (2nd)	& 6 - Flap L fwd
Reverse	7 - Step R bk

MILITARY TIME STEP	
(A) & 8 & - Sh R, Hop L	& 8 & 1 - Sh Hop St R
1 2 3 - Step R, L, R	& 2 & 3 - Sh Hop St L
1 M Reverse (A)	& 4 & - Sh R, Hop L
	5 6 7 - Step R, L, R

Double Military Time Step

Similar to the military time step as shown in the chart above, but change every step to flap.

Triple Military Time Step

Similar to the military time step as shown in the chart above but change every step to shuffle step (very seldom used).

RUBY KEELER TIME STEP	
(A) 8 & - Shuffle R	2 M Repeat (A)
1 2 - Hop L, Hop L	(B) BREAK:
& 3 - Flap R fwd	8 & - Shuffle L
& - Step L bk	1 2 - Hop R, Hop R
4 & 5 - Shuffle R, Hop L	& 3 & - Shuffle Step L & R
6 & 7 - Step R, Flap L fwd	4 & 5 - Shuffle BC L
	& 6 & 7
& - Step R	
2 M Reverse (A)	

TIME STEP (continued)

SOFT SHOE TIME STEP #1		SOFT SHOE TIME STEP #2	
1	- Step R to R	(A) 1	- Step R to R
& A	- Frt Shuffle L	& a2	- Br BC L frt R
2 &	- Bk Shuffle R	3 & a4 - Reverse (A)	
A 3	- BC L bk R	(B) 5	- Step R to R
& 4	- Flap L to L	& a6	- Br BC 3 Xs L frt,
		& a7	bk, frt of R
		& a8	
1 M	Repeat		

ADVANCED SOFT SHOE TIME STEP			
(A) & 1	- Sp St R Xd bk L	(C)	& a5 - Sh St bk R L R
			& a6
			& a7
& a	- Flap L to L	&	- Step L Xd bk R
2	- Step R ip	a8	- Flap R to R
(B) & 3	- Sp St L bk R	Reverse (A), (B), (C)	
& 4	- Stamp R & L (2nd)		

Waltz Clog Time Step

SINGLE		DOUBLE		TRIPLE	
1	- Leap (Step) R	& 1	- Flap R to R,	& a1	- Sh St R to R,
&2	- to R, Sh BC L	& 2	- Sh L	& 2	- Sh BC L bk R
&3	- bk R	& 3	- BC L bk R	& 3	

Barrel Roll Traveling Time Step
[11 sounds] [8&1&2&3&4 5 6 7]

TO EXECUTE:
Begin stage left, face frt, shuffle step R to R [8&1] shuffle L, 2 bcs L R L R traveling to R [&2&3&4], execute a L outside leaning fwd barrel roll, ending with [5], step L R L to L [6], reverse

Bombershay Time Step
[18 sounds] [&1 2&a3 &4 &5 &a6 &a7 &a8]

Not a legitimate time step because of its last section, but extensively used in vaudeville.

TO EXECUTE:
Back brush R (spank), hop L [&1], hop L, shuffle R to R side, step R [1] shuffle R, step R back L [2&a3], step L, scuff R fwd [&4], (flap) flap R to R side [&5], 3 L toe bombershays [&a6&a7&a8] reverse

Bombershay Traveling Time Step
[15 sounds] [8&1 2&3&4 &5&6&7]

Not a legitimate time step because of its last section, but extensively used in vaudeville.

To execute:
R shuffle step [8&1], L shuffle ball change [&2&3&4] 2 L toe bombershays [&5&6&7]

TIME STEP BREAK. See BREAK: Standard, Buck, Half, Full

TIMES SQUARE. See BROADWAY SQUARE

TOE (Toe Hit, Toe Tip, Toe Tap, Toe Strike)

Striking the very tip of the toes of one foot on the floor with no weight.

TOE BEAT
[1 sound] [1]

Striking the top of the toes on the floor with no weight. May also refer to a toe drop, which carries no weight.

TOE BRUSH. See BRUSH

TOE CHANGE. See BALL CHANGE

TOE CLICK
[1 sound] [1]

Standing on the heels of both feet (heel stand), toes raised and turned outward, turn toes sharply inwd and click the toes tog. See CLICK

TOE CLIP

The toe of one foot striking a part (toe, heel, ball, etc.) of the other foot in passing.

TOE CRAMP. See TOE DROP

TOE DIG. See DIG

TOE DOWN. See BALL CHANGE

TOE DRAG. See DRAG

TOE DRAW. See DRAW

TOE DROP (Ball Drop, Ball Cramp, Ball Beat, Ball Beat Down, Toe Beat, Toe Cramp)
[1 sound] [1]

With R heel on floor, toes raised and flexed, using heel as pivot pt., forcibly lower toes. Infers to carry wt.; if not then it should be stated as no wt. Many times no statement is made, but the step to be executed next will disclose which foot is to be used.

TOE FLAM. See TOE HEEL

TOE HEEL (Ball Heel, Step Heel, Tap Heel, Toe Flam)
[2 sound] [1 2]

Usually executed: place ball R on floor, heel drop R with wt. May also mean to tap R bk L, then place bk edge R heel fwd on floor.

TOE HEEL BALANCÉ

Execute a balancé and substitute toe heels for all the steps. [&1&2&3].

TOE HEEL CATCH. See TOE HEEL CLIP

TOE HEEL CLICK
[1 sound] [1]

Standing on ball L (L heel raised), strike toe of R to heel of L. Click indicates that both the toe and the heel strike each other with equal force.

TOE HEEL CLIP

Clip and catch mean that as one part of the foot, for example the toe, passes another part of the foot, such as the heel, a sound is created and that the initiator of the movement is named first. This would be termed a toe heel clip (or catch), as the toe is initiating the movement and sound.

TOE HEEL HEEL (Step Heel Heel, Ball Heel Heel, Tap Heel Heel)
[3 sounds] [1&2]

To execute:
- Step ball R, drop L and R heels. Reverse [1&2]

or

- Step ball R, drop R heel 2 times or drop L heel 2 times [1&2]

or

- Step ball R, drop R and L heels. Repeat [1&2]

TOE HEEL TURN. See TURN: Traveling

TOE HIT. See TOE

TOE JAB. See JAB; DIG

TOE JUMP
[1] or [2] [1 2] OR [&1]

Old term for rising into a double toe stand. Relevé on both toes ast to the exact top of the toes. Feet in are par and close tog.

TOE LEAP
[2 sound] [1 2] or [&1]

Tap tip of R toe bk L, leap onto R. Reverse.

TOE LIFT
(Movement)

Stand on both feet, flat and par, lift R toe off floor, leaving the back edge of the R heel on the floor.

TOE SCRAPE

A sliding or scraping sound executed by standing on one foot or both. Execute by scraping outside edge of R to R. Foot ends in air, wt. remains on L. See SCRAPE; WING: Scrape shuffle

TOE SLIDE

A prolonged sliding sound. Literally, to slide on the very tip(s) of the toes in any direction. See Slide

TOE SNAP
[2 sounds] [&] or [a1]

Literally, a ball snap.

> TO EXECUTE:
> Begin with the edge of R heel on floor and fwd, brush the ball of the R bkwd

TOE STAB

To hit the top of the toe quickly and then raise the leg bent and immediately. No weight. See TOE

TOE STAB STEP. See TOE STEP

TOE STAND
[w/wo sound]

Traceable to vaudeville.

> TO EXECUTE:
> Suspend wt. of body on very tip(s) of toes

Single Toe Stand: Stand on toes of only one foot, the other being raised in air or placed on floor.

Double Toe Stand: Stand on the tips of both toes, simultaneously.

TOE STAND WING

Toe stand on one foot and execute a wing on the free foot.

TOE STAND WINGS. See WING: OTHER TYPES, Toe Stand Wings

TOE STEP (Tap Step, Toe Tip Step, Step, Toe Stab Step)
[2 sounds] [1 2]

Strike toe (tip) R Xd bk L, step R. Reverse.

TOE STRIKE. See TOE

TOE TAP. See TAP

TOE TAP TIME STEP. See TIME STEP: Toe Tap

TOE TIP. See TOE

TOE WING. See WING: Wing Toe

TOGETHER. See CLOSE

TOMMY GUN. See PARADIDDLE

TORNADO
[10 sounds] [8&1e&a2&a3]

> TO EXECUTE:
> Begin with R heel on floor to R, R toe raised. Spank bk R, heel drop L, stand on ball R (turned in), (body faces L), spank L, alt. pickup R to L, 2-ct. riff R (turned out) to R, heel drop L, heel dig R to R

(Courtesy of Barbara Denny).

TOUCH

Extending and placing any part of foot (toe, heel, etc.) on floor, no wt. The word implies lightness. May also mean to touch one part of body to or with another part (for example, the foot to the head or the hand to the shoulder.) The choreographic touch implies that a certain recognizable style or attitude surrounds the work, thus labeling it as belonging to a certain choreographer, or group.

TOUCH STEP
[2 sounds] [1 2]

Touch any part of foot (toe, ball, heel, etc.) to floor in any direction and step on same foot.

TOUR

Literally, "a turn," such as tour en l'air, a turn in the air.

TOUR EN L'AIR

A turn that is executed in the air, not on the floor
See AERIAL; TURNS: En l'air

TRADING FOURS, EIGHTS

Two dancers or a dancer and a musician alternate improvising four or eight measures each in a little challenge. One can trade twelfths, sixteenths, etc. See CHALLENGE

TRAIN STEP

Old vaudeville step

✿ May be a patter step See PATTER

✿ This train step was used many times for entrances and exits:

[4 sounds] [1&2&]

TO EXECUTE:
Face sl, stamp R frt L, step L ip, step R bkwd R, step L ip. May remain ip or travel fwd

✿ This combination is also used in a train step because of its repetitive pattern:

[16 sounds] [&8&1&2&3&4&5&6&7]

TO EXECUTE:
Shuffle ball change L, shuffle ball change, ball change L, shuffle ball change, ball change, continue to repeat

TRANSPOSE

To change the pitch of the music to a higher or lower key.

TRAVEL

✿ To move or to progress in a certain dir., fwd, sdwd, etc.

✿ To travel on the road, as with a road company or show.

✿ A traveling step (e.g., the parallel travel, a traveling cramproll, etc.).

Single Travel

A pivoting movement on the heel and toe of one foot.

TO EXECUTE:
Stand on L, R raised, L plié and flat, using L heel as pivot pt. lift L toe and drop it to R, then using L ball as pivot pt., lift and drop L heel to L

DOUBLE TRAVEL. See PARALLEL TRAVEL: 2

TRAVELING BARREL ROLLS. See BARREL ROLLS: Traveling

TRAVELING CRAMPROLL. See CRAMPROLL: Traveling

TRAVELING FOUETTÉ. See FOUETTÉ: Traveling

TRAVELING RENVERSÉ. See RENVERSÉ: Traveling

TRAVELING TIME STEP. See TIME STEP: Traveling

TRAVELING TURN. See TURN: Traveling

TREADMILL
[3 sounds] [&a1]

A running pickup keeping knees bent and high in the air. See PICKUP: Running and Treadmill

TREMBLE

A constant, rapid execution between the ball and the heel of the same foot, which creates a trembling sound. Part of the roll family.

TRENCH (Trench Step, Pulling the Trenches, Through the Trenches)
[w/wo sound]

Traceable to the World War I era. A form of slide and a well-known flash step. With wt. on one foot and the free leg straight and raised diagonally to the back corner or directly to the back, slide on the outside edge of the supporting leg, landing on the free foot in the same spot that has been vacated by the standing

TRENCH (continued)

leg. The body leans fwd; if standing leg is the L, then the R arm is frt arm. Alternate arms with each slide. The step theoretically mimicked the soldiers, staying low and running through the trenches. When executed, the feet trace a v pattern on the floor.

Outside: Trench moves from spot directly under body, away from body (i.e., when standing on R, slide R to R bk cor).

Inside: Trench starts from pos. away from body and moves to spot directly under body (i.e., when standing on R, slide to L), or it may start from spot directly under body and cross to opp. side (i.e., stand on R and slide to L). Trenches were so called because they subscribed groovelike patterns on the floor, and if correctly done, forming a v. Usually the body is in an inclined pos. to the frt, arms swinging in rhythm adding movement and lift to the trench. Originally these arm movements were executed to make the step appear difficult to perform and draw applause. Thus, trenches are classified as a flash or trick step.

TRENCH STEP. See TRENCH

TRICK STEP. See FLASH STEP

TRIPLE. See SHUFFLE STEP

TRIPLE DRAWBACK. See DRAWBACK: TRIPLE; CINCINNATI: Single

TRIPLE ESSENCE. See ESSENCE: Triple

TRIPLE ONE STEP RHYTHM. See ONE STEP RHYTHM: Triple

TRIPLE RIFF. See RIFF: Pendulum, Triple Parallel and Turned Out

TRIPLE SHUFFLE. See SHUFFLE: Triple

TRIPLE TIME STEP. See TIME STEP: Buck, Standard, Triple

TRIPLE VIRGINIA ESSENCE. See ESSENCE: Virginia, Triple

TRIPLE WALTZ CLOG. See WALTZ CLOG STEP: Triple

TRIPLE WALTZ CLOG TIME STEP. See WALTZ CLOG STEP: Triple; TIME STEP: Waltz Clog, Triple

TRIPLET

✿ A triplet is a grouping of only three beats or sounds executed within one beat of music and is counted **[&a1]**

   or

✿ Leap R, step L to L step R ip **[&a1]**

TRIPLET RHYTHM

Triplet rhythm occurs when one note is divided into three equal parts. Its basis is the $\frac{1}{8}$ th note and is counted a **[1 & a]**.

TURN ⚲

Turn is a broad term for a movement that revolves. It encompasses 5 or 6 turns (pirouettes) executed on one foot, chaînés which step from foot to foot and turns, that take place on the floor or in the air. Because tap has now absorbed ballet and its technique, we can be much more specific about the exact type of turn to be executed. Below is listed some general information regarding the category.

NOTE:
All tap turns are inevitably linked to the ballet or jazz concept of en dedans or en dehors, pirouettes, and/or chaîné turns.

All tap turns are either right or left and may be classified as:

En dedans (inside): Turning on the supporting leg in the direction of the supporting leg.

En dehors (outside): Turning on the supporting leg in the direction of the working leg.

On center: Turning in a vertical alignment to the floor.

Off center: Turning while the body and/or its parts are at an angle to the vertical alignment.

Turned out: The turning out of the whole leg from the hip socket, the feet then creating a 180-degree angle.

Oblique: The feet and legs creating an acute or obtuse angle.

Parallel: The feet and legs face directly front with no turnout.

Degree of Turn: ¼, ½, ¾, one revolution to multiple revolutions.

Relevé: Fully elevated on the balls of the feet with legs straight and stretched.

Relevé/Plié: Fully elevated on the balls of the feet with the legs in a plié position.

Flatfooted: Standing on the full foot, legs straight or bent.

Stationary: The turn(s) remain in the spot in which they began.

Traveling: Turns do not remain in one space but cover distance in a specific direction.

Floor Turns: Any turns that are executed on the floor (e.g., seat spins, knee spins, etc.).

Standing Turns: The position in which most turns are executed, while standing on the feet.

Tour en l'air (Air Turns; Aerial Tour; Aerials): Any turn in which the major portion of the turn is airborne, even though the preparation and ending must take place on the ground.

With or Without Sound: The tap dancer has the choice of creating sounds and rhythms or not as he/she chooses.

Please keep the following points in mind

1 Gravity opposes vertical alignment and its energy is to pull a mass in a downward direction; therefore, the performer must always make a conscious effort to stretch the body upward.

2 The best balance is obtained when the weight is equally distributed over the base support, whether it be equalized between two feet or placed directly over one.

3 Dancers are required to balance on a small surface of the foot, the ball, and tap dancers must also deal with the surface of the tap as well. Taps, because of their addition to the shoe, do not allow the foot to have a normal friction point with the floor, and are slippery and add thickness to the ball, which is especially felt in the relevé position.

4 Once the relevé has been established, don't distort the alignment or placement in any way, unless an off-center effect is desired.

5 The supporting leg must remain in a vertical position to the floor, unless the turn is inclined through the leg.

6 Each pirouette, especially those in which the working leg is extended away from the body in 2nd, 4th, arabesque, attitude, etc., must come to a pause at the end of each turn for clarity and to decrease the acceleration process, for the closer the working leg is to the body, the faster the pirouette. If, however, a number of successive turns are being executed (i.e., doubles, triples etc.), the pause must be present at the conclusion of each series.

7 Creating certain sounds causes the toes to flex and/or the heels to rise, forcing the dancer to find ways of staying within the confines of technique, yet produce the tap sounds required.

8 The lack of proper friction with the floor has the tendency to increase the speed of turns, a point the tap dancer must always remember.

9 Never forget: spotting is as important to the tap turn as it is to the turn executed in ballet jazz. See SPOTTING

Stationary (Spot) Turns

Below are listed only a few of the more recognized spot turns, there are many more. Most of them may be executed as either inside or the outside pirouettes. The explanations given turn to the right side.

Arabesque or Attitude: The more popular and easier execution of either of these two turns is on the inside. The sound produced is from the supporting leg only and may be accomplished with heel drops while in plié, toe heels, flap heels, etc. The spot may be fwd or to the side in line with the turn itself, with no snapping of the head involved. Be careful that the relationship between the body and the working leg is maintained throughout the turn and that the lifted leg does not lower. See ARABESQUE; ATTITUDE

Barrel Rolls: As previously stated, barrel rolls may be leaned, arched, straight, spotted on the floor, etc. See BARREL ROLLS

Outside Barrel Rolls: Very popular and may begin with spank R; spank toe R; or spank R, heel drop L, toe R; etc. [&]; [&1]; or [&a1] and end with stamp R and L; spank toe heel R, step L; or a R cramproll; [&2]; [&a2]; or [e&a2].

> **TO EXECUTE:**
> **Riff barrel rolls, spank R, drop L heel on turn, end with 3-ct. conventional riff R fwd, [&1&a2]**

Pump Barrel Rolls: are executed with a heel drop on each turn.

Inside Barrel Rolls ending in stamp and **aerial barrel rolls** ending in stamp R and L are used frequently. See BARREL ROLLS

Compass and Pencil Turns: In either turn, the only sound that usually occurs is from the supporting leg and its accenting with heel drops, continuously executed or one per turn. These pirouettes are very popular in their double or triple form and are often executed with a leaned or inclined line and/or in r/p. They seem to be preferred on the inside, rather than on the outside. See: COMPASS TURN; PENCIL TURN

Fouetté Turns: Fouetté turns are exciting and difficult to control and perform within technical boundaries. They are a combination of an outside (or inside) pirouette, which picks up momentum, followed by an extension to 4th or 2nd, which is a slowing-down process. Thus, one must have control awareness. Be sure that a momentary stopping or pause occurs upon each facing to the front and that the working leg begins its circular passage before the turn. Heel drops are one answer to sound. Riff fouettés end with a conventional 3-ct. riff to the front or to 2nd. However, the working leg must be lowered each time to produce the riff sounds, thereby creating a different look and execution. See FOUETTÉ

TURNS (continued)

Outside Turns: In executing an outside turn, which receives its major momentum from the grounded supporting foot, it is necessary to add propulsion and impetus from that foot alone, in this case the right. The following tap sounds represent only a few of the possibilities:

TO EXECUTE:

1   Spank toe heel R on turn, step to 2nd on ending [e & a1]

2   Chug both feet to 2nd, face frt, execute double pickup turning bkwd [1e & a2]

3   Outside par passé turn bk R, end stamp R and L to 2nd [1 & 2]

4   Spank R bk, drop L heel on turn, end with flap R, heel drop R and L (called an Eleanor Powell) [&1e&a2]

5   Spank R, drop L heel on turn, end frt with 3-ct. riff R to 4th or 2nd [&1&a2]

6   Heel drop L, begin to turn bk R, ball R, heel drop R L [1ea2]

NOTE:
The heel drop L is the movement that makes the turn remain in one place, while the ball, heel, heel propels the turn around.

Paddle Turns: Inside or outside paddle turns seem to be equally popular and the sounds that seem to be most executed are ball changes and brush or spank ball changes. If the turn is inside they are usually begun with a step R to R; if they are outside, the preparation step is step L to the L.

Inside Paddle Turn: Two of the most popular executions are:

TO EXECUTE:

1   Step R to R, 3 bcs (L to R) to complete turn [1&2&3&4]

2   Step R to R, brush L fwd, bc (L - R) 3 times [1&a2&a3&a4]

Outside Paddle Turn: Two of the most popular executions are:

TO EXECUTE:

1   STEP L, (SPANK BC R) 3 TIMES [1&A2&A3&A4]

2   STEP L (SPANK TOE HEEL R, STEP L) 3 TIMES [1E&A2E&A3E&A4]

Renversé Turns: The renversé turn is a popular spot turn in tap and is usually done by accenting sounds that are already present, such as hop L, ball R and step L [1&2]. However, after the hop spank toe heel R, step L may be substituted for ball R, step L [&a2] or spank ball change R may be executed in place of the final step R and L [&a2]. See RENVERSÉ

Spinarounds: No doubt one of the first stationary turns we teach a student because it is inside, easier, and ends with a firm stamp L to 2nd; therefore, the control is maximum.

TO EXECUTE:
Place ball of R on floor in r/p position. Turn may be executed in r/p or the supporting leg remains straight or straightened each time.

NOTE:
The speed is far faster when remaining in plié. Spot directly fwd and stamp in 2nd position in plié each time upon its completion. [1 2]

Turns in 4th and/or 2nd: The underneath heel drop is, technically, the usual sound executed. However, pickups and wings may also be used. Turns such as these, in which the working leg is extended in a position away from the body, are more difficult to control and to execute than those in which the working leg is close to the body. They are also slower turns in performance and require a momentary stop or pause each time upon reaching front. The working leg must never be allowed to lower or raise higher than in the original opening picture.

Other Stationary Turns: Other turns that may be performed in one spot include pivots, corkscrews, pas de bourrée, aerials, and inside and outside fan turns (all of these may be found under their proper names, e.g., fan turns, aerials, etc.).

Traveling Turns

Inside Chaîné Turns: Below are listed some general rules concerning the chaîné-based tap turn. The execution is given for a right inside (en dedans) turn. In the example below, the dancer begins the turns on sl, spotting sr and continuing in a str. line to the spot.

❂ Consider each step as accomplishing ½ of a turn. Step R to R, body faces front, head and eyes are focused on the spot to sr. Arms are open to 2nd position. Step L to beside R, body rotates ½ turn to the R and is now facing the back. Feet are beside each other and arms are closed. Head has held onto the spot at sr and is now over the L shoulder. This is actually the completion of the first turn. Turn bk R and Step R to the R, the head will snap and arrive at the spot before the body arrives at the front. Arms will have reopened. Thus, the second turn has begun.

❂ Think of each turn as creating a link in this chain of turns.

❂ Do not allow the body to overturn. It should never face the spot, but remain flattened to the front or the back of the room.

❂ The body should remain with the weight equally distributed over both feet, as each foot steps twd the lod.

The following sounds are commonly used with these Chaîné-based turns. This is a minor listing compared to the number of possibilities that exist.

NOTE:
When the R foot is being used, the body is facing or in the process of facing the front. When the L foot is being used, the body is facing or in the process of facing the back.

Stamp R, Step L (flat toe)	[1 2]	Br Hop St R and L	[&a1&a2]
Stamp R, Toe Heel L	[1 &2]	Drawback R and L	[&a1 &a2]
Stamp R, Sh St L	[1 &a2]	Cincinnati R and L	[&a1&a2 &a3&a4]
Sh St R, Sh St L	[&a1 &a2]	Hop St R and L	[a1a2]
Sh Toe Heel R and L	[e&a1 e&a2]	Hl Dr L, St R, Rev. L	[&1&2]
Sh Hop St R and L	[a1a2 a3 a4]	Stamp R Alt. CR L	[1e&a2 3e&a4]
Sh R, Hl Dr L, St R, Rev. L	[a1a2 a3a4]	Waltz Clog R and L	[1&2&3 4&5 &6]
Toe Heel R and L	[a1 a2]	Leap R, Sh Leap Toe L	[1&2&3]
Fl Heel R and L	[&a1 &a2]	Maxie Ford w/ Graboff R	[1 ie&a2]
Fl Hl Hl R and L	[a1a2 a3a4]	Leap R, Tap L Bk R Rev.	[&1&2]
Fl BC R and L	[a1a2 a3a4]	4-ct. Flat Riff R and L	[e&a1 e&a2]

Outside Chaîné Turns: This execution is given for a right outside (en dehors) turn. The dancer begins the turns on sr, spotting sl and continuing in a str. line to the spot, step L to L, head over L shoulder to the spot, body faces frt and arms in 2nd, turn bk R, eyes focus on spot, body faces bk, arms closed and head is now over R shoulder. This is the completion of the first turn. Step L to spot as body turns bk R face frt head is now over the L shoulder. This is the beginning of the 2nd turn.

NOTE:

1 The outside chaîné is not as popularly used as the inside chaîné.

2 The sounds presented for the inside chaînés are usable for the outside chaîné as well, but one must begin with the L, not the R.

3 One may use a traveling spot rather than the spot on the opposite side of the stage. See SPOTING: TRAVELING

Listed below are other popular R outside turns. Begin at sr and progress to sl while using a traveling spot. See SPOTING: Traveling

Outside R Barrel Rolls: These turns may be executed with a varied amount of tap sounds. See BARREL ROLLS

TO EXECUTE:
Spank bk R, start to turn bk R, tap R bk L (head frt and over L shoulder), complete turn, face frt, stamp R and L in 2nd position [&1&2]

TO EXECUTE:
Heel drop L (turn bk R), toe heel R and step L to L (face frt) [1&a2]

TO EXECUTE:
Relevé L, ast turn bk R, execute R cramproll to face frt (turn on L, cramproll) [e&a2]

TURNS (continued)

Outside/Traveling Renversés

After hop on ct. 1, the ending may be made with the following tap sounds, to complete the turn. See RENVERSÉ: Traveling

> TO EXECUTE:
> Step R and L [&2]

> TO EXECUTE:
> Toe heel R, step L to L
> [&a2]

> TO EXECUTE:
> Spank toe heel R, step L to
> L [e&a2]

> TO EXECUTE:
> R leaping cramproll R
> [e&a2]

Outside R Traveling Turns

Many sound patterns can be executed by crossing the R foot behind the L, turning bkwd to the R and upon the completion of the turn, placing L foot to the L. Such sounds are listed below:

> TO EXECUTE:
> St L to L, St R Xd bk L,
> (face frt), heel drop R, turn
> bk R, St L to L [&1&2]
> Toe heel R bk L (face frt),
> turn bk R, St L to L [1&2]
> Spank toe heel R bk L (face
> frt), turn, toe heel L to L
> [&1&2]
> Spank R, heel drop L (face
> frt), toe heel R, Xd bk L,
> turn bk R, step L to L
> [&1&a2]

Other Traveling Turns

Traveling turns may also be executed by facing the line of direction and traveling directly toward and to the spot. One very effective use of this might be to have a dancer begin usc facing the audience and repeat a straight line of turns that would end dsc and close to them. Traveling renversés, fouettés, turns in 4th, barrel rolls, and aerial fouettés might well be used in this manner. Another turn that might be considered is the inside/outside turn.

Inside/Outside Turn

Begin at sl and face sr or begin us and face ds. Spot directly ahead of the body. For turns executed on the right side, prepare in 4th position with R foot forward, relevé and execute a R inside, parallel passé pirouette. Step forward L into a 4th position as a preparation for the next turn. Execute a R outside, parallel passé pirouette and step forward R into 4th position to repeat the series again [1234] or [&1&2].

Combining Traveling and Stationary Turns

Many interesting combinations are possible by placing traveling turns together with spot turns. Usually a change of spot would be involved: in executing a straight line of R chaîné turns, which begin at sl, the spot would be taken at sr. If spinarounds were to be introduced upon the arrival at cs, the spot would have to shift to the front during the execution of the last chaîné.

Tour en l'air (Air Turn, Aerial Tour, Aerials)

- ✿ Involve a rotation of the body around a central axis.

- ✿ After the initial pushoff and lift from the floor, it is necessary for another force or impetus to enter, thus adding a further lift. In an aerial barrel roll, it is the first knee being thrust into the air, followed by the second knee, thus adding a second impetus.

- ✿ In most aerial tours, the transition or high point of the turn must take place at the high point of the elevation, for example, in the switch split turning, the switch split must be visible at the greatest height of the elevation.

- ✿ The gaining of this elevation must never show in the body, but be accomplished with the legs, etc.

- ✿ The timing of the arm movements is extremely important to the tour and the appearance of it, as well as to its sustaining quality.

- ✿ A wider preparation base is required for the elevation and should be experimented with.

Air turns include stag turns, grands jetés, aerial renversés, fouettés, barrel rolls, and axels. They are a very advanced form of turning and should be carefully taught and executed.

Turns in Circles and Patterns

Turns may be executed in circles and patterns such as a v, zigzag, or triangle. Always think of the pattern to be performed as a geometric figure with straight lines, even if the pattern is curved. For example, think of a circle as a square with rounded corners or as 4 dots, one at each corner, with connecting lines that represent the direction of travel. Once the decision is made as to whether the circle is to be inside (clockwise), or outside (counterclockwise), and the starting point has been determined, one merely follows the imaginary line. See SPOTTING

Floor Turns

Any turns where the body or a portion of the body such as a knee, foot, shoulder, etc. is in contact with the floor and turned upon.

Knee Spins: Begin in kneeling position on R knee. L foot placed to L with arms to L in preparation for a R turn. From this position one might do the following turns:

Three Step Turn to R: Spin on R knee to R, place L knee beside R. Now facing bk with knees close together, spin bk R on L knee and step R foot out to R side to complete and stop the turning process. End in kneeling position on L knee with R foot to R.

NOTE:
When spinning on the knee, one must bend the supporting lower leg to keep the foot off the floor. Spot is in the direction of the turn **[123 hold 4].**

R Knee Spin(s): Using the same preparation position as in #1, execute an inside R turn on R knee with L held in bk attitude, arabesque, etc. Two or three turns are very possible. Upon completion of the turn(s), L leg could step into 4th croisé or end in a jazz croisé jazz split. L outside pirouettes could be executed from this same preparation.

Knee Chaînés: Knee chaînés are very possible in a straight line or in a circle. Execute as a regular chaîné turn but on the tips of the knees.

Other floor spins are possible, such as seat spins, shoulder spins, etc.

TURNED IN

The legs or feet are in an inverted or pigeon-toed position. It is the opposite of being turned out.

TURNED OUT

Turning out the entire leg from the hip bone. Therefore, when one stands in 1st position, the feet theoretically form a 180-degree angle or a straight line. In tap, turned out may also mean that the feet are placed on a less severe angle, such as oblique.

TURNING CRAMROLL. See CRAMPROLL; TURNS

TWIST DROP
[2 sounds] [12]

A step done in a pigeon-toed manner, frequently used in Charleston. Drop the toes to R, using heels as pivot pt., then drop heels to R, using toes as pivot pt. Both toes or heels are dropped tog ast.

TWISTER

Origin is in social dance, a step used often in the jitterbug or Lindy.

TO EXECUTE:
Two partners face each other, clasping hands. First partner kicks legs over the clasped hand, hunches over, steps on lifted foot and is now facing backward from partner. Second partner does the same, but with the opposite leg. Partners are now back-to-back, hunched over, and still clasping hands. The process is then reversed by the first, then the second partner until they are face-to-face.

TWISTING CRAMPROLLS. CRAMPROLL: Twisting

TWO (2). See SHUFFLE

TWO BEAT. See Fast 2/4 music

TWO COUNT (TAP) RIFF. See RIFF: 2 Count

TWO STEP
[3 sounds] [1&2]

Traceable to character and folk dancing. Really misnamed, for it involves 3 steps, but named as such for it uses 2 cts. of music. It is actually our step ball change or side close step.

UP-BEAT

An unaccented beat in a musical measure, usually the 2nd, or the raising of the hand when beating time.

UP SYNCOPATED STEP
[18 sounds] [&a1&2&a3&4&5&6&7&8]

TO EXECUTE:
(A) Shuffle step R, ball change (L - R) [&a1&2], shuffle step L, ball change (R - L) [&a3&4], (B) scuff R, chug L, step R and L [&a5&6], repeat (B) [&7&8]

UP TEMPO

To play in a tempo that is quite rapid and/or faster than the original tempo.

UPSTAGE

- ✿ The very back of the stage proper, the part farthest away from the audience.
- ✿ A performer drawing attention to himself and away from the rest of the cast, or "upstaging" another performer.

UPWARD RHYTHMIC PROGRESSION

RHYTHMIC PROGRESSION: Upward.

VAMP

A short musical phrase played repeatedly in anticipation of a cue.

VAUDEVILLE

A popular form of family entertainment that began in the early 1900s and began to disappear in the late 1920s. See AN HISTORICAL LOOK AT TAP

VIRGINIA ESSENCE. See ESSENCE: Virginia

VIRGINIA REEL

A country-style group dance.

WALK AROUND
[18 sounds] [&a1&2&a3&4&5&6&7&8]

TO EXECUTE:
Shuffle R, step R, L, R [&a1&2], shuffle L, step L, R, L [&a3&4], heel toe R, ball change (L - R) [&5&6], heel toe L, ball change (R - L) [&7&8]

- ✿ In the closing number of a minstrel show, all the cast would sing, dance, and improvise as they paraded in a circle around the stage.
- ✿ A master of ceremonies (M.C.) or comedian would often do a step or tell a joke, then walk in a circle and allow time for the audience to applaud.

WALKIN' TO CHURCH
[6 sounds] [&a1 &a2]

TO EXECUTE:
Turn feet out, move fwd while doing heel click R to L in passing, drop L heel, step fwd R [&a1], reverse [&a2], continue forward while repeating

Courtesy of Ron Sawyer, London, England.

WALKING FLAPS. See FLAP

WALKING GRAPEVINE (Cross Walk, Weaving)
[4 movements] [1 2 3 4]

TO EXECUTE:
Step R to R, step L frt R [1 2], step R to R, step L bk R [3 4]

NOTE:
May be done with or with out sounds.

WALKING PENDULUM RIFF. See RIFF: Pendulum, WALKING

WALKING RIFF. See RIFF: Walking

WALKING SHUFFLE. See ALTERNATING SHUFFLE

WALKING THE DOG
[6 sounds] [8 12 3 hold 4 5 hold 6 7 hold 8]

TO EXECUTE:
Hit R thigh with R hand [8], touch R fwd [1], hit R thigh with R hand [2], touch R bkwd [3], walk fwd R and L [5, hold 6, 7, hold 8]

WALKING TURN. See THREE STEP TURN

WALKING WING. See WING: Walking

WALTZ

Began as a very popular European ballroom dance, brought to this country from Vienna and Germany.

Its basic step was the waltz step: step forward R, step L to L and close R to L. Reverse. The music and the feeling became the basis for the waltz clog.

WALTZ CLOG (STEP) (Waltz Clog Time Step, Five, 5, Clog Step)
[5 – 7 sounds] [1&2&3] or [&1&2&3] [&a1&2&3]

Traceable to clog dancing, where it took its name from the wooden shoes that were worn and the waltz music used for its accompaniment. It is incorrectly known as a time step, since it fits none of the time step criteria and is probably best known in its single form. The waltz clog was popularized by Pat Rooney, but Eddie Rector is credited with its smooth and elegant performance.

TO EXECUTE:

Single: leap R, shuffle ball
    change L [1&2&3]
Double: flap R, shuffle ball
    change L [&1&2&3]
Triple: shuffle step R, shuffle
    ball change [&a1&2&3]
Quadruple: shuffle toe heel R,
shuffle ball change L
    [e&a1&2&3]

Running Waltz Clog: A waltz clog done springing from foot to foot and covering a large amount of space in its execution. Waltz clogs may also be done turning.

Advanced Waltz Clog:

TO EXECUTE:
Step (flap or Sh St R), Sh bc
L frt R, drop R heel
[1&2&a3]
or
Step (flap or Sh St R), Sh bc
L frt R, drop L & R heels
[1&2e&a3]

WALTZ CLOG TIME STEP. See WALTZ CLOG STEP; TIME STEP: Waltz Clog

WALTZ PICKUP (WALTZ PULLBACK)
[5 sounds] [&12&3]

TO EXECUTE:
Spank step R frt L, brush
battement L to L, pickup R.
reverse

WALTZ PULLBACK. See WALTZ PICKUP

WALTZ TAP

Any tap routine that uses a waltz, or ³/₄, tempo for its accompaniment. Previously, it leaned heavily on the Waltz Clog step. In the 1930s, it became much more complex and involved in syncopation and accenting.

WALTZ TURN
[6 sounds] [1&2&3&]

TO EXECUTE:
(1) Leap R, shuffle leap L,
tap R bk L turn R, drop
L heel. Repeat.
(2) Execute the waltz step
while turning.

WALTZ WING. See WING: Waltz

WARMUP

A group of exercises and/or movements to properly prepare the feet and the body for a further dance event, such as a class, a performance, etc. There are many different kinds of tap warmups, four of which are presented here:

Followed Warmup: The student or the dancer follows the exercises presented, without knowing in advance the sequence of the steps or movements to be given.

Learned Warm up: This warmup has been previously taught and the student or dancer uses it as a warmup and as a means of perfecting the various movements and tap sounds contained therein.

Individual Warmup: The student or dancer decides on and performs his own movements and steps which he deems satisfactory for his requirements. He/she does this alone and it is usually performed without the music so that tempo and syncopations may be made or changed as desired.

Barre Warmup: These tap exercises are performed at the barre. They may be based on technique from another form, such as jazz or ballet, or they may be in the logical order for the progression of tap sounds and movements from the basic to the advanced: single sounds to multiple; slow to fast, etc.

WEAVE
[8 sounds] [1&2&3&4&]

TO EXECUTE:
Step L to L, brush step R to L,
shuffle step L Xd frt R, tap R
bk L, heel drop L. Rev.

WEAVING. See WALKING GRAPEVINE

WIGGLE STICKS

This is the basic foot movement of the Charleston: the toes turn in toward each other and then are turned outward as the heels turn in.

> TO EXECUTE:
> Begin with the feet parallel and apart. Using the L heel as a pivot point, lift the L toe and swivel it outward, ast, place the ball of the R, Xd in back of the L, ball facing outward. Heels are now in and toes are facing out. Using the L heel as a pivot point, drop the L toe inward, ast, step ball R inward, feet are now in pigeon-toed position. Reverse or Repeat.

WILE-A-WAY
[9 or 13 sounds] [1234567&8] or [&12&34&56&7&8]

A step created so that the dancer or dancers remained moving but in one spot. Basically, it was used by chorus girls when they were backing a star act. It was originally dig step R, L, R, followed by a step ball change L. Repeat. It later became brush dig step R to L, reverse and repeat and spank step ball change L open to 2nd, which in turn became the third step of the shim sham shimmy called the tack annie.

WINDMILL. See BARREL ROLL

WINDSHIELD WIPER

A step in which one foot taps out and in.

> TO EXECUTE:
> Stand in par 2nd, position, while maintaining weight on L foot, tap R foot outward, then inward in an even rhythm.

WING

Stage: The area lying on either side of the stage, usually curtained or hidden by tormentors, flats, etc., to block audience vision into the backstage area. Serves as exit and entrance for the performers.

Dance: The wing has a long history. Although its first American appearance was in the buck and wing, of which the wing was the new ingredient, its first tracing, according to Marshall and Jean Stearns in their book *Jazz Dance*, may be found in a movement called the pigeon wing. In this, a foot was scraped or shaken to the side, while the arms created a flapping and/or fluttering motion in direct imitation of a bird. This same event occurred in the buck and wing, when on the wing section the arms were flapped or circled wildly to add to the excitement of the step.

Some say that Jack Wiggins was the first to use the wing; others contend, that it was already part of John Durang's hornpipe. The final credit has been given to James McIntrye, who brought the buck and wing to the New York stage in 1880. This new dance quickly replaced the clog.

In the beginning, the wing was part of a time step and it did not leave the floor or spring into the air; it was merely a flinging of one foot to the side in an imitative movement. By the 1920s, the 3-point (count) scrape-shuffle wing came into existence. By 1922, Frank Condos, one of the famous Condos brothers, at age 17 had developed the 5-point wing which involved scraping the working foot out to the side, executing 3 sounds on the way back and, finally, landing on the ball of the same foot. Still later, with the exploration of classical tap, the shuffle wing was created. In this, the scrape-spank sounds were replaced with two clear taps in the form of a nerve shuffle. Both types of wings are recognized today.

Wings have always been considered a flash step. At present, the pride of achievement lies not in applause-getting but in their technical execution and presentation. In discussing wings, the words point, count, and tap are often used. They are all interchangeable terms that refer to the number of sounds to be executed. Thus, a 4-point, tap, or count wing would produce 4 sounds.

The Wing category is a huge composite of steps. The ones described below are those most prevalently found in research.

Single Scrape Shuffle Wing
[3 sounds] [&a1]

> TO EXECUTE:
> Standing on ball of R foot, in r/p, with the R heel well lifted and with the R toes straight fwd and/or slightly turned in; L foot in passé, parallel or turned out; spring off supporting leg (L knee may be jabbed into air, for appearance sake or to aid in lifting of the body), ast roll

onto outside edge of R toes (thus rolling the ankle) and execute the scrape sound of the wing. As R foot completes the scrape, spank R, returning it to a position directly under body and landing on ball R in the starting position [&a1]. In scrape shuffle wings, the working foot goes directly to 2nd.

NOTE:

1 The great danger in the execution of these wings lies in the possible injury to the ankle in the rolling process. Be extremely careful that all weight has been removed from the supporting leg so that an injury will not occur.

2 When learning the execution of these wings, students may find that placing their hands on a high surface, such as a table, the back of a chair, or a corner where two ballet barres meet will aid in removing the weight from the ankle until the step has been learned.

Single Shuffle Wings
[3 sounds] [&a1]

TO EXECUTE:
Stand on the ball of the R, in r/p, with the R heel well lifted and the R foot turned out on a 45-degree angle. The L knee is in a passé position, turned out or parallel. Spring into the air and execute a clear shuffle with the R—a brush and a spank—returning to the ball of the R in the starting position.

In its more advanced form, the first two sounds would become a nerve shuffle.

All the wings presented below may be executed as either a scrape shuffle or shuffle wings.

Single Wing
[3 sounds] [&a1]

While standing on the supporting leg in r/p, execute the 2 sounds of the wing and return to the supporting leg.

Double Wings
[3 sounds] [&a1]

Double wings are executed by standing on both feet and executing single wings on both the R and L foot simultaneously (i.e., both the outgoing sounds and, the incoming sounds as well as the sounds on the landing take place together, thus creating three sounds).

NOTE:
There are no R and L double wings if both outward brushes, inward spanks, and landings are executed on both feet simultaneously. However, scatter or splatter wings are classifiable as R or L because one foot takes the lead-off brush, (e.g., on a R double scatter wing, the order of the feet is Br R to R, Br L to L, Sp R to L, Sp L to R, land on R, land on L **[6 separate sounds] [i e a & a1]).**

Alternating Wings (Changing Wings, Swap Wings, Wing Changes)
[3 sounds] [&a1]

While standing on the R, execute a single R wing, either scrape or shuffle, but land on the L foot. Then reverse the action to regain standing on the R.

Drum Wing

Whenever a heel drop(s) is added to the landing of a wing, it is called a drum wing: if a R drum single wing were to be executed, one would perform a single wing on the R and add a heel drop R after the landing **[4 sounds] [e&a1].** A R drum alternating wing would begin on the R foot, execute the wing ending on the L and heel drop L **[4 sounds][e&a1],** and a drum double could begin and end on both feet and both heels could be dropped simultaneously and together or separately, one heel, then the other **[4 sounds] [e&a1].**

Wing Toes

Any wings in which a toe tap is added after the wing is executed.

NOTE:
1 Additional sounds such as heel drops, toe drops, toe taps, riffs, shuffles, etc. may be added before or after any wing.

2 Most wings may be executed ip, fwd, sdwd, or turning.

Fake Wing

Any wing that does not create all the sounds, illegitimately executed, or that does not fulfill the requirements of a single, double, or alternating wing.

WING (continued)

OTHER TYPES OF WINGS

Alternating Wing Toe
[4 sounds per Wing Toe] [e&a1]

Execute an alternating wing from the R foot to the L foot and add a toe tap R. Reverse

Cramp Wings (Drum Wings). See WING: Drum

Five-Sounded (Count) Wing
[5 sounds] [ie&a1]

> TO EXECUTE:
> Begin in par 1st position, spring into the air, brush (tap) R to R, brush (tap) L to L, spank R to L, under boot, land both feet tog. in par 1st position [ie&a1].

Flash Rattle
[5 sounds] [1e&a2]

> TO EXECUTE:
> Stand L frt R, ball R Xd bk L, spring upward in toe stand L, ast execute a scrape shuffle wing R, drop L heel, tap R bk L

Heel Stand Wing
[3 sounds] [&a1]

While standing in a heel stand on L, execute a wing with R.

Hip Wing

The hip wing is executed by tapping the free foot (in this case the L Xd bk R), followed by the wing on the R. When the wing is performed, the L knee is bent, raised, and twisted across the front of the body to add a lift to the wing. Presented below is a short combination involving a hip wing: cts. [8&a1] are the preparation step; cts. [2&a3] the actual hip wing, and cts. [4-7] a repetition of the hip wing.
(From Glenn Shipley's *The Complete Tap Dictionary*)

> TO EXECUTE:
> 8 Hop L 4 toe tap L bk R &a1 Sh St R F of L &a5 wing R
> 2 toe tap L bk R 6 toe tap L bk R
> &a3 wing R &a7 wing R

Passé Wings
[3 sounds] [&a1]

Execute any single or alternating wing with the working leg held in a turned-out passé position.

Pendulum Wings (Cloche Wings)

These wings may be executed in two different manners:

> TO EXECUTE:
> ✪ Stand on the R, brush battement L fwd, L leg straight, wing R, brush battement L bk, L straight, wing R [e&a1e&a2]
> ✪ Stand on R, brush battement L fwd, L leg straight, wing R, brush battement L bk, L bent, wing R, tap L bk R [e&a1ie&a2]

Pump Wings

Any wing in which the passé leg pumps up and down as each wing is executed.

Running Wings

Brush L fwd, execute an alternating wing from R to L and rev. Brushing leg may be straight or bent. The execution should be done by springing from foot to foot, as though running [4 sounds] [1e&a].

Russian Wings

> TO EXECUTE:
> Begin either from a deep squat on the floor or standing and plié to a deep squat position. Upon coming to a standing position execute a scrape or regular Brush out and upon returning to the floor execute the spank and land in plié squat position. Both feet are done simultaneously as though it were a double wing. A scuff may be substituted for the scrape or brush out [3 sounds] [1&2]

> ✪ Execute the above, the same way, but exclude the squat position; go only to a deep plié.

Saw Wing
[4 sounds] [1e&a 2]

TO EXECUTE:
Stand on R, execute single
wing on R   [1e&a]
tap L toe bk R   [2]

Scatter Wings (Spatter, Splatter,
Echo)
[6 sounds] [1ie&a2]

The sounds in a Double Wing can also be staggered, thus
producing 6 sounds.

TO EXECUTE:
Prepare as for double wing
(regular). Scatter wings can
be either R or L footed,
depending on which foot
leads off. For R scatter
wings, as body lifts brush (or
scrape) R to R, then L to L,
spank R then L, and land R
and L in starting pos.

NOTE:
All double wings may be alternated by placing no wt.
on the last foot to land and beg. w/ that foot next.

Fake Scatter Wings
[6 sounds] [1ie&a2]

In this type, the whole scrape-shuffle or shuffle is
completed on one foot before the next scrape-shuffle or
shuffle is executed on the second foot. Therefore, the order
would be shuffle R, shuffle L, land R, land L.

NOTE:
The same number of sounds are created, but in the
wrong order.

Scissors Wings
[8 sounds] [e&a1e&a2]

TO EXECUTE:
Stand R, wing R, tap L toe
bk R, turned out, wing R,
tap L frt R, turned out lift L
into higher passé on each
wing.

Swap Wing
[6 sounds] [a&e&a2] or [&a1&a2]

TO EXECUTE:
Stand on the L. Shuffle with
R, execute an alternating
wing from L to R, add toe
tap L bk R

The swap wing is part of the alternating wing family.

Thrust Wing
[3 sounds][&a 1]

Stand in par 1st position.

TO EXECUTE:
Thrust or shoot both feet
straight fwd and bkwd while
executing a par double wing
[&a].
Land on both feet ast [1].

Toe Stand Wings
[3 sounds] [&a1]

TO EXECUTE:
Standing in toe stand pos. on
L foot, execute either a
scrape-shuffle or shuffle
wings with R foot. Other
sounds may be added before
or after the wing, such as
heel drop, toe tap, etc. Rev.
for wings on L foot

NOTE:
This is a form of a flash rattle.

Treadmill Wings
[4 sounds] [e&a1]

Treadmill wings are running wings done with the legs
parallel and the knees bent. Stand on L, brush R leg fwd,
parallel and bent, execute alternating wing from L to R.
Reverse movement to continue to run. Knees should be
high and step executed with a real springing action.

Triple Wings (Paul Draper)

TO EXECUTE:
Scrape outside of both ball taps
to sides at same time   [a]
Brush both ball taps inward [&]

WING (continued)

Brush both ball taps
inward   [a]
Land on both ball taps
together at the same time

Walking Wings
[5 sounds] [1e&a2]

Brush R fwd, execute Scrape-Shuffle or Shuffle
Wing on L. Step fwd R. Reverse to continue. Brush
may be a low or high Battement.

Waltz Wings
[6 sounds] [&12&a3]

Brush Step R frt L, Brush Battement L to 2nd,
execute Scrape-Shuffle or Shuffle Wing R. Rev.

WING HEEL. See DRUM WING

WING CHANGES. See WING: Alternating

WING HEEL. See WING: Drum

WING TIME STEP. See TIME STEP: Wing

WING TOE. See WING: Wing Toes

WORKING LEG

The working leg refers to the leg that is performing a
movement or being held in air. The supporting leg is
the one upon which the dancer is standing.

WRIGHT SYSTEM

A system of tap notation developed by Dexter
Wright that combines musical notes, tap
abbreviations, and directional indications for the
various movements. For example, a W indicates a
weight change.

YACHT STEP
[5 sounds] [1&2&3]
Usually done in Waltz tempo

TO EXECUTE:
Leap R to R, Shuffle L, Leap
L   [1&2&]
Step R frt L   [3]
Reverse

ZANK
[1 sound] [1]
(From *The Tap Dance Dictionary* by Mark Knowles)

TO EXECUTE:
Slide R foot bkwd, ast Chug
L foot fwd   [1]

ZIGZAG PICKUP. See PICKUP: Double,
Zigzag.

ZIG ZAG PULLBACK. See PICKUP: Double,
Zigzag

ZINC
[1 sound] [1]
(From *The Tap Dance Dictionary* by Mark Knowles)

TO EXECUTE:
Slide R foot fwd, ast Chug L
foot bkwd   [1]

PART IV

A REFERENCE MANUAL FOR TAP

PERFORMING

THE STAGE AREA

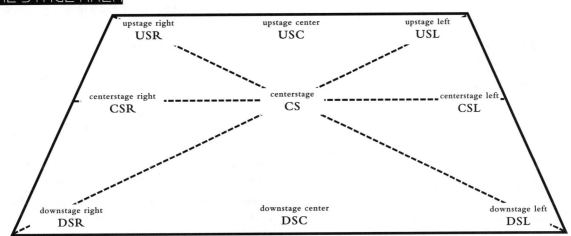

upstage right
USR

upstage center
USC

upstage left
USL

centerstage right
CSR

centerstage
CS

centerstage left
CSL

downstage right
DSR

downstage center
DSC

downstage left
DSL

STAGE DIRECTIONS

ll stage directions are given from the point of view of the performer standing center stage while facing the audience.

Center Stage (CS)
The exact center of the performance area where all the sightlines converge.

Center Stage Left (CSL)
The area lying directly to the left of the performer standing CS.

Center Stage Right (CSR)
The area lying directly to the right of the performer standing CS.

Downstage (DS)
The area closest to the audience and below CS.

Downstage Center (DSC)
The area lying in a direct line from CS to the edge of the stage.

Downstage Left (DSL)
The area lying at the front part of the stage and to the left of the performer.

Downstage Right (DSR)
The area lying at the front part of the stage and to the right of the performer.

Upstage (US)
The area farthest away from the audience and above CS.

Upstage Center (USC)
The area lying in a direct line from CS to the back of the stage.

Upstage Left (USL)
The area lying at the back part of the stage and to the left of the performer.

Upstage Right (USR)
The area lying at the back part of the stage and to the right of the performer.

Stage Left (SL)
The area lying from CS anywhere to the performer's left.

Stage Right (SR)
The area lying from CS anywhere to the performer's right.

DANCERS' GUIDE TO THEATER TERMINOLOGY

A.S.C.A.P.: American Society of Composers and Publishers. A nonprofit organization based in New York City that protects the rights of composers and publishers of music.

Act Call: The call issued by the stage manager to assemble the cast in their positions for the opening of an act or a scene.

Act Curtain: The front curtain, in view of the audience, that goes up at the beginning of an act or scene and down at its conclusion.

Act Warning: The stage manager's "half hour," "fifteen," or "five-minute" call that announces the amount of time remaining until the production is to begin.

Ad-lib: To improvise, create, or make up on the spot, dialogue, a routine, etc. because of a lapse of memory, a late cue, or intentionally.

Apron (Forestage): That part of the stage, beyond the curtain, or grande drape, line that projects forward into the audience and beyond the proscenium arch.

Arena Theater (theater-in-the-round): A stage in which the audience is seated around the total performance area, the shape of which may be round, square, oblong, etc.

Asbestos: The fireproof curtain, mandatory in most professional theaters, that is hung between the stage and the audience.

Backing: A drop, drape, or piece of scenery that is placed behind a window, door, or open space to mask the backstage area from the view of the audience.

Back Light(s): Lighting behind the performer to produce a special, usually mysterious effect.

Backstage: Any area that lies back of and around the performing area and out of view of the audience. It may includes storage rooms, wings, dressing rooms, or production apparatus.

Back Wall: The rear wall of the set or of the theater itself.

Battens: Pipes or pieces of wood used in the top and bottom of drapes and cloth scenery to make them hang smoothly.

Blackout: All lights out simultaneously to create a dramatic or needed effect.

Blocking: The directed movement of the performers on the stage.

Book: The story and dialogue for a musical or a play.

Border: A width of black cloth, canvas, etc. hung as a valance to hide the upper part of the stage.

Box Office: The business office of the theater where tickets are kept and sold, or a production that has become a large success.

Breakaway: A costume, prop, or object that will fall apart or break away easily.

Business: What a performer does on stage, such as shut a door, pick up a hat, etc., all of which is part of the play's action.

Call Board: A bulletin board where the stage manager, director, or choreographer can post notices, rehearsal times, corrections, and other information that affects the company.

Choreographer: The dance director and creator of all the dances and musical numbers that are part of the production.

Clear Stage: A stage manager's call that requests all crew and performers to leave the stage area.

Crew: The backstage members of the team who do the physical and technical work connected with the production.

Cross: When the performer moves from one area of the stage to another or exits on cue.

Cue: The spoken line or movement that signals the next action to take place.

Curtain: The raising and lowering of the front curtain that signals the beginning or ending of the play, or the curtain itself.

Curtain Line: The imaginary line that marks the position of the front curtain on the stage floor when it is lowered or closed.

Curtain Time: The time the performance is scheduled to begin.

Cycle (Cyclorama): A curved background surrounding the sides and back of the performance area, which may be painted to act as a scenic background or for atmosphere.

Dance Director: Old term for choreographer.

Dimout: A planned, orderly dimming of the stage lights to create a special mood or to add a softer ending to the scene.

Director: The person responsible for the entire production as well as for the blocking, rehearsing, and coordination of all the elements.

Dress Parade: A parade of the entire cast, wearing their costumes, for perhaps the first time, to check for fit, colors, hairstyle, etc.

Drop(s): Any canvas, drapes, or fabric painted as part of the set and scenery; usually hung from the grid.

Encore: To return to the stage to perform again, owing to the loud and continuous applause or response from the audience.

Ensemble: The entire group of performers in the production or a specialized group such as a chorus of singers, dancers, or both that make up the cast.

Exit: The performer leaving the stage, or the physical place where he/she leaves.

Flat(s): Wooden frame(s) covered by canvas that acts as scenery and is easily transportable.

Flies: An area above the stage, out of view of the audience, where scenery is hung and stored.

Fanfare: A large and exciting musical interlude that creates an atmosphere of expectancy and excitement and that acts as an announcement that someone or something wonderful is going to happen.

Follow Spot: A special spotlight constructed to follow the dancer, action, actor, etc. throughout the routine. This is used especially in the case of solo performers.

Footlights: A strip of lights placed on the DS area of the stage, the basic purpose of which is to light the faces of the performers, and which in reality defines the stage area and those on it. Used extensively in vaudeville; many theaters of today are built without them.

Front of House: The front of the audience and/or the lobby, box office, etc. used to conduct the theater's business.

Gel(s): A thin sheet(s) of colored plastic placed over a light to cast color onto the stage.

Grande Drape: The frontmost curtain in a theater, often very beautiful and made of heavy material.

Grid (Gridiron): The frame resembling a grid that is suspended above the stage for the handling of the scenery.

Grips: Stagehands who handle the scenery.

Green Room: The performers lounge, where they can visit with friends, etc.

House: The audience itself and the place where they sit to observe the performance.

House Left: When seated in the audience, to the audience's left and the performer's right.

House Right: When seated in the audience, to the audience's right and the performer's left.

In One: The performing area in front of the downstage curtain.

Legs (Leg Drops): Narrow drapes or flats used in pairs to obscure the audience view into backstage.

Lights: All the lights, spots, floods, etc. used on and off the stage to create special effects.

Off Stage: The area around and behind the stage that is not visible to the audience.

On Stage: The area of the stage that is visible to the audience and upon which the performers work.

Out Front: The audience and the auditorium.

Paper the House: To give away tickets so that the audience will look full.

Places: A call from the stage manager, usually at the five-minute call, telling the performers to assume their proper positions for the beginning of the act or the show.

Practical: Any piece of scenery or a prop that is functional and workable, such as a door that opens or food that can be eaten.

Prompt Book: A book containing all the cues, exits, lines, and lights used by the stage manager to run the show.

Properties (Props): Includes scene props used as stage dressing as well as hand-held props.

Property Table: Table or tables placed off stage near the performance area where hand props are placed in a specific order for the performers.

Proscenium: The architectural structure that frames the stage and separates it from the house.

Rake(d): An inclined stage surface, usually higher in the back and slanted downward toward the audience.

Ring Down: A signal for dropping or closing the curtain at the end of the performance.

Royalty: The money paid to the publisher and author for the rights to perform the play.

Set: The scenery, which provides the environment in which the production appears.

Scrim: A gauze or transparent drop used in the transformation of scenes, projections, as bleedthroughs May or may not be painted.

Stand By: A stage manager's call to get ready, or (as standby) another performer paid to be prepared to perform in the case of an emergency.

Strike: A taking down of the entire set, props, and scenery by the crew.

Tech Rehearsal: For the technical crew to coordinate cues, refocus lights, and in general tend to the technical running of the production.

Thrust Stage: An auditorium in which the audience sits on three sides of the performing area.

Tormentor: Scenery of either flats or drapes set at right angles to mask the audience view into backstage.

Traveler: A draw curtain that travels from one side of the stage to the other, usually positioned downstage.

Wing(s): A space off stage right or left, beyond the performing area, for storage of scenery or props and for performers to make their entrances and/or exits.

THEATER TAP TALK

The following slang statements and sayings are recorded here for the sake of preservation and out of respect for all those performers and tap dancers of the past and present. Many of the terms are outdated, others are still in use, but regardless of their antiquity or current status, they show the love, devotion, and dedication of tap dancers and performers everywhere.

Angel: A backer for a show.

Black-up: Blacking the face with burnt cork, as in minstrelsy.

Blue Stuff: Risqué comedy.

Boff: A box-office hit.

Boomer: A talent scout.

Break a Leg: Take a lot of bows; superstitious way to wish a performer good luck.

Brodie: A complete flop.

Bury the Show: Club talk. Performers switch roles; audience is unaware.

Burning up the Floor: Tapping well.

Challenge: Two or more dancers entering into competition with each other.

Copasetic: Everything's great.

Cutaway: Film term meaning to switch camera angles.

Deucing: Receiving second billing.

Doing an Eddie Leonard: Making a speech, singing, etc. in response to applause when your act is already completed.

Downtown End: Wall Street.

Exit Stage Right: Make a fast exit.

Flop(Flopped): An act, play or performance that has failed.

Flora Dora Girls: A group of seven female dancers of the Gay Nineties who performed in vaudeville.

Goin' Home: Cue to band to wind up the number.

Gyp 'n' Take: A larcenous show; one for money only.

Handcuffed: An audience that won't applaud readily.

Hang(ing) 4: Tap your best 4 measures, often used in connection with challenges.

Hang(ing) 8: Tap your best 8 measures, often used in connection with challenges.

Hitting It: Getting it right.

Hitting the Timber: Tap dancing.

Hold Your Screws: Good luck in your tap routine.

Hoofer: A traditional tap dancer.

Hoofing: Tap dancing with no other dance influence, such as from ballet or jazz.

Hype: Publicity to stimulate the sale of tickets.

Indie: Independent manager, performer, etc.

In One: Performing in a DS area, very close to the audience.

Jobreened: A cleaned–up script.

Keep Your Screws: Good luck in your tap routine.

Kickin': Great, terrific.

Laying down Iron: Straightforward hoofing.

Layoff: Unemployed.

Leblang: Profit through cut-rate tickets.

Legit: It's legal, or pertains to dealing with the legitimate theater.

Mazda Lane: Broadway.

N.S.G.: Not so good.

Obit: (short for obituary). A bad review and/or a bad play.

Olio: Scenery behind an act.

Pacted: Signed a contract.

Pad the House: Complimentary tickets to help fill the house.

Pix: A motion picture.

Pound the Wood: Tap dancing.

Prima: Someone who expects to be treated well, or like a prima ballerina.

Pro-Am: A professional amateur.

Pulling Focus: Drawing the attention to yourself when on stage with others.

Pulling a Houdini: Getting out of a tight spot.

Rave: A wonderful review.

Round Heels: A pushover.

Scram: Exit.

Scrim: A very sheer, see-through curtain, used for special effects.

Shoestringer: A cheap theatrical production.

Showmanship: What every person needs to have, according to the three Ps: personality, projection, pizzazz.

Shubert Alley: A private street off of Broadway between 44th and 45th streets.

Sleeper: A boring show.

S.R.O.: Standing Room Only.

Tab Show: Abbreviated vaudeville show.

Tad Comic: An Irish comic.

Take Me Away: Cue to band to finish the song or performance.

Take Me Home Boys: Cue to band to wind up the number.

Terp Team: A ballroom team.

Terps: Dancing.

Tin Pan Alley: Music publishers' neighborhood in New York City.

Trading 8's: An exchange of 8 measures between two dancers or a dancer and a musician.

Treading the Boards: Dancing on the stage.

Twofers: Two theater tickets for the price of one.

Vaudery: Vaudeville.

Vidpic: Films made for TV.

Washed Up: A nonusable performer or act.

Wickered: Wastebasketed.

W.K.: Well known.

Many of the terms were contributed by performers; many others come from the following sources: Rosemarie Boyden, well-known dance teacher and educator; *American Vaudeville* by Charles W. Stein (New York: Henry Holt and Company, 1951); *Show Biz* by Abel Green and Joe Laurie Jr. (New York: DaCapo, 1984).

TEACHING

STUDIO OR TEACHING AREA

The diagrams below represent the Cecchetti and Vaganova methods of numbering the fixed points of the dance studio. All students should visualize themselves as standing in the center of the space while facing the mirror, relating each number to themselves (e.g., in the Cecchetti method, #8 is to the student's right, while #7 covers the area behind; in the Vaganova method, right is #3 and #7 is to the left). Students should be equally acquainted with both methods.

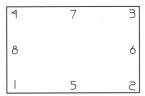

Mirror/Audience

Mirror/Audience

CECCHETTI		VAGANOVA	
1	Right front corner	1	Mirror
2	Left front corner	2	Right front corner
3	Left back corner	3	Right wall
4	Right back corner	4	Right back corner
5	Mirror	5	Back wall
6	Left wall	6	Left back corner
7	Back wall	7	Left wall
8	Right wall	8	Left front corner

CLASSES

This section of the manual is meant to be a broad, generalized guide for the teacher, and in no way implies that this is the only material that could or should be taught on each level. Much of the determination for the work presented is reliant upon the students' age, ability, and previous dance experience. There is no preschool work in this manual. In the lower levels, the theory of dance, understanding of music, body development, coordination, and presentation begins. As the levels advance, so should the dancer, for learning is a building-block procedure.

Primary: Beginner work for the young student

Level I: Beginner

Level II: Beginner-Intermediate

Level III: Intermediate

Level IV: Advanced

PRIMARY

This section is directed toward the very young child, and is not concerned with the older beginner, teenager, or adult.

General Characteristics

The student basically has had limited exposure to the outside world and to formal education. He or she is more interested in "I" than "we"; has a rather short attention span; must be taught the responsibilities of learning as well as being taught the subject; has not developed a fine sense of coordination; is meeting, perhaps for the first time, a field dealing with the arts; thinks in simple, realistic, short-thought sentences, and does not think in abstract terms.

Suggested Procedures

- ✪ Offer a combination class, recognizing tap as the primary subject but includes within the class structure the basic rudiments of dance: leaping, hopping, marching, or walking.

- ✪ Stress counting, coordination, ability to follow directions, responsibility to self and class, etc.

- ✪ Generally, the student needs a great deal of repetition; the design of the work and directions for it must be orderly, logical, and simple.

- ✪ Write the new step, its counts and its correct name on a black board or on cards; have them repeat it after you.

- ✪ Praise is essential.

Body Placement

Foot and leg positions: Basically parallel, even when crossed.

Body: The body moves in one piece. Further development hinges on the ability to control the smaller muscle groups. Torso can bend forward, backward, or side to side. There is minimal isolation at this stage.

Head and Arm: Pupils feel geometric patterns best (i.e., straight lines, circles, or vees). Arm positions might include placing hands on hips, holding arms in 2nd position, swinging them from side to side, airplane arms, crossing them at chest, high vees, low and high 5th position. Head can move up,

down, side to side (profile). Arms and head work best when coordinating in the same direction as feet or step.

Stage and Room Directions

The tendency is to think of the front and back of the room, or to right and left of oneself. The pupil is capable of thinking in circular patterns, involving the whole class, or turning himself around. Straight lines and very simple floor patterns, such as squares and circles, can easily be mastered.

Rhythms and Tempos

Keep rhythms and tempos basically moderate, simple, not overlapping, and strongly accented. Use quarter-notes and the occasional eighth-note.

Routines and Combinations

These must be short concise and logical. Repetition is necessary and expected, as are some forms of open, or rest, counts (eg., 4 heel steps R L R L followed by 2 slow shuffle steps R & L [1 2, 3 4, 5 6, 7 8][1 2 3 (4), 5 6 7 (8)], repeat all (4M)).

Class Procedure

At the primary level, the student is capable of working at the barre, in the center, and across the floor. It is advisable, because of the student's short concentration span, to change room position, often. The barre is used for new or old work, where balance is difficult to maintain. The proper term should be connected to the proper step, even though descriptive words might be used at first.

Suggestions

Good communication is important at this level. Different explanations or wording may be needed to impart knowledge. Patience and tolerance are essential. You may find that conducting the class in approximately the same manner for each lesson is beneficial, for example, begin in center, review old work, introduce new work, etc.

Some of the basic steps that might be expected of the primary level follows, grouped in families.

Taps	Ball (leg extended forward, strike tap plate)
	Heel (leg extended forward, strike back edge of heel)
Toe (Tip)	(cross leg front or back of supporting leg, strike tip of toe)
Dig	(strike ball of foot close to supporting foot)
	(strike heel of foot close to supporting foot)
Heel Stand	(extend R forward, dig heel edge, place wt. on heel temporarily step bkwd L ip)
Heel Change	(place weight on heel of one foot, then step on ball of other foot,

	similar to ball change)
Heel Drops	May be done alternately or simultaneously, with or without weight
Toe Drops	May be done alternately or simultaneously, with or without weight
Twisted Toe Drops	(drop toe in tno position, then repeat toe drop with same foot in tni position)

Point step, heel step,

toe(tip) step, dig step	Shuffle step, shuffle	Step ball change
toe heel, heel toe	hop step	shuffle ball change
brush R fwd, spank R	slap, flap, spank step	flap ball change
bkwd (shuffle)	flap heel, spank toe	
	heel	
	ball change	

Movements on the primary level might include the following:

hop	march	step, clap
jump	bourrée	step kick
leap	pas de bourrée	side close
skip	3-step turn	relevé
slide	battement	plié

LEVEL I - BEGINNER

The beginner level embraces a wide age range, which may include the child in grammar school through the teenage beginner to the adult. Work from the primary level must be included here (i.e., flaps, shuffles, ball changes, and other basics), but using a different approach covering material in a shorter length of time. The older beginner probably takes in an hourlong tap class.

General Characteristics
At Level I, communication is obviously quicker and easier, as is the assimilation of new material. However, other elements will infiltrate the learning pattern, some a deterrent, others an aid. The student may be frustrated by things he does not do well, or inhibited if the execution of new material is not immediate. The general pattern at this level is to feel quite secure when performing in a group and insecure when asked to demonstrate alone.

Body Placement
The basic principles of body placement and alignment should be presented and incorporated into the class from the first lesson onward.

Stage and Room Direction
At this level, patterns and formations from the Primary level are more easily absorbed, plus the principles of diagonal lines, split lines, and groups, working in opposition rhythms, steps, and formations could be introduced to some classes. The idea of the numbering of the room and stage directions might also be introduced, depending on the level of maturity of the class.

Rhythms and Tempos
Tempos may become faster or slower, basic yet more intricate. Rhythms and patterns should be introduced along with different time signatures, (e.g., waltz, softshoe, etc). Continue the use of the quarter-note rhythm, but begin to explore the eighth- and, in the case of the older student, the sixteenth-note patterns.

Routines and Combinations
These should be logical but longer in length, and require more reasoning, concentration, and practice. They may cover more space, be rhythmically more demanding, and certainly more stylistic. At this stage, it is necessary to discuss the performance and the presentation of the work as well.

Suggestions
Reviewing old work before presenting new work is usually a sound procedure. However, in the Primary and in the Level I grades, it is a necessity for ensuring a sound foundation. Reviewing may be done out of order, context, or room positioning from lesson to lesson, depending on the group. Always use the proper terminology when addressing the class.

Class Procedure
Each class should have a goal to achieve. This could involve the following: to learn a certain grouping of steps; to clean up the routine; to review the past work. Progress takes planning and the beginning levels are crucial for they contain the basic knowledge, the foundation on which all other work will be drawn. Combinations offered in class are essential, since they help to solidify the work that has already been presented. Pointing out sameness, likeness, opposite, etc. (shuffle hop step is to hop shuffle step; flap ball change is to shuffle ball change) is also important.

Some of the steps that are associated with the Beginner Level follows. Remember to include the Primary terminology as well.

Heel drops and toe drops (w/wo), **alternating heel drops, alternating toe drops, alternating heel and toe drops** on each beat of the music, using the **&** count, etc.

Buck and catch (both feet), **chug and hitch** (1 foot)

Scuff, scuffle (sciffle), shuffles Xd in frt and in bk, **double shuffles, shuffles** to 2nd (tno or parallel),

Shuffle steps R & L

Hop step, hop toe, toe hop, leap toe, toe leap, toe hop step, shuffle hop toe,

shuffle leap toe, dig hop toe, **scuff hop step, brush hop toe** (ip, fwd, bkwd), **shuffle hop step** (ip, fwd, bkwd), **single and double Irish,** etc.

Hop shuffle step (ip, fwd, bkwd) (2 or 4 counts)

Flap close step, running flaps (a1, 2, a3, 4), **spank steps, flap heels, spank toe heels**

Paddle step (w/ step or flap) (ip, fwd, bkwd, turning R or L) (a1, a2, a3, a4)

Ball, stomp, slam
Ball change, shuffle ball change (traveling s/s) (a1, a1, a2)
Buffalo, waltz clog (time step), **chaîné turns** (w/wo sound)

LEVEL II - BEGINNER-INTERMEDIATE

A large gap exists between the beginner and the intermediate levels. Level II requires the student to explore the use of the smaller muscles of the feet and body, as well as the larger ones, to articulate the tap sounds and perform them closer to the floor and to increase the tap vocabulary to include steps such as shim sham, cramrolls, bombershay, toe and heel clicks (see list below). In general, dancing will take on a new look and form.

General Characteristics
The student is now familiar with learning, at the studio level and has progressed to a higher emotional and educational plateau. His or her communication and response time to learning have been established and he or she is ready to accept new challenges. Unfortunately, many students find these challenges overwhelming, and as a result drop out of dance entirely or prefer a class on a lower technical level. Other fields of dance should be pursued.

Foot and Leg Positions
Parallel, turned out, oblique.

Moment of the Body
The use of isolated body movement, the incorporation of the principles of ballet and jazz, and alignment and placement should continue to be reinforced.

Head and Arms
Isolations that are both fluid and percussive are explored. More advanced port de bras, reintroduction of the principles of body design and form. Attention to style and presentation becomes more important.

Stage and Room Patterns
More intricate patterns, such as figure 8's, zig-zag patterns, and S designs are used. Room numbers and stage directions should be fully understood.

Rhythms and Tempos
A continuation of the beginner level, plus faster and more intricate rhythmic patterns are introduced. Some off-beat and syncopated phrasing, time steps, and breaks are also introduced.

Class Procedure
At the beginner-intermediate Level, one may introduce a tap barre, which includes pliés, (executed w/wo heel beats), relevé, beginning of rond de jambe. Jazz tap movements and a jazz barre are also possible. Changing room positions during the course of a class adds interest and stimulates thinking. Proper terminology should always be placed. Emphasis should be made on the retention and accuracy of the work presented.

Some of the tap steps learned at the beginner-intermediate level follow:

Steps	Movements
falling off a log	pivot (outside)
Maxie Ford	sauté arabesque
cramrolls	jump Sissonne
drawbacks	jump stag
spank step heel heel	calypso jump
running flaps	drag
running shuffle steps	draw (edge of foot)
shuffle ball change (frt & bk)	grapevine
heel clicks	hitch kick
toe clicks	
essence	*Turns*
basic time step	stamp shuffle step
heel grind time steps	toe heel (flap heel)
shuffle toe heel	leap toe (tip)
waltz clog	flap ball, change
military time step	Introduction to different inside
bombershay	and outside turns
bells	
falling off a log	*Attention to*
	Clean sounds of taps
	Body placement
	Rhythms: double, triple
	Counting and phrasing

LEVEL III - INTERMEDIATE

Level III concentrates and refines the principles introduced in Level II. Increased emphasis is placed on expanding tap terminology and its technical execution, presentation, and performance. The serious student should be involved in other areas of dance at this time.

Characteristics
The intermediate student has attained a level at which he or she is capable, to a degree, of using the finer muscles of the

body and of executing longer and more complex work. This student has also developed a sense of presentation and style, not only during a performance, but also during class. At this level, a great deal of emphasis may be placed on body alignment, line, level, accenting, shading, and delving into more abstract theories and thoughts.

General

The student is working on technical proficiency, style, presentation, and integrating other dance areas into tap work. Repetition, new challenges, information, criticism, and praise are essential.

Foot and Leg Positions

The principles of parallel, turnout, and oblique will be used more and further defined. The addition of inverted and distorted usage of the foot and leg on the floor should be initiated.

Body Movement

An intermediate student will have more control over isolations, rhythms, and footwork. The use of the body is stressed in accenting, starting, stopping, and posing. The expansion and contrast of various qualities of movement, such as fluid, sharp, or lyrical improves the student's style and understanding.

Rhythms and Tempos

Progressive and overlapping rhythm patterns are introduced at this level. Many varied tempos and musical arrangements along with work in stop time and in tacit are employed at this time.

General Attention To

- ✿ Control of the feet to produce accenting, shading, and clusters of sound.

- ✿ The amalgamation of tap with the fields of jazz, modern dance, primitive, etc.

- ✿ The application of barre work to center floor and vice versa.

- ✿ The ability to analyze, criticize, and transfer information, either new or previously given.

- ✿ The concentration on technical execution, presentation, and performance.

Class Procedure

It is recommended that the intermediate student devote his entire class time (one to one-and-a-half hours) to tap and that allied dance subjects be allotted their own special class. Many classes on level III must be devoted to the extensions of isolated techniques, such as turns, pickups, riffs, and other more advanced movement. As a result, class procedure may vary considerably. Nonetheless, the intermediate student must not be deprived of combinations, routines, and center floor and barre work, or the alliance of the theories of other dance techniques. The introduction of seminars and workshops are of great value to a student of this level. Level III presupposes that the student is more keenly interested in dance and therefore finds more outlets for his or her abilities. This may take the form of extra classes with small groups, solo work, demonstrating and assisting the teacher, the development of dance projects, and more frequent public performances.

The following list of tap steps and movements are recommended for the intermediate student:

Jab	toe & heel
Clicks	toe heel, or heel toe
Rolls	heel-toe; alt. heel & toe; alt. toe & heel, side travels
Scuffles	double and triple
Scuff heel	
Shuffle toe heel	
Waltz clogs	with heel drop
Essences	short, long, Virginia
Drawbacks	single, double, triple, one sided, alternating
Cincinnati	single, double, triple
Take aways	
Flash steps	
Trenches	
Fake splits	
Floor work	
Leaps/jumps	
Air work	
Cramprolls	in place forward backward traveling, turning R and L (reg); alternating shuffle cramproll shuffle alternating, flap cramproll fake cramproll progressive standing
Riffs	walking riffs back riff riffle pendulum leaping riffs turning
Wings	double single toe stand wings
Paradiddles	
Tangle foot	
Turns:	
Stationary	(w/wo taps) spin arounds - s, d, t inside/outside - s, d barrel rolls renversé, etc.

Turns:
Traveling   barrel rolls
                       attitude
                       brush ball changes

LEVEL IV - ADVANCED

Tap students who have arrived at level IV are technically proficient, experienced in performance, and quite knowledgeable about themselves and their work. They have been exposed to other kinds of dance—ballet, jazz, modern—and to other teachers and choreographers. They are considered mature, responsible, reliable, quick to learn, memorize, and adapt, emotionally and aesthetically. They are on a new and different level from that of the intermediates.

General Characteristics

- The work tools have been assembled and understood.

- There is a great deal of consciousness toward line, level, shading, accenting, clarity, direction, and rhythmic patterning.

- There is a clear understanding of the finer points of technique, plus a good understanding of the total work and design.

- There is a development of individualism.

- There is a personal understanding of one's own abilities and limitations with a desire to perpetuate the first and correct the second.

- There is a keen need for competition with oneself and others.

- There is pride of accomplishment and a feeling of responsibility toward the field and oneself.

- There is an acceptance that perfection is more meaningful than any collection of steps and styles.

Class Procedure

On this level, the procedure of the class is not as important as the worth of the class. Class procedure may vary from week to week, but each lesson must carry in its presentation a meaningful goal and an awareness of the students' needs and abilities. Bringing in a guest teacher from time to time is exciting for the class and beneficial for you, as it allows you to observe how the class absorbs the material and learns collectively and individually. Other interesting types of classes might be:

- A tap class where tap exercises and combinations are based solely upon another type of dance such as ballet, jazz, or modern dance.

- A class in which a complete routine must be assimilated and absorbed by the student within the space of the class time.

- A class in which the student does not dance, but is presented with a discussion on, or lectures concerning allied, subjects (e.g., choreography, anatomy, dance, drama, etc).

- A class in which the student exhibits a short, original choreographic piece of his own, which is analyzed by the teacher and fellow classmates.

- A class, out of the studio, to observe someone else's class, a professional company in rehearsal, etc.

- A class where you don't speak or explain the steps, merely do them.

- A class whose primary intent is the art of improvisation, the creating of rhythms, steps, and combinations, which all must learn and in turn contribute to.

Obviously, the technical training should be continued in tap as well as in the allied fields. Sometimes, one must return to the basics and review the proper technique by which a step is executed. For example, close to the floor work, such as pickups, riffs, wings, etc. are often muffled because concentration is on the total step and not its separate parts. Clarity becomes lost in the presentation. The broader focus is on rhythmic and complex patterns, longer and perhaps more difficult combinations, the quality of the presentation, the dynamics of the performance, and a general pulling together of all the past information.

Much time of the teacher's time will be spent on individual suggestions and criticism, for each dancer is now quite different from other. That is what will be expected of them if they choose a professional dance career. Teachers are often placed in the position of mentor or adviser, and at this level of advancement the student might have to make certain choices: Do I pursue dance as a career—especially in tap? Do I want to continue my dance training at a college or university? Is teaching dance a possibility or should I choose another profession and allow dance to become an advocation or a hobby? It might be helpful if, as a teacher, you had available information about colleges and universities, especially those with majors in dance, some current information about possible careers in dance, and perhaps a list of professional classes or teachers in New York, Los Angeles, or other major dance cities.

Listed below are some of the possible exercises for the advanced student, all of which are found in various sections of *TAPWORKS*.

- Review all the large families of steps and their variations. They may be found under the following term names:
  Breaks; Cramprolls; Pickups; Riffs; Time Steps; Turns; Wings.

Procedure

A. Review all in their pure or proper form.

B. Combine the family variations in combinations, eg.:

4 alternating cramprolls (move bend)	1 - 8 ct.
2 hop cramprolls R (turn bk R, ip)	1 - 4 ct.
1 brisé cramproll R	5 - 6 ct.
1 assemblé cramproll R	7 - 8 ct.
REVERSE **B**	4 M

C. Mix some family members with another family

1 crossing pendulum riff R, St R & L	1 - 4 ct.
2 double wings and a scissors riff	

✪ Refer to the dictionary: dynamics (tap sounds). Listed below are some exercises pertaining to the principles of the dynamics of tap sounds. These principles also pertain to the dynamics of presentation and performance.

A. **Rhythm:** Choose a step like a buck timestep and execute it.

On beat: The normal way—stomp a ct. of 8.

Off beat: Place the stomp on a ct. of 2 or 3.

B. **Rhythm:** Using a paradiddle, execute the following rhythms:

Duple: ct. 1 & 2
Triplet: ct. 1 & a (overlapping)
Quadruple: ct. 1 e & a (accent on 1)

C. **Rhythm:** Using shuffle toe heel, execute the following rhythms:

Single time: ct. & 1 & 2
Double time: ct. e & a1
Triplets: ct. 1 & a , 2 & a (overlapping)

D. **Syncopation:** Using stamps and claps, execute the following counts:

ct. 1 & 2 & 3 & 4 or 1e & a2e & a3 & 4 or 1 2 & hold3 & a4 5 & a6 7 8

E. **Accent:** Using shuffle alternating pickup:

1. Place the accent on the landing - e & a **1**
2. Place the accent on the shuffle - **e** & a 1
3. Place the accent on the pickup - e & **a** 1

F. **Shading:** Using running flap heels as the step:

1. Crescendo in ct. 1 - 8 (soft to loud)
2. Decrescendo in ct. 1 - 8 (loud to soft)
3. Crescendo for ct. 1 - 4 and decrescendo ct. 5 - 8.

G. **Contrast:**

1. Execute 3 buck timesteps loudly; do break softly.
2. Execute railroad step:

a & a1 e & a2 e& a3 e& a4
shuffle ball change, shuffle ball change
ball change, shuffle ball change ball change
do set (1 - 4) loud, second time (5 - 8)
soft, etc.

✪ See Performing: The Stage Area: Each stage has different dimensions and sightlines, but all stages have certain properties that are alike, for example, the downstage areas are theoretically more human, friendlier; corners are a little more mysterious than center downstage.

A. Create a simple routine and try it on the stage in various areas, at various angles and levels, with different port de bras, and see how these principles work.

✪ Create 8 to 16 M combinations in tacit.

✪ Have the class improvise 8 or more counts individually and on the spot, one after another.

The levels given here are only suggestions. Each teacher must present work based upon the structure of the class, one's own previous training, and personal philosophy. Although all of us may arrive from different paths, with care and education we all arrive at the same meeting place.

BIBLIOGRAPHY

Ames, Jerry and Jim Siegelman. THE BOOK OF TAP. New York: David McKay Company Inc., 1977.

Anbinder, Tyler. FIVE POINTS: THE 19TH-CENTURY NEW YORK CITY NEIGHBORHOOD THAT INVENTED TAP DANCE, STOLE ELECTIONS, AND BECAME THE WORLD'S MOST NOTORIOUS SLUM. New York: The Free Press, 2001.

Andrews, E.O. CHRONICLES OF AMERICAN DANCE. New York: Henry Holt and Company, 1948.

Atwater, Constance. TAP DANCING. Vermont, Tokyo, Japan: Pub. unknown, 1971.

Audy, Robert. TAP DANCING: HOW TO TEACH YOURSELF TAP. New York: Vintage Books/Random House Inc., 1976.

Ballwebber, Edith. TAP DANCING: FUNDAMENTALS AND ROUTINES. London: A. Weekes and Co. 1930.

Buckman, Peter. LET'S DANCE: SOCIAL, BALLROOM AND FOLK DANCE. London/New York: Paddington Press Ltd., 1978.

Carlos, Ernest. TIPS ON TAP. New York: Edward Marks Music Corporation, 1937.

Clarke, Mary & Clement Crisp. THE HISTORY OF DANCE. New York: Crown Publishers Inc., 1980.

De Mille, Agnes. AMERICA DANCES. New York: Macmillan Publishing Company Inc., 1980.

Denis, Paul. OPPORTUNITIES IN THE DANCE. New York: VGM Career Horizons, 1980.

Draper, Paul. ON TAP DANCING. New York: Marcel Dekker Inc., 1978.

Ellfeldt, Lois & Carnes. DANCE PRODUCTION HANDBOOK. Mountain View, CA: Mayfield Publishing Company, 1971.

Emery, Lynne Fauley. BLACK DANCE: FROM 1619 TO TODAY. Princeton NJ.: Princeton Book Company, Publishers, 1988.

Feldman, Anita. INSIDE TAP. Hightstown, NJ.: Princeton Book Company, Publishers, 1996.

Fitt, Sally S. DANCE KINESIOLOGY. London / New York: Schirmer Books Macmillan, 1988.

Fletcher, Beale. HOW TO IMPROVE YOUR TAP DANCING. New York: A. S. Barnes & Company, 1957.

Frank, Rusty E. TAP! New York: William Morrow and Company, 1990.

Frost, Helen. TAP. CAPER AND CLOG. New York: A.S. Barnes, 1932.

Gottfried, Martin. BROADWAY MUSICALS. New York: Harry N. Abrams, 1980.

Glover, Savion and Bruce Weber. MY LIFE IN TAP. New York: William Morrow and Company Inc., 2000.

Gray, Acia. THE SOULS OF YOUR FEET: A TAP DANCE GUIDEBOOK FOR RHYTHM EXPLORERS. Austin, TX:Grand Weaver's Publishing, 1998.

Green, Abel & Joe Laurie Jr. SHOW BIZ FROM VAUDVILLE TO VIDEO. New York: Henry Holt Company, 1951.

Green, Stanley. RING BELLS! SING SONGS! BROADWAY MUSICALS OF THE 30'S. New York: Galahad Books, 1971.

Hirschhorn, Clive. THE HOLLYWOOD MUSICAL. New York: Crown Publishing Inc., 1981.

Humphrey, Doris. THE ART OF MAKING DANCES. New York: Holt, Rinehart and Winston, 1959. Rpt: Hightstown, NJ: Princeton Book Company, Publishers, 1987.

Kinney, Troy & Margaret West. THE DANCE: IT'S PLACE IN ART & LIFE. New York: Tudor Publishing Company, 1936.

Kislan, Richard. HOOFING ON BROADWAY. New York: Prentice Hall Press, 1987.

Knowles, Mark. THE TAP DANCE DICTIONARY. North Carolina and London: McFarland & Co. Inc., 1998.

Kobal, John. GOTTA SING, GOTTA DANCE. New York/Sidney/Toronto/London: Hamlyn Publishing Company Ltd., 1971.

Laurie, Joe Jr. VAUDEVILLE: FROM THE HONKY-TONKS TO THE PALACE. New York: Henry Holt & Company, 1953.

Laws, Kenneth. THE PHYSICS OF DANCE. New York: Schirmer Books/Macmillan Inc., 1984.

Martin, John. AMERICA DANCING. New York: Dodge Publishing Company, 1936.

Ormonde, Jimmy. TAP DANCING AT A GLANCE. New York: Brewer, Warren & Putnam Publishing, 1931.

Raffé, W. G. DICTIONARY OF THE DANCE. New York: A. S. Barnes & Company, 1964.

Ryman, Rhonda. DICTIONARY OF CLASSICAL BALLET TERMINOLOGY. London: Royal Academy of Dancing, 1995.

Ryman, Rhonda. DICTIONARY OF CLASSICAL BALLET TERMINOLOGY. London: Royal Academy of Dancing, 1995.

Sennett, Ted. HOLLYWOOD MUSICALS. New York: Harry N. Abrams Inc., 1981.

Stearns, Marshall and Jean. JAZZ DANCE: THE STORY OF AMERICAN VERNACULAR DANCE. New York: Schirmer Books, 1968; rpt. New York: DaCapo Press, 1994.

Stein, Charles W. AMERICAN VAUDEVILLE. Rpt. New York: DaCapo 1984.

Stern, Lee Edward. THE MOVIE MUSICAL. New York: Pyramid Publication, 1974.

Tanner, Averett / Fran. BASIC DANCE PROJECTS. Idaho: Clark Publishing Company, 1972.

Tutterow, Gayle. "TAP" THE DANCE AND SOUND FROM THE 20'S TO THE 90'S. Available from Gayle Tutterow, 13225 101st Street S.E. #372, Largo, FL.: 34643.

Vaganova, Agrippina. BASIC PRINCIPLES OF CLASSICAL BALLET (RUSSIAN BALLET TECHNIQUE). Rpt. New York: Dover, 1969.

Wilk, Betty. THE FILM MUSICAL. MD: Digon Press Inc., 1979.

Woll, Allen. BLACK MUSICAL THEATER: FROM COONTOWN TO DREAMGIRLS. Baton Rouge: Louisiana State University Press, 1997.

Dictionaries, Syllabi, and Technical Manuals

Cholerton, Judy. HINTS ON TAP DANCING. Friar Gate, Eng.: Association of American Dancing, 1936.

_____. THE THEORY OF AUTHENTIC TIME STEPS AND BREAKS. Friar Gate, Eng.: Association of America Dancing, 1936.

_____. THE THEORY OF TAP DANCING FOR THE MEMBERS. Friar Gate, Eng.: Association of American Dancing,

_____. TIME STEPS: VARIATIONS AND BREAKS. Frier Gate, Eng.: Association of American Dancing.

Dance Magazine. December, 1988.

Dance Masters of America. ABC'S OF DANCE TERMINOLOGY. New York: Dance Masters Assoc. Press, 1949.

_____. TAP TERMINOLOGY. New York: Dance Masters Assoc. Press, 1975.

_____. JAZZ SYLLABUS. New York: Dance Masters Assoc. Press, 1979.

Daniels, Ronn. FAPA MANUAL. CA: Fred Astaire Performing Arts Assoc., 1955.

Gilbert, Al and Phil Mayfield. JAZZ - TAP TECHNIQUES. CA.: Theatrical Duplicating Service, 1994.

_____. TAP DICTIONARY & ENCYCLOPEDIA OF TAP TERMINOLOGY AND RELATED INFORMATION (1998). Available from Stepping Tones Ltd., P.O. Box 352336, Los Angeles, CA, 90035.

Gudat, Diane. THE TIMESTEP DICTIONARY. 1121 East Edgewood Ave. Indianapolis, IN: Self Published, 1990.

Hoctor, Danny, Art Stone, and Gayle Tutterow. THE ENCYCLOPEDIA OF TAP. 1964.

Grant, Gail. TECHNICAL MANUAL AND DICTIONARY OF CLASSICAL BALLET. New York: Dover, 1967.

Hoctor, Danny. GRADED EXERCISES FOR TAP DANCING . NJ: Dance Records Inc., 1971.

Kelley, Charles. AMERICAN TAP DANCING DICTIONARY. Dance Educators of America, Publisher unknown.

Knowles, Mark. THE TAP DANCE DICTIONARY. Jefferson, NC:McFarland and Company Inc. Publishers, 1998.

Kraines, Minda Goodman and Kan Ester. JUMP INTO JAZZ, 2nd ed. Mountain View, CA: Mayfield, 1990.

Kriegel, Lorraine Person, and Kim Chandler-Vacaro. JAZZ DANCE TODAY. St. Paul, MN: West Publishing Company, 1994.

Long, Camille. TEXTBOOK FOR TEACHERS OF DANCING. Publisher unknown, 1954.

Mahoney, Billie. INTERNATIONAL TAP ASSOCIATION NEWSLETTER. Vol. 5, No.4, March—April, 1995.

_____. INTERNATIONAL TAP ASSOCIATION NEWSLETTER. Vol. 5, No. 6, 1996.

TAPWORKS

National Council of Dance Teachers Organization. TAP DANCING. Publisher unknown, 1965.

Ralabate, Tom. JAZZ SYLLABUS, REV. ED. Dance Masters of America, July 1995.

Raye, Zeila. AMERICAN TAP DANCING. Eng. Publisher unknown, 1936.

Schlaich, Joan and Betty Dupont. THE ART OF TEACHING DANCE TECHNIQUE. Reston, VA. National Dance Association, 1993.

Sutton, Jimmy. FASCINATING RHYTHMS. Place unknown, Sam Enterprises, 1985.

Sutton, Tommy. TAP ALONG WITH TOMMY: A TECHNICAL GUIDE FOR TAP DANCE TEACHERS. Volume I, Volume II, Volume III. Publisher unknown, US, 1986.

Tutterow, Gayle: FOR TAP LOVERS ONLY (1986). Available from Gayle Tutterow, 13225 101st Street S.E. #372, Largo, FL 34643. FL, Self-published, 1986.

_____. THE TAP TALE DICTIONARY. (1986).

Videos

GREAT FEATS OF THE FEET: A video portrait of jazz and tap dance. Directed by Brenda Bufalino, A Dancing Theater Production, 1977.

HONI COLES TRIBUTE: In association with WNET, New York, NY. Narrated and hosted by Gregory Hines. Distributed by Dave Davidson and Amber Edwards, Hudson West Productions, 1991.

JAZZ HOOFER: BABY LAURENCE: Rhapsody Film Inc. Funded by grants from the Maryland Committee for the Humanities, the National Endowment for the Arts and the D.C. Commission on the Arts and Humanities, 1966.

LEONARD REED'S THE SHIM SHAM SHIMMY: Presented by Rusty E. Frank. On Tap Enterprises, 8564 Chalmers Drive, Suite 2, Los Angeles, CA, 90035.

TALKING FEET: Produced by Mike Seegar with Ruth Pershing. Flower Films and Videos, 10341 San Pablo Avenue, El Cerito, CA, 94530.

TAP DANCE IN AMERICA: *Great Performances*. Funded by Texaco, Martin Marietta, the National Endowment for the Arts, and the Corporation for Public Broadcasting.